AF763203

Evaluating Sustainable Food System Innovations

This book presents Urbal, an approach that applies impact pathway mapping to understand how food system innovations in cities, and their territories, change and impact food system sustainability.

Around the world, people are finding innovative ways to make their food systems more sustainable. However, documenting and understanding how these innovations impact the sustainability of food system can be a challenge. The Urban Driven Innovations for Sustainable Food Systems (Urbal) methodology responds to these constraints by providing innovations with a simple, open-source, resource-efficient tool that is easily appropriated and adaptable to different contexts. Urbal is designed to respond to the demands of field stakeholders, whether public or private, to accompany and guide them in their actions and decision-making with regard to sustainability objectives. This book presents this qualitative and participatory impact assessment method of food innovations and applies it to several cases of food innovation around the world, including the impact of agricultural districts in Milan, chefs and gastronomy in Brasilia, e-commerce in Vietnam, eco-friendly farm systems in Berlin and the Nourish to Flourish governance process in Cape Town. The book demonstrates how food innovations can impact different dimensions of sustainability, positively and negatively, and identify the elements that facilitate or hinder these impacts. The volume reflects on how to strengthen the capacity of these stakeholders to disseminate their innovations on other scales to contribute to the transition towards more sustainable food systems.

This book will be of great interest to students and scholars working on sustainable food systems, urban food, food innovation and impact assessment, as well as policymakers, practitioners and funders interested in these areas.

Élodie Valette is a geographer and a senior researcher at CIRAD (French Agricultural Research for Development) in Montpellier, France. She is the coordinator of the Urbal project.

Alison Blay-Palmer is the UNESCO Chair in Sustainable Food Systems, the founding director of the Laurier Centre for Sustainable Food Systems, and a professor at Wilfrid Laurier University, Canada. She is the co-editor of

Sustainable Food System Assessment (Routledge, 2019) and the scientific coordinator of the Urbal Project.

Beatrice Intoppa is a project manager at the UNESCO Chair in World Food Systems at L'Institut Agro Montpellier, France. She holds an MA in Local Development from the University of Padua, Italy.

Amanda Di Battista is the project coordinator of the Laurier Centre for Sustainable Food Systems, Canada. She produces the Handpicked: Stories from the Field podcast and is the co-editor of *Food Studies: Matter, Meaning, Movement* (2022) and *Sustainable Food System Assessment* (Routledge, 2019).

Ophélie Roudelle is a project manager at the UNESCO Chair in World Food Systems in L'Institut Agro Montpellier, France. She is in charge of the valorization, dissemination, and popularization of research results of the Urbal project.

Géraldine Chaboud holds a PhD in economics from Université de Montpellier, France, and has been a former project manager at the UNESCO Chair in World Food Systems in L'Institut Agro Montpellier, France.

Routledge Studies in Food, Society and the Environment

Food Loss and Waste Policy
From Theory to Practice
Edited by Simone Busetti and Noemi Pace

Rewilding Food and the Self
Critical Conversations from Europe
Edited by Tristan Fournier and Sébastien Dalgalarrondo

Critical Mapping for Sustainable Food Design
Food Security, Equity, and Justice
Audrey G. Bennett and Jennifer A. Vokoun

Community Food Initiatives
A Critical Reparative Approach
Edited by Oona Morrow, Esther Veen, and Stefan Wahlen

Food Futures in Education and Society
Edited by Gurpinder Singh Lalli, Angela Turner, and Marion Rutland

The Soybean through World History
Lessons for Sustainable Agrofood Systems
Matilda Baraibar Norberg and Lisa Deutsch

Urban Expansion and Food Security in New Zealand
The Collapse of Local Horticulture
Benjamin Felix Richardson

Evaluating Sustainable Food System Innovations
A Global Toolkit for Cities
Edited by Élodie Valette, Alison Blay-Palmer, Beatrice Intoppa, Amanda Di Battista, Ophélie Roudelle, and Géraldine Chaboud

For more information about this series, please visit: www.routledge.com/Routledge-Studies-in-Food-Society-and-the-Environment/book-series/RSFSE

Evaluating Sustainable Food System Innovations

A Global Toolkit for Cities

Edited by Élodie Valette, Alison Blay-Palmer, Beatrice Intoppa, Amanda Di Battista, Ophélie Roudelle, and Géraldine Chaboud

Routledge
Taylor & Francis Group
LONDON AND NEW YORK

earthscan
from Routledge

First published 2024
by Routledge
4 Park Square, Milton Park, Abingdon, Oxon OX14 4RN

and by Routledge
605 Third Avenue, New York, NY 10158

Routledge is an imprint of the Taylor & Francis Group, an informa business

Funded by Institut Agro.

British Library Cataloguing-in-Publication Data
A catalogue record for this book is available from the British Library

ISBN: 978-1-032-25881-2 (hbk)
ISBN: 978-1-032-25883-6 (pbk)
ISBN: 978-1-003-28544-1 (ebk)

DOI: 10.4324/9781003285441

Typeset in Times New Roman
by SPi Technologies India Pvt Ltd (Straive)

Contents

Contributors

Giulia Bartezzaghi is the director of the Food Sustainability Lab at the School of Management of Politecnico di Milano (Italy) and PhD Candidate in Management Engineering.

Jane Battersby is an urban geographer based at the Department of Environmental and Geographical Science, University of Cape Town (South Africa). Her work focuses on urban food security, food systems, and their governance from local to global scale with a particular focus on African Cities. DPhil (Oxon).

Valerio Bini is an associate professor of Geography at the Department of Cultural and Environmental Heritage, University of Milan (Italy), where he teaches Development Geography and Environmental Politics. His main areas of research include development cooperation, political ecology, and agri-food policies.

Alison Blay-Palmer is the UNESCO Chair on Food, Biodiversity and Sustainability Studies, the founding director of the Centre for Sustainable Food Systems, and an associate professor at Wilfrid Laurier University (Canada). She works in the Department of Geography and Environmental Studies where she does research on resilient food systems and sustainable communities. She is the scientific coordinator of the Urbal project.

Michaël Bruckert is a researcher at UMR Innovation, CIRAD (French Agricultural Research Center for International Development), posted at FAVRI (Fruit and Vegetable Research Institute) in Hanoi (Vietnam). He is the coordinator of the Malica (Markets and Agriculture Linkages in Asia) research platform. He works in the field of political economy and ecology focuses on food system transformations in Asia (mainly in India and Vietnam).

Federico Caniato is a full professor of Supply Chain and Purchasing Management at the School of Management of Politecnico di Milano (Italy), where he is also the Rector's Delegate for Lifelong Learning. His research interests are in the field of Supply Chain Finance, Supply Chain Sustainability, and Supply Chain Resilience.

Mauro G. M. Capelari is an assistant professor at the Center for Sustainable Development at the University of Brasília (CDS/UnB) and at the Graduate Program in Sustainable Development (PPGCDS/UnB), Brazil. He is also a postdoctoral fellow in Socio-Environmental Policy and Management and a PhD in Public Administration and Public Policy. His researches focus on socio-environmental public policies, public policy analysis, institutions, and sustainability.

Géraldine Chaboud is a PhD in economics from Université de Montpellier, France, and a former project manager at the UNESCO Chair in World Food Systems in L'Institut Agro Montpellier, France.

Amanda Di Battista is the project coordinator of the Laurier Centre for Sustainable Food Systems and the UNESCO Chair in Food, Biodiversity and Sustainability Studies, Canada. She produces the research podcast, *Handpicked: Stories from the Field* podcast and has co-edited *Food Studies: Matter, Meaning, Movement* and *Sustainable Food System Assessment: Lessons from Global Practice*.

Janaína D.A.S. Diniz is an associate lecturer at the University of Brasília (Brazil) in the Graduate Program in Environment and Rural Development and in the Professional Master in Sustainability alongside Traditional Peoples and Territories. She holds a PhD in Logistics and Strategy (Aix-Marseille University, France) and in Sustainable Development (University of Brasília).

Undine Giseke has been a professor at the Technical University Berlin (Germany), Department of Landscape Architecture + Open Space Planning from 2003 to 2022. In 1987, she founded the landscape architecture office BGMR. From 2005 to 2014 she led the inter- and transdisciplinary research project UAC, focusing on urban–rural linkages, urban metabolism and systemic design.

Stéphane Guéneau is a researcher at CIRAD (Agricultural Research Centre for International Development), Montpellier Interdisciplinary Centre on Sustainable Agri-food systems (MOISA), France. PhD in Environmental Sciences from Agroparistech, Paris, MSc in Economics from Montpellier University, France. His research topics encompass both quality in food supply chains (sustainability certification) and agri-food policies analysis.

Gareth Haysom is a senior research officer at the African Centre for Cities at the University of Cape Town (South Africa). Gareth co-leads the Urban Food Systems Research Cluster at the ACC. He holds a PhD in Environmental and Geographical Science from the University of Cape Town and an MPhil in Sustainable Development from Stellenbosch University.

Lucas Hövelmann (M Sc) is a landscape architect and has worked at the Technical University Berlin (Germany) at Prof. Undine Giseke from 2017 to

2022. In 2020, he founded OTTL.LA, an office for landscape architecture. His work is focusing on communication techniques, urban metabolism and urban planning, as well as strategic landscape projects in multiple scales.

Beatrice Intoppa is a project manager at the UNESCO Chair in World Food Systems at L'Institut Agro Montpellier, France. She holds an MA in local development from the University of Padua, Italy.

Julie Le Gall is a geographer and a lecturer at Ecole Normale Supérieure in Lyon (France), seconded to the French Embassy in Santiago (Chili). Her research has focused on agri-food justice, agri-food education, and on young people facing global change.

Héloïse Leloup is a post-doctoral researcher at INRAE (National Research Institute for Agriculture, Food and the Environment), within the AGIR (Agroecology, Innovations, and Territories) unit, France. Her research focuses on the transformation of farmers' practices in the face of changes in their environment.

Olivier Lepiller is a researcher at CIRAD, Montpellier (France), Montpellier Interdisciplinary Center on Sustainable Agri-food Systems – Social and nutritional sciences (MoISA). Olivier holds a PhD in sociology (University of Toulouse Jean Jaurès, France).

Jessica Pereira Garcia is a PhD student at the Center for Sustainable Development at the University of Brasilia (Brazil). She holds a master's degree in Environment and Rural Development from the University of Brasília and undergraduate degree in Forestry Engineering from the University of Brasília (2013).

Marlène Perignon is a research engineer in nutrition and public health at INRAE (National Research Institute for Agriculture, Food and the Environment), UMR MoISA (Montpellier Interdisciplinary Centre on Sustainable Agri-Food Systems) in Montpellier (France). Her research focuses on nutritional security and sustainable diet.

Ophélie Roudelle is a research assistant at the UNESCO Chair in World Food Systems at L'Institut Agro Montpellier, France. She holds an MSc in social sciences and food studies, Toulouse University, France.

Denis Sautier is a researcher in agri-food economics at CIRAD (Agricultural research for development) in Montpellier, France since 1991. His work deals with food systems, focusing on localized agri-food systems, land-based food labelling and Geographical Indications. He worked for 7 years in Latin America and 6 years in Vietnam on markets and agriculture linkages for cities.

Nguyen Thi Sau is a researcher at the Fruit and Vegetable Research Institute (FAVRI) in Economics and Marketing Department in Hanoi (Vietnam).

She holds a master's in Economics and her major is market, value chain, and consumption. Recently, she is actively involved in new research topics related to digital transformation, circular economics, and consuming food away from home.

Nguyen Thi Tan Loc is the Head of the Economics and Marketing Department at the Fruit and Vegetable Research Institute (FAVRI) in Hanoi, Vietnam. She holds a PhD in Agricultural Economics and has 30 years of experience in this sector. She has experience in researching fruit and vegetable value chains and proposing interventions to upgrade the chain.

Élodie Valette is a geographer and a senior researcher at CIRAD (French Agricultural Research for Development) in Montpellier (France). Her main research works have addressed territorial development and the rural–urban interface in France and in the Mediterranean. She is the coordinator of the Urbal project.

Amélie Wood is a PhD candidate in political science at CIRAD, Montpellier (France), Montpellier Interdisciplinary Center on Sustainable Agri-Food Systems – Social and Nutritional Sciences (MoISA), and at Université Gustave Eiffel, LISIS, Marne-la-Vallée (France). She works on public health nutrition policies in Sub-Saharan Africa, evidence-informed decision-making and agnogenic practices.

Tainá Bacellar Zaneti is a professor at the University of Brasília (UnB) at the Center for Excellence in Tourism (CET), Brazil.

Giacomo Zanolin is a tenure assistant professor in human geography at the University of Genoa (Department of Educational Sciences), Italy, and a PhD in Cultural Heritage and Environment. His work focuses on tourism in protected areas and rural spaces, geo-literary representations, and didactics of geography.

Acknowledgments

Urbal (N° 1507-200 AF; N° FC 2015–2440, N° FDNC Engt 00063479) was supported under the 'Thought for Food' Initiative of Agropolis Foundation (through the 'Investissements d'avenir' programme, reference number ANR-10-LABX-0001-01'), Fondazione Cariplo and Daniel & Nina Carasso Foundation. For further information, please refer to: www.urbalfood.org.

Our warm thanks to all the researchers and practitioners around the world who were involved in the Urbal project from 2018 to 2023. This book would not have been possible without their enthusiasm, ingenuity, and attention to detail.

In particular, the editors and authors would like to thank Nonta Libbrecht-Carey and her brilliant work translating and reviewing the book. Finally, special thanks to Nicolas Bricas who initiated the project.

1 Mapping change

The Urbal approach

Élodie Valette, Alison Blay-Palmer, Olivier Lepiller and Amanda Di Battista

1.1 Introduction

This book describes the Urbal (Urban Driven Sustainable Food System Innovations) research approach that was developed by a multidisciplinary, international team of food system researchers and experts between 2018 and 2023. The Urbal research project, supported by the Agropolis, Carasso, and Cariplo Foundations' *Thought for Food* initiative,[1] provided the time and resources necessary to explore how innovations can produce short-term changes and longer-term impacts on multiple dimensions of urban food system sustainability. Urbal enables and activates a better understanding of the flows in food system innovation processes and the impediments and enablers to increasingly sustainable food systems.

Urbal emerged as a response to the multiple challenges that arise from industrial food systems that generate enormous exploitation, externalities, and cascading socio-environmental damage. On top of increasing food insecurity, environmental degradation, and inadequate livelihoods (Biovision Foundation for Ecological Development & IPES-Food, 2020; FAO et al., 2022; Lacerda et al., 2020), climate change, the COVID-19 pandemic, and conflicts including the war in Ukraine add extra strain for those already marginalized by this globalized food system (Moustier et al., 2023; Lang & McKee, 2022; Blay-Palmer et al., 2021; Kaiser et al., 2021). Confronting these challenges demands a multi-scale approach that addresses multiple sustainability issues at the same time so polyvalent solutions can help improve food and nutrition security, livelihoods, and preserve biocultural diversity, among other co-benefits (Tribaldos & Kortetmäki, 2022; Hebinck et al., 2021).

Calls from policy and decision-makers to understand food systems at the regional scale are growing, with a recognition of the need for evidence to support the transformation of the existing global food system to one that is more regionally focused and sustainable. In the fall of 2022, the United Nations Committee on World Food Security set its 2-year goals and directions for its High-Level Panel of Experts on Food Security and Nutrition. These goals and directions focus on creating more regional food systems through improved urban, peri-urban, and rural linkages with a mandate to "provid[e] independent,

DOI: 10.4324/9781003285441-1

comprehensive and evidence-based analysis, and elaborat[e] its studies through a scientific, transparent and inclusive process" (High Level Panel of Experts, 2023, np). The Convention on Biodiversity COP15 meeting in December 2022 and the resulting Global Biodiversity Framework (GBF) which includes 23 targets and associated indicators further demonstrates the need to monitor and map out food system changes and impacts. Urbal can contribute to developing and tracking regionally relevant evidence about meaningful change brought about through more sustainable food systems, including agricultural and ecosystem biodiversity, improved livelihoods, and increasing gender equity, all included in the GBF.

Urbal's urban focus is also important given the fast pace and extent of urbanization. While urbanization can be a challenge for future sustainability given the complexity of urban spaces, it can also open up opportunities for solutions. Key questions in applying Urbal are whether existing innovations are broad enough or too narrow to bring about food system transformation within urban regions and how public policy can enable sustainable food system transitions. This can be particularly important when local city authorities are increasingly involved in developing food policies to support more sustainable food systems (Moragues-Faus & Morgan, 2015). It is also important to understand when and how food system innovations result in significant and/or unintended consequences for urban and social landscapes and to note that change is not always positive, intentional, or governable.

Attention to systems is equally relevant for sustainability where the inherent complexity means that solutions often only address one dimension of sustainability. A uni-dimensional approach can result in unanticipated conflicts or require trade-offs with other sustainability dimensions. For example, direct sales from producers to consumers through farmers' markets can eliminate the need for distributors so that producers earn more revenue while consumers may pay lower prices. However, from an environmental perspective, direct sales don't guarantee pesticide-free food production, and from an economic perspective it may adversely affect the viability of livelihoods for distributors who work between the farmer and retail spaces. Mapping impacts can help us understand how innovation contributes to sustainability by analysing these complex interactions that result in positive outcomes as well as identify areas for improvement.

This introductory chapter describes the key components of the Urbal approach and provides collective insights from the case studies, called Urban Food Innovation Labs (UFILS), which helped to test and refine this approach. It was written using many internal and publicly available resources developed and gathered during the Urbal process from 2018 to 2023, including author participation in workshops and interviews, participant exit surveys, internal Urbal webinars and meetings, training workshops, and key reflections from the chapters in this book. The subsequent chapters focus on developing the Urbal process and lessons learned. Chapter 2 describes how Urbal was developed across all the 16 UFILs (Figure 1.1) and highlights lessons learned from the

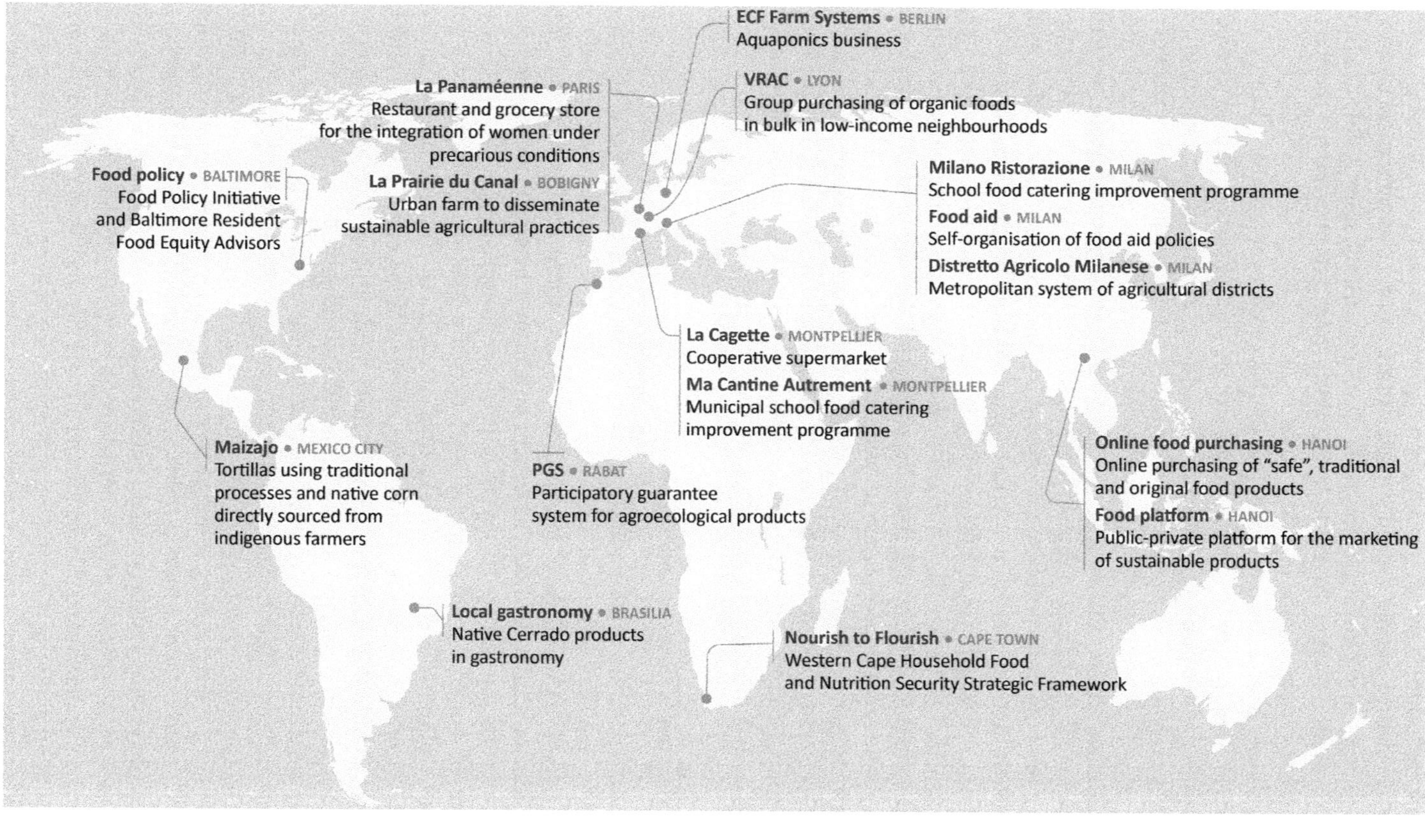

Figure 1.1 Map of all 16 Urban Food Innovation Labs (UFILs).

research including how, by working on the ground with communities, Urbal was developed to enable a deeper understanding of governance, food system supply chains, and consumer practices. Starting with Chapter 3, 8 UFILS out of 16 present insights from their adoption and adaptation of the Urbal approach for their specific context.

The book is structured according to the three over-arching themes that guided the research project and were used, as relevant, to organize, consider and report our findings: (1) consumer practices, (2) value chain organization, and (3) governance. Explicitly differentiating the three themes helped ensure there was a cross section of case studies from different sources. Given the interconnectedness that is inherent to food systems, UFIL missions were nevertheless obviously found to overlap in many cases, so drawing clear thematic lines was not possible in several cases. Chapters 3–5 present three case studies which focus on initiatives that aim to transform consumers' practices, from social gastronomy in Brasilia and Mexico City (Chapters 3 and 4) to school canteens in Montpellier (Chapter 5). Chapters 6–8 explore various innovations focused on value chain organization, from the impact of the use of short food supply chains in the school food system in Milan (Chapter 6) to that of e-commerce in Hanoi (Chapter 7) and that of a private urban farm in Berlin (Chapter 8). Chapters 9 and 10 focus on governance innovations in Milan (Chapter 9) and Cape Town (Chapter 10). The book concludes with a discussion about applying Urbal as a monitoring and tracking tool (Chapter 11).

1.2 The possibilities in applying Urbal

While questions of sustainable food system assessment have been addressed elsewhere (see Blay-Palmer et al., 2019), this work has focused mainly on developing indicators to measure urban food system sustainability. Many of these approaches are time- and cost-intensive and cannot be easily adopted by local authorities or innovators to better inform decision-making processes. In the absence of accessible tools to support decision-making, policymakers may engage in planning without a clear idea of their context and/or the impacts they can expect from food systems innovations (Callon et al., 2001). To address this gap, Urbal offers a simple, participatory methodology that fosters learning in the context of public policy and improved sustainability.

This qualitative, participatory evaluation approach can help build consensus, empower stakeholders, and create agency to support actors as they strive to increase sustainability (Ciaccia et al., 2019; Ceasar et al., 2017). Urbal uses a participatory research approach as it enables community members to identify the outputs, barriers, and enablers of change and impacts on their food system. This approach builds on the foundations of impact pathway assessment, allowing the identification of pathways for action that are relevant to stakeholders (Tribaldos et al., 2020) and that can reach across scales. As an evolving, field-tested approach, Urbal can help innovators, policymakers, researchers, and funders understand how urban innovation unfolds in place-specific, sustainable food systems (Lever et al., 2022; Rees 2019; Sonnino et al., 2016). By mapping the pathways of sustainability from the possible five dimensions—governance, health, environment, socio-cultural, and economic—the enablers and barriers to sustainable innovation can be made more apparent, helping to activate the benefits of using a systems approach (Hebinck et al., 2021; Gliessman, 2013). As a whole, Urbal can support the decision-making process undertaken by organizations and funders and the creation of policy and programmes by policymakers.

Following the initial development of the Urbal approach, it was tested in 16 UFILs, including 1 in each of Baltimore, Berlin, Brasilia, Cape Town, Lyons, Mexico City, Rabat; 2 in Hanoi, Montpellier, and Paris; and 3 in Milan. To ensure that the approach is widely accessible and adopted, a free, detailed, and adaptable Urbal guide and resource toolkit is available online at http://urbalfood.org.

1.3 The Urbal process: A participatory impact pathway analysis

The Urbal approach builds on theory of change and impact pathway assessment. Impact pathway maps have been used and refined for decades, emerging from and alongside other assessment and project management resources such as theory of change, project management tools, and causal modelling concepts and tools. Impact pathway maps were originally created to assess agricultural development projects (Padilla, 2002; Thornton et al. 2017) and initially developed to map out how research projects unfolded and what researchers observed about the impact of their work. In the early 2000s, ex-post impact pathway maps were developed to assess project impacts in complex circumstances (Douthwaite et al., 2003) and used to evaluate agricultural research in response to increasing pressure from funders to provide evidence of social impact (Springer-Heinze et al., 2003). Building on this work, CIRAD, the French Agricultural Research Centre for International Development, launched the ImpresS (IMPact of RESearch in the South) project in 2011 to assess the impact of public institutional research on innovation. ImpresS used a participatory approach to get answers to questions about the value of agricultural research through 13 projects that were either completed or in process (Hainzelin et al. 2017; Faure et al., 2020). ImpresS created impact pathway maps to describe how research impeded or supported the emergence of an innovation, uncovering where power imbalances existed in the process. Urbal takes up and refines the tools developed by ImpresS and others by expanding the focus from assessing academic research to creating tools for innovators working within food systems. These tools can be used to understand and improve sustainability changes and impacts of their work.

Urbal builds on and contributes to these approaches by providing a qualitative and participatory approach and a suite of tools to help innovators, policymakers, funders, academics, and practitioners improve the sustainability of an innovation. The aim of the Urbal approach is to help disentangle the chain of actions and strategies that push an innovation towards or away from sustainability. Urbal invites a diversity of actors to co-design impact pathway maps that make explicit the changes and impacts of innovations on sustainability dimensions. Impact pathway maps identify three key types of information about an impact: (1) the actual changes produced by the innovation on sustainability; (2) how changes are generated by innovation activities; and (3) the ways that actions and sustainability are interconnected, from short-term changes (outputs) to medium-term (outcomes) and to long-term changes (impacts). The approach therefore assesses not only the intended and unintended impacts on sustainability but also the pathways that lead to change, in some cases addressing multiple scales from the local to the global. It is important to understand that these pathways are not necessarily linear and are often winding or circuitous. There can also be divergence between the various changes and pathways as to how the innovations contribute to different sustainability dimensions. As such, Urbal focuses primarily on the process of change rather than the final result and does not measure the innovation's impact. Impact pathway maps can help identify positive and negative feedback loops as well as unforeseen changes, trade-offs, and contradictions between pathways, which can be particularly relevant when examining complex sustainable food systems.

1.4 A 3+1-step approach

Urbal helps answer one central question: what are the actual changes that result from the innovation? To address this question, Urbal unfolds as a three-step methodology, with an optional fourth step. Step 1 is dedicated to the collection of background information through interviews with key informants that help to raise awareness about the innovation, document the context, develop a timeline and network diagram for the innovation, and in some cases, draft a preliminary impact pathway map. In Step 2, a participatory workshop is organized with practitioners and experts to understand the innovation and map the pathways of activities through changes to impacts. Step 3 offers the opportunity to reflect on the outputs from Step 2 during another workshop or meeting according to needs and constraints. Finally, Step 4 is an optional step that extends the impact pathway maps developed during the workshop to specify indicators to measure and, perhaps, track change over time (see Chapter 11).

This 3+1-step approach was undertaken in various forms in the 16 UFILs over 3 years. These first three steps were outlined at the beginning of the research project in 2018. As the research project developed, we adapted the thematic foci, the terms of reference and the details of how to use the Urbal approach. While we provide an exemplary UFIL process in Box 1.1 that features the work undertaken in Ma Cantine Autrement (MCA) in Montpellier (see also Chapter 5), other UFILs and their learnings are presented in the subsequent chapters of this book.

Box 1.1 Ma Cantine Autrement (MCA)

Ma Cantine Autrement (MCA) was exceptionally well suited to engage in and actively use the Urbal approach. The enabling conditions included a clear request from the local authority in charge of the MCA programme for a long and thorough evaluation; the active and committed participation of faculty and graduate students at CIRAD and the active and thoughtful contributions from people working at MCA. The Fact that MCA operates in Montpellier, where the researchers live and work also made this UFIL more robust and iterative. As a result, the MCA research extended the Urbal approach beyond original expectations, and, in some cases, facilitated revisions to the Urbal approach in time to share with other UFIL, especially the Lyons, Paris, and Mexico projects.

Notable insights from MCA include the need to:

- clearly identify relevant and meaningful activities from the interview process and use these to animate the workshop. As a key informant from MCA explained in the exit interview,

  > During the workshop we used the chronogram and the map we made during the workshop in Step 1, because at that time we mapped all the activities of innovation, and also different actors/ stakeholders. In step 1 we had to describe very precisely all the activities of the innovation, and identify all the actors.

- Distinguish between *outputs, or direct effects*, and *outcomes* as the intermediate changes from the innovation. As noted in Chapter 5 (the MCA chapter), outcomes help spread activities to more actors than direct outputs. Outcomes result in positive changes but also some (un) avoidable negative changes. The unavoidable changes often result as trade-offs from implementing the innovation. For example, there was an increased workload for staff at MCA as they prepared more meals from scratch that, in turn, required pay adjustments for staff. This effect, among others, needed to be taken into account if this innovation is adopted in other places. *Impacts* are long-term shifts in sustainability as a result of the innovation such as policy changes. There are practical considerations during workshops where it can be fairly straightforward to determine "changes" or "effects" while it is more challenging to locate them on the causal chain as, for example, direct or indirect changes. This distinction between three possible effects produced by an innovation is a key contribution from the MCA UFIL and consistent with classic distinction made in the impact pathway literature (Hainzelin et al., 2016, 2017). As the Urbal approach explores the sustainability dimensions for each activity, MCA researchers and participants suggested that the sub-dimensions be clearly specified and made consistent as much as possible to improve the clarity and readability of the IP.

- The final recommendation from MCA researchers is the opportunity to

> …identify the *brakes and enablers along the IP*, and classify them into: i) *conditions for success* (required to reach the expected impact), ii) *impact facilitators* (not necessary to reach the impact but favourable to its achievement), and iii) *brakes* (i.e. factors that limit the efficacy/performance of the program).
>
> (Chapter 5, p. 92)

There is also the need to distinguish between the conditions needed for success and others that are facilitators but not required, "and to identify if they are *context-related, material or organisational inputs*" (Chapter 5, p. 97). As relevant, with respect to the *outputs and outcomes step*, MCA notes the importance to be clear about,

> which group of actors these effects occur, and to classify them in *positive or negative effects*. In addition, negative effects should be classified as *"avoidable" or "unavoidable" effects*, in order to subsequently identify how the first could be avoided, and how the second could be compensated.
>
> (Chapter 5, p. 97)

While providing valuable insights, MCA is not universally representative as other innovations come to the process with various capacities. In other cases, this level of precision may not be possible or even desirable as the impact pathway mapping process may be more exploratory.

Social dimensions, such as food access and equity, were a foundational component in the development of specific tools for each step in the Urbal method, including actor network diagrams, interview questions, guidelines for choosing and engaging with participants, and impact maps. Urbal's participatory approach helps to ensure that the social dimensions of sustainability are incorporated throughout the process, especially during the co-creation of impact pathway maps in Step 2. While the extent of participation in the Urbal process varied from one UFIL to another depending on the resource availability, capacity, and project goals in each context, overall it was broadly inclusive of key actors implicated and affected by the innovation process. While the overarching Urbal approach itself was developed prior to the research in each lab, it was modified based on input from the various UFILs over the course of the project. The emergent and adaptive nature of the Urbal approach facilitated increased consideration on social innovation in UFILs where the social dimensions of sustainability were not a key consideration at the outset of the project (see Berlin UFIL, Chapter 8).

1.4.1 Step 1: The context

Step 1, as the foundational basis for the Urbal approach, begins with a literature review to provide a context for the innovation and the impact pathway map in Step 2. This includes grey literature and academic sources where applicable to ground the UFIL innovation in both theory and practice. The literature review provides the information necessary to craft effective questions for interviews with innovators and other stakeholders about the development of the innovation and helps to make decisions about the workshop. General categories of questions put to key informants include the following: (1) Was there a clearly defined innovation statement at any point in the process?; (2) How was the challenge defined as an innovation problem?; (3) Was sustainability a consideration?; and (4) How did the innovation develop over time into a range of defined activities meant to directly or indirectly propose alternatives to the dominant food system's regular activities? In general, UFILs interviewed between 4 and 10 people, including innovators and stakeholders representing different stages of the process and experts to help understand the different aspects of sustainability and the larger context.

The interview results typically described the mission and activities of the innovation and enabled the creation of a case description, timeline, actors network map, list of activities created by the innovation and, sometimes, a draft impact pathway map. A key goal was to produce knowledge useful for: (1) the Urbal workshop; (2) innovation stakeholders to help them understand and promote their innovation; and (3) decision-makers and other supporting actors to help them make informed decisions about the innovation.

It is important to note that the Urbal approach—including the interviews in Step 1—is not intended to question innovation objectives, values, drivers for action, or future directions. Rather, the aims are to uncover the actual contribution of the innovation to the various dimensions of sustainability, to build reflexively from these observations, and to identify the various changes and impacts produced by the innovation activities. The interviews and other Step 1 activities provide the context needed to plan and conduct an effective workshop in Step 2.

1.4.2 Step 2: The workshop

The findings from Step 1 create interest, awareness, and understanding about the innovation and help to generate more support for the Urbal initiative. As the key activity of Step 2 of the Urbal approach, the workshop builds on this momentum using a participatory exercise that draws on the collective intelligence to enable discussion about the innovation processes and pathways that lead to changes. The workshop may look very different in different contexts, but it should provide the time and space for key stakeholders and experts to engage in co-creation of impact pathway maps that help to uncover the changes, impacts, enablers, and barriers for selected innovation activities. More information about planning and facilitating the workshop can be found in Chapters 3 through 10 and in the Urbal guide and toolkit. The workshop provides many other benefits including gathering community support for the innovation and capacity-building that, in some cases, can ultimately lead to a Community of Practice.

1.4.3 Step 3: Sharing results

The third step in the Urbal approach provides the opportunity to consolidate the findings from Steps 1 and 2 and share these back to the participants and other stakeholders. Since knowledge sharing goals and capacity are much variable across contexts, Step 3 is the least prescribed step in the Urbal approach. As a result, the UFILs described in this book each found a unique and context-specific way to report their findings from their engagement in the Urbal process back to their communities. In some cases, UFILs prepared reports that were shared directly with key stakeholders (e.g., Berlin, Chapter 8) while in others, UFILS established new relationships and adopted the Urbal approach as part of on-going evaluation (e.g., Cape Town, Chapter 10 and MCA, Chapter 5). These reports are available at http://urbalfood.org.

1.4.4 Step 4: Indicators

Urbal can provide a jumping off point for identifying place-specific metrics based on existing indicators (e.g., Milan Urban Food Policy Pact, Sustainable Development Goals, etc.) or support the creation of new initiatives (see Chapter 11 for a more detailed discussion). Impact pathway maps can be used to community-relevant indicators that can help better align global, regional, and local priorities.

Given the policy/decision-maker interest in indicators, Urbal can provide both the inclusive relationships and tools necessary for an iterative process to develop and refine indicators and use them to monitor changes and impacts over time. As observed in Chapter 11, "practitioners can identify metrics that embrace complexity and specificity of where they work and are making change, so the results are place-specific" (pp. 225). Equally important, Urbal provides the local knowledge and relationships needed to develop relevant indicators for sustainability changes and impacts. While it can be difficult to operationalize meta-indicators and there are challenges in moving between scales, indicators developed using Urbal may offer an important opportunity to benchmark, monitor, and compare innovation over time. That said, there are challenges in moving between scales and it can be difficult to operationalize meta-indicators.

1.5 Considerations when using Urbal

The trial phase for Urbal allowed the researchers to identify some key considerations for people using Urbal. These include Urbal as a flexible and adaptable approach, power asymmetries, the value of engaging with experts, as well as place-based considerations, sustainability dimensions in the context of food systems, innovation, and social innovation (see Chapter 2).

1.5.1 Urbal as a flexible, adaptable approach

Urbal is flexible in many ways and, as a result, it has been, and can be, applied to a variety of innovations. We also expect that Urbal can be used in other circumstances including monitoring and tracking changes and impacts over time (Chapter 11). What is possible depends on stakeholder needs, the time available, the result expected, and the capacity for organizing participatory meetings, among other considerations. Given its flexibility, Urbal can be carried out very quickly or more extensively, researchers can be included or not at all, final results may be formalized as a report or utilized in more informal ways, and key findings may be communicated to the general public or only used internally. All this depends on the initial reasons for using Urbal, the organizational needs and capacity, and on budgetary, time, and organizational constraints.

The relevance of Urbal for diverse circumstances became more evident in the last phase of Urbal. As the project wound down, the scope of UFILs expanded to include practitioner led UFILs where project leads were willing to apply the Urbal approach to their own innovation with little help from researchers. These UFILS each offered a unique opportunity to live-test the Urbal approach with great success. The results confirmed the possibility to adapt the method to the particular needs and constraints of UFILS. In the case of one of the UFILs in Paris, la Panaméenne, the impacts were distinguished according to the type of social impact on different public participants enabling the results to be refined with precision. In this case, as well as in the UFIL in Lyons, researchers were only involved in the process to explain the steps and answer questions, while the practitioners selected the interview questions and innovation activities to be mapped based on their interests and needs vis-à-vis the assessment. In the case of the other UFIL in Paris, Bobigny, preliminary impact pathway maps were merged with those produced during the workshop resulting in a very rich summary map. In the UFIL in Lyons, every decision about applying the methodology, particularly those related to the workshop, including appropriate participants and the innovation activities selected for building the impact pathway maps, was discussed collectively by the team of innovators to better fit the expectations of the evaluation.

1.5.2 Taking power asymmetries into account

It is crucial to consider power relationships when selecting participants for the workshop and work to avoid power asymmetries where one or a few voices dominate the conversation at the expense of others (Gray et al., 2022). Flexibility and reflexivity are also key to successful engagement using the Urbal approach. It is crucial to the production of relevant impact pathway maps that all voices are included in the discussion and a concerted effort must be made to include everyone who has been either directly or indirectly impacted by the innovation. And, as participation does not equal inclusion, it is critical that participants feel they can provide feedback and input throughout the process so that their voices are heard, and they have the opportunity to build additional capacity through engagement. In practice, this may require more than one workshop and/or breakout sessions during the workshop to provide opportunities for all participants to express their perspectives and ideas. For example, it may be difficult for new members to speak honestly if innovation leaders are in their group and organizing breakout groups can allow more open conversations. A mix methods approach can also help. For example, it is possible to conduct interviews with more/less vocal people followed by a workshop that might be more stakeholder focused. Interviews can supplement the workshop results for those who might either dominate a workshop or be too intimidated to participate. Clear, plain language that avoids jargon can also help participants feel engaged. As all knowledge and experiences should be treated as equally valuable and valid, lived experience, scientific knowledge, and policymaker contributions need to be given the same consideration.

More generally, engaging participants and ensuring their free and inclusive participation might be a challenge, as participatory approaches might not be commonly used and/or encouraged by the authorities (see Hanoi, Chapter 7). Language issues should also be addressed. In the UFIL in Brasilia, Brazil (Chapter 3), communication challenges arose in Step 2 as workshop as not all participants spoke the same language with the same fluency, and some could not read or write. To make the workshop as inclusive as possible, the UFIL leaders adapted the process accordingly:

> Although they [workshop participants] speak and understand Portuguese, some of the participants from traditional populations express themselves more easily in their own languages. For this reason, guiding questions were pre-established by the researchers and organized into four impact pathways: social inclusion, economic justice, nutritional aspects

> and environmental dimension. In order to ensure full engagement of all participants, the food system actors were invited to answer questions orally and interact with others in the workshop. Video and sound recordings were collected for the production of a summary video and the audio recordings were transcribed for content analysis.
>
> (Chapter 3, pp. 42)

Concerns around language barriers to full participation in the Urbal process reinforce the importance of inclusion and the need to attend to power asymmetries based on people's capacity to engage in participatory processes. While there was a very explicit effort made from the start of the research to be as inclusive as possible across all UFILs, most UFIL teams were working together for the first time and the trust-based relationships required for participatory research processes to excel were in their initial stages. Accordingly, in some cases the research results may not reflect the needs of all the actors being affected by the innovation.

1.5.3 The value and role of experts and facilitators to the Urbal process

An expert facilitator can enable an inclusive-, smoothly-run workshop by making people feel comfortable, keeping discussions on topic, and creating the space where all participants can express their perspectives, including any concerns or negative observations they may want to share. Sustainability experts, as participants to the workshop, can help provide context for the innovation, insight on the sustainability dimensions and other research, raise gaps or missing questions, and provide support in the dialogues.

Experts in various capacities, not necessarily academics, helped to streamline the Urbal process and uncover important information with participants. As we developed the Urbal approach, especially in the UFILs where core Urbal academics were involved in the interviews and workshops, the findings about the Urbal process were clear and easily interpreted (Box 1.1). In other cases, the results from interviews and workshops were not so obvious and their interpretation required consultation with academic and community leaders. The role of researchers as experts in applying the Urbal approach has varied substantially and we expect this trend to continue as Urbal is adopted more widely. For several reasons including the amount of time available for case studies, the expressed needs by UFIL leaders, and the type of expected outputs, the Urbal approach was tested in multiple UFILs and exceeded the initial expectations about impact pathway maps for Urbal (e.g., MCA and their elaborate maps), or was applied in a shorter period of time than anticipated (e.g., UFILs in Paris and Lyon). In the case of MCA (Box 1.1), there was important iteration between practice and theory by adding insights from the academic literature to the Urbal process. During the analysis phase, great effort was made to ensure interpretations were true to the intentions of workshop participants.

The UFIL in Cape Town also benefited from the deep knowledge of academic experts with the credibility to both provide information and lead the Urbal consultation process. This meant that

> When the Nourish to Flourish [the key document that was part of the governance innovation] process started its final phase, that of building the Western Cape Western Cape Food and Nutrition Working Group, URBAL researchers were asked to play a role in the Working Group as independent specialists. Not only were voices from the URBAL researchers included in the process, the figures and tables derived from the methodology were key tools used to build consensus, to shift overly simplistic views, and to demonstrate the long-term evolution of the process.
>
> (Chapter 10, pp. 207)

These examples point to the role of various experts including academic, researchers, and practitioners in facilitating various iterations of Urbal. Accordingly, the results differ based on the expectations and processes adopted and developed by each group, and this flexibility is a hallmark of the Urbal approach. And while experts can help, the UFILs in Paris and Lyons were undertaken successfully by community members on their own.

1.6 Conclusions: The benefits of using Urbal

Given the flexibility and adaptability of Urbal, it is no surprise the benefits of using the approach varied from one innovation and UFIL to another. For stakeholders in urban-driven innovations across the UFILs—including producers, processors, commercial businesses, consumers, citizens, environmentalists, or officials working in government—the Urbal process provided valuable insights about innovation processes and how the changes and impacts on sustainability dimensions emerged from the innovation. Urbal also resulted in the creation of several resources including reports and diagrams that can be used by the organization to be more strategic about the innovation pathways and enable deeper understanding of the innovation process. These materials can also enable clearer communications with others, including funders, policy and decision-makers, and the public. In some cases, the process of creating innovation impact pathway maps contributed to the development of a local food system sustainability network and emergence of as some form of a Community of Practice (CoP) to support the innovation as it grew and changed (see MCA Chapter 5 and Cape Town Chapter 10) (Mohtar & Lawford, 2016; Wenger & Snyder, 2000).

For policymakers, Urbal provides a step-by-step process and related tools to help create a deeper, evidence-based understanding about existing and proposed urban food innovations, including useful insights for the development of programmes and policies. We expect that improved insights about the actual contribution of innovations to the sustainability of food systems could be a valuable asset in the conceptual development of local food policies that promote and foster innovations in an integrated way (Moragues-Faus & Morgan, 2015). For researchers, Urbal has expanded what is understood about the interactions between urban food system innovations and sustainability dimensions, and the extent to which innovations build towards more sustainable food systems (Blay-Palmer et al., 2022). For funders, Urbal offers a way to assess projects and the extent to which and how they create sustainable changes. The insights from Urbal can also enable more evidence-based and strategic decisions for a range of innovators and organizations (Faure et al., 2020). As demonstrated by the UFILs presented in this book, the flexibility of Urbal allows it to be adapted to the unique constraints and opportunities in each urban food system innovation. The experiences in the UFILs also demonstrate the ability of Urbal to make relationships more dynamic, build capacity, and envision future directions for Urbal users. And, as discussed in the subsequent chapters, each UFIL also provides insights into how to improve Urbal.

Note

1 The project Urbal (N° FC 2015/2440 • N° FDNC Ellgt 00063479) was supported under the Thought for Food⁰ Initiative of Agropolis Fondation, Fondazione Cariplo and Daniel & Nina Carasso Foundation, through the "Investissements d'avenir" programme with reference number ANR-10-LABX-0001-01.

References

Biovision Foundation for Ecological Development & IPES-Food. (2020). *Money flows: What is holding back investment in agroecological research for Africa?* [Executive Summary]. Biovision Foundation for Ecological Development & International Panel of Experts on Sustainable Food Systems. www.agroecology-pool.org/MoneyFlowsReport

Blay-Palmer, A., Conaré, D., Meter, K., Di Battista, A., & Johnston, C. (Eds.). (2019). *Sustainable food system assessment: Lessons from global practice* (1st ed.). Routledge. https://doi.org/10.4324/9780429439896

Blay-Palmer, A., Halliday, J., Santini, G., Carey, J., Malec, R., Taguchi, M., van Veenhuizen, R., & Young, L. (2022). The city region food system: Broadening space for urban governance. In *Routledge handbook of urban food governance*, Edited by Ana Moragues-Faus, Jill K. Clark, Jane Battersby, Anna Davies. Routledge.

Blay-Palmer, A., Spring, A., Nelson, E., & Valette, E. (2021). Food systems—Beyond the buzz. *Rural 21*, *56*(3), 7–9. https://www.rural21.com/fileadmin/downloads/2021/en-03/rural2021_03-S07-09.pdf

Callon, M., Lascoumes, P., & Barthe, Y. (2001). *Agir dans un monde incertain: essai sur la démocratie technique*, Seuil.

Ceasar, J., Peters-Lawrence, M.H., Mitchell, V., & Powell-Wiley, T.M. (2017). The communication, awareness, relationships and empowerment (CARE) model: An effective tool for engaging urban communities in community-based participatory research. *International Journal of Environmental Research and Public Health*, *14*(11), 1422.

Ciaccia, C., Di Pierro, M., Testani, E., Roccuzzo, G., Cutuli, M., & Ceccarelli, D. (2019). Participatory research towards food system redesign: Italian case study and perspectives. *Sustainability*, *11*(24), 7138.

Douthwaite, B., Kuby, T., van de Fliert, E., & Schulz, S. (2003). Impact pathway evaluation: An approach for achieving and attributing impact in complex systems. *Agricultural Systems*, *78*(2), 243–265.

FAO, IFAD, UNICEF, WFP, & WHO. (2022). *The state of food security and nutrition in the world 2022*. FAO; IFAD; UNICEF; WFP; WHO. https://doi.org/10.4060/cc0639en

Faure, G., Blundo-Canto, G., Devaux-Spatarakis, A., Le Guerroué, J.L., Mathé, S., Temple, L., Toillier, A., Triomphe, B., & Hainzelin, E. (2020). A participatory method to assess the contribution of agricultural research to societal changes in developing countries. *Research Evaluation*, *29*(2), 158–170.

Gliessman, S. (2013). Agroecology and food system transformation. *Agroecology and Sustainable Food Systems*, *37*(1), 1–2.

Gray, B., Purdy, J., & Ansari, S. (2022). Confronting power asymmetries in partnerships to address grand challenges. *Organization Theory*, *3*(2), 26317877221098765.

Hainzelin, E., Barret, D., & Faure, G. (2016). Agriculture research in developing countries: From a" culture of promise" to a" culture of impact". ImpresS Policy Brief. CIRAD. https://agritrop.cirad.fr/583241/1/Impress%20Policy%20Brief.pdf

Hainzelin, E., Barret, D., Faure, G., Dabat, M.H., & Triomphe, B. (2017). Agricultural research in the Global South: Steering research beyond impact promises. *Perspective*, *42*, 1–4.

Hebinck, A., Selomane, O., Veen, E., De Vrieze, A., Hasnain, S., Sellberg, M., Sovová, L., Thompson, K., Vervoort, J., & Wood, A. (2021). Exploring the transformative potential of urban food. *NPJ Urban Sustainability*, *1*(1). https://doi.org/10.1038/s42949-021-00041-x

High Level Panel of Experts. 2023. About the HLPE of the United Nations food and agriculture committee on world food security. https://www.fao.org/cfs/cfs-hlpe/en

Kaiser, M., Goldson, S., Buklijas, T., Gluckman, P., Allen, K., Bardsley, A., & Lam, M.E. (2021). Towards post-pandemic sustainable and ethical food systems. *Food Ethics*, *6*(4), 1–19. https://doi.org/10.1007/s41055-020-00084-3

Lacerda, A., Hanisch, A.L., & Nimmo, E. (2020). Leveraging traditional agroforestry practices to support sustainable and agrobiodiverse landscapes in Southern Brazil. *Land*, *9*(6), 176. https://doi.org/10.3390/land9060176

Lang, T., & McKee, M. (2022). The reinvasion of Ukraine threatens global food supplies. *BMJ*, 376. https://doi.org/10.1136/bmj.o676

Lever, J., Blake, M., Newton, D., & Downing, G., 2022. Working across boundaries in regional place-based food systems: Triggering transformation in a time of crisis. *Cities*, *130*, 103842.

Mohtar, R.H., & Lawford, R. (2016). Present and future of the water-energy-food nexus and the role of the community of practice. *Journal of Environmental Studies and Sciences*, *6*, 192–199. https://doi.org/10.1007/s13412-016-0378-5

Moragues-Faus, A., & Morgan, K. (2015). Reframing the foodscape: The emergent world of urban food policy. *Environment and Planning A: Economy and Space*, *47*(7), 1558–1573.

Moustier, P., Holdsworth, M., Anh, D.T., Seck, P.A., Renting, H., Caron, P., & Bricas, N. (2023). The diverse and complementary components of urban food systems in the global South: Characterization and policy implications. *Global Food Security*, *36*, 100663.

Padilla, E. (2002). Intergenerational equity and sustainability. *Ecological Economics*, *41*(1), 69–83.

Rees, W.E. (2019). Why place-based food systems? Food security in a chaotic world. *Journal of Agriculture, Food Systems, and Community Development*, *9*(A), 5–13.

Sonnino, R., Marsden, T., & Moragues-Faus, A. (2016). Relationalities and convergences in food security narratives: Towards a place-based approach. *Transactions of the Institute of British Geographers*, *41*(4), 477–489.

Springer-Heinze, A., Hartwich, F., Henderson, J.S., Horton, D., & Minde, I. (2003). Impact pathway analysis: An approach to strengthening the impact orientation of agricultural research. *Agricultural Systems*, *78*(2), 267–285. https://doi.org/10.1016/S0308-521X(03)00129-X

Thornton, P., Schuetz, T., Förch, W., Cramer, L., Abreu, D., Vermeulen, S., & Campbell, B. (2017). *Responding* to global change: A theory of change approach to making agricultural research for development outcome-based. *Agricultural Systems*, *152*, 145–153. https://doi.org/10.1016/j.agsy.2017.01.005

Tribaldos, T., & Kortetmäki, T. (2022). Just transition principles and criteria for food systems and beyond. *Environmental Innovation and Societal Transitions*, *43*, 244–256. https://doi.org/10.1016/j.eist.2022.04.005

Tribaldos, T.M., Oberlack, C., & Schneider, F. (2020). Impact through participatory research approaches: An archetype analysis. *Ecology and Society*, *25*(3), 15.

Wenger, E.C., & Snyder, W.M. (2000). Communities of practice: The organizational frontier. *Harvard Business Review*, *78*(1), 139–146. https://hbr.org/2000/01/communities-of-practice-the-organizational-frontier

2 Urbal

A research project

Alison Blay-Palmer, Élodie Valette, Olivier Lepiller and Amanda Di Battista

2.1 The evolution of the Urbal approach and related tools: The unfolding research process

In applying principles of participatory research to Urbal, we engaged in an iterative, co-created, loosely prescribed, and much adapted research process as we worked our way towards a place-based approach for mapping the changes and impacts from sustainable food system innovation and identified the outcomes, enablers, and impediments to sustainability impacts (Ceasar et al., 2017; Ciaccia et al., 2019; Faure et al., 2020; Tribaldos et al., 2020). We tested our draft approach in 16 case study Urban Food Innovation Labs (UFILs), adapting key features of the Urbal approach to ensure that it is relevant in the greatest diversity of contexts possible (Chapter 1).

The process of developing and refining the Urbal approach was iterative and engaged with both the insights and vision of and materials developed by the core research group and the activities of the UFILs. Initially, our vision, the Urbal guide, and supporting material were developed and refined by the core research team through online and in-person meetings and a test case UFIL. This process allowed us to continuously refine the Urbal approach and add new key components and information such as: 1) reviewing interview findings to narrow the activities to be considered at the workshop as the starting point for the impact pathway map; 2) providing a clear, defined role for experts; and, 3) incorporating participatory research processes in the Urbal approach to explicitly enable social inclusion and the consideration of relative power and voice for various participants in the UFILs. Building on the work of Bricas (2017), we reviewed and expanded the dimensions and sub-dimensions for sustainable food system considerations. We also worked to ensure that Urbal is adaptable to a diversity of contexts. Throughout the process we also held online webinars for Urbal participants to present guiding material to our UFILs teams and report their research findings. Simultaneously, each UFIL conducted their own Urbal process with new insights incorporated into the general methodological research as appropriate.

Urbal was then interrupted by the COVID-19 pandemic. While some UFILs had concluded their interview process (Step 1) and workshops (Step 2), several

DOI: 10.4324/9781003285441-2

had not held public meetings and others were not yet part of the project. While this presented challenges, the onset of COVID-19 demonstrated the value of Urbal as a flexible and adaptable tool. In some cases, Urbal workshops were held online with minimal in-person interaction under these circumstances. Despite this, lively conversations and significant engagement took place online, highlighting the importance of having these discussions and opening the doors for engagement. In other cases, researchers held smaller in-person workshops that respected social distancing needs and/or conducted online focus groups and interviews. In two cases, academic researchers developed the impact pathway maps from existing data and then shared the maps for comment with innovators and practitioners.

2.1.1 *Evolving terms of reference and lessons learned from the Urbal research process*

The flexibility and iteration that is a hallmark of Urbal extended to the terms of reference for the project as they too evolved throughout the research. What became clear as the UFILs used the Urbal approach was the iteration that occurred between the steps and how, with each round, the information gained and understanding about the interaction between the innovation and sustainability deepened. For example, in Brasilia (Chapter 3) UFIL leaders used their literature review in Step 1 to determine relevant sustainability criteria for chefs and restaurants. This was then the basis to select restaurants for interviews based on their willingness to engage in sustainability and interview guides were developed and adapted to each group of key informants. Particularly notable changes in our terms of reference occurred for place-based considerations, sustainability dimensions in the context of food systems, innovation, and social innovation.

2.1.1.1 *Place-based insights*

The breadth of the case study selection themes (governance, value chain, and consumer practices) and the intended audiences (policymakers, funders, academics, and/or practitioners), makes Urbal widely relevant. This breadth also works well as a place-based approach to identify and develop relevant sustainability innovations. This proved to be the case as Urbal was trialed across the UFILs and resulted in unique findings and insights into the Urbal approach based on place-based interpretations of and alignment with Urbal. For example, in the case of Berlin (Chapter 8), the ECF-Farms had a start-up culture and goal of changing the way cities produce food but also the requirement to build a self-sustaining company that can compete in the marketplace. The openness and flexibility of the Urbal approach permitted unique findings to emerge for the ECF-Farm such as the need for more flexible regulations for specifics such as compost. At the time of the research, regulations required that fish waste be dumped so this source of nutrients was lost to the food cycle.

However, Urbal helped uncover that regulatory improvements permitting composting of the Yellow Perch fish waste from the ECF production cycle to produce usable fertilizer could help ECF become even more ecologically sustainable.

The relevance of Urbal as a useful place-specific approach also emerged for UFILs exploring the governance theme and raising important insights about the innovation to policy. In the case of the Agricultural Districts in Milan, "the existence of districts makes farmers more visible to other actors in the area, facilitating the creation of partnerships with institutions and civil society organisations in order to produce projects that develop and protect the territory" (Chapter 9, p. 183).

These particular territorial conditions allowed the UFIL participants to become active agents of change for regional and national policy as they were able to

> …reflect on the role of agricultural districts from the point of view of land governance: through the districts, farmers transcend their role as workers of the land and become protagonists of a proposal for a radical change in land use policies. The districts work to promote access to the tools and funds of the Common Agricultural Policies, provide technical support for the implementation of projects that have concrete effects on food production and distribution, and contribute to the maintenance and production of local environment and landscape. Their impact, measured [previously] from the merely econometric point of view, is still very limited and today the agricultural districts can be considered emerging actors that are playing a crucial role as innovators of metropolitan food systems governance, and forerunners of a change in progress.
>
> (Chapter 9, p. 184)

An important contribution of Urbal to the Mexico City UFIL (Chapter 4) was identifying the need to include producers in value chain considerations. Prior to Urbal, the innovators' focus was largely on food processors but engaging in the Urbal process allowed them to better understand that farmer's income is important to the viability of their supply chain, particularly as a point where interventions could increase sustainability. The Urbal approach helped uncover concerns about the fragility of relationships between food processors and producers in the region by providing a more complete picture of the supply chain and identifying possible pathways to help improve supply chain viability.

In the Cape Town UFIL (Chapter 10), the timelines developed as part of Urbal demonstrated how the different components of their project, Nourish to Flourish (N2F), aligned with and captured the iterative processes associated with the development of project outcomes. The flexibility and ease of using Urbal meant that, despite several impediments—including limited budgets, mandate disputes, contested policy and strategy development interactions, leadership changes, and conflicting views about who is responsible for food and nutrition—it was possible to get the strategy accepted. As a result of initial Urbal consultations and follow-up processes, the N2F authors were asked to present the Urbal documents to the emerging Provincial Food Systems Working Group as an external, independent review. The Urbal researchers were then asked to draft a summary version of the Urbal Project Assessment Report that further supported the N2F consultation processes. The Urbal approach and methodological process supported the needs of the N2F strategy evolution and refinement from concept through to implementation in a mutually reinforcing and beneficial iterative process. As well as providing an operational framework for N2F, groups such as the City of Cape Town Food Working Group, the Western Cape Community of Practice and the Western Cape Food Forum all used the Urbal report as both an internal working document and to support their own processes of mandate deepening.

Urbal also enabled the development of methodologies adapted to the needs of each UFIL circumstances. For example, in the Milano Ristorazione UFIL (Chapter 6) for Step 1, the researchers tailored the approach so that they conducted semi-structured interviews and meetings with only two key informants. They then developed their own network map using a grid with the interest of stakeholders along one axis and power/influence along the other axis. The impact pathway map was then adjusted by academics following the workshop as participants found it challenging to identify the impacts of the relatively new innovation. As changes from the innovation had not been in place long enough to have lasting effects, in the end, they were able to identify potential or anticipated sustainability impacts.

2.1.1.2 *Sustainability dimensions and food systems*

The Urbal project began by framing the research so it combined both food systems *and* sustainability considerations. The food systems lens means that Urbal researchers looked across the various points along the food chain to include as many aspects as possible from seed to waste heap. While the project did begin with urban innovations, applying a food systems lens also led us to broaden the geographic scope and use a more territorial/regional focus.

At the beginning of the project, we used six sustainability dimensions, including food security, nutrition, governance, environment, social-cultural, and economic dimensions (Bricas, 2017). As we moved to the end of the pilot project research phase, we collapsed nutrition and food security into one 'health' category to provide a broader dimension for food systems analysis. Accordingly, the relevant sustainability dimensions and key sub-dimensions that emerged over the course of the Urbal project are:

1) **Health**: food security (access, quality, regularity), nutrition, well-being, physical activity
2) **Governance**: transparency, power dynamics, people's participation, accountability

3) **Environment**: protection of biodiversity, renewable resources, energy efficiency, climate resilience
4) **Social-cultural**: equity, community building, confidence in the system, positive expression of social and cultural identity, culture
5) **Economic**: equity, resilience, fair work and remuneration, local economies, circularity

The sub-dimensions listed are those that arose most prominently or frequently during the course of the research. However, the above list is not intended to be normative and the identification and use of other sub-dimensions are feasible and encouraged. It is important that users of Urbal ensure that the approach meets the needs and goals for each innovation being studied.

The features of a sustainable food system may vary according to regional or territorial contexts (Chapters 3–10). To reflect place- and context-specific considerations, each UFIL used the five-dimensional diagram to define and focus on their own definition of food system sustainability so that it reflected their values and objectives.

2.1.1.3 Innovation

Beginning with the idea that innovation is an umbrella term for initiatives that result in change, we developed an innovation typology to guide how we framed the Urbal project. This typology included a range of innovation characteristics used to select the UFILs to help ensure the widest diversity of UFILs within the project. Social innovation was a key consideration as we developed the Urbal project. This focus allowed us to begin to explore whether the innovation satisfied human needs, brought about changes to social relations through process, and/or increased levels of socio-political capability and access to resources (Kirwan et al., 2013). Another parameter was the type of actors leading the innovation, including whether innovations were led by individuals from civil society, the private sector, and/or by public authorities. Next, we considered who was impacted by the innovation and whether it was linked to consumer practices, value chain organization, or governance related to urban food policies. These categories were the basis for the three research themes previously discussed. Sustainability dimensions were taken into account and, as described in the previous section, included food security, nutrition, governance, environment, social-cultural, and economic at the outset of the research. We considered the presence of participatory approaches, classifying them as high or low to begin to include equity and power considerations. To ensure that Urbal would have global appeal at the end of the project, we considered location by global region, including Europe, Northern America, Latin America, Northern Africa, Sub-Saharan Africa, and Asia. Finally, we considered the progress of the innovation, including if the innovation was at the planning stage, newly launched and experimental, fully in service, or completed and focused on the dissemination of information and results. Not surprisingly, the stage of innovation made a difference to the impact pathway mapping in that the more established the innovation, the more complex and detailed the impact pathway maps.

It is interesting to note that the innovations were not necessarily perceived as such by the innovators themselves. The purpose and vision of what was being done was sometimes unclear to the innovators, so Urbal was able to bring some precision to their processes. Other times, the innovation was a work in progress that Urbal helped fine-tune. For example, an innovation may have originated and be guided by innovators, such as in the Berlin UFIL (Chapter 8), where a private company had a clear vision for more localized, environmentally sustainable production of protein and greens. In other cases, that the innovation was less clearly specified was identified as part of the research at the outset with ideas being refined as the project evolved. This was the case of the Brasilia UFIL (Chapter 3) where the concept of sustainable gastronomy emerged as a framing research concept and was then refined more precisely as the project developed. In that case, the interview questions and the activities were easily aligned with sustainability goals as sustainability was a key consideration of the innovation at the outset. This led to the determination of specific sustainable gastronomic practices including the use of traditional food in menus and locally produced and/or organic food as well as waste minimization initiatives. The researchers also identified food activism and social inclusion as both emergent opportunities and challenges, particularly in terms of inclusion.

2.1.1.4 Social innovation

In addition to innovation as an umbrella concept, Urbal intentionally focused on different aspects of social innovation (SI). We grounded this work in Bouchard et al.'s definition of social innovation as:

> [A]n intervention initiated by social actors to fulfil an aspiration or need, provide a solution or seize an opportunity for action in order to modify social relations, transform a framework for action or propose new cultural orientations. From this perspective … social innovation aims to modify the institutional frameworks that shape relationships in society.
>
> (Bouchard et al., 2015, p. 9)

Social innovation generally involves social transformation based on the introduction of novelty into the established order. To identify UFILs engaged in a diverse range of social innovations to include in the Urbal project, we used Richez-Battesti et al.'s (2012) types for social innovations, in which social innovations can be: 1) tools to enable more responsive public policy with respect to social issues. In these cases, policy is shaped into new forms of interventions, usually based on public-private partnerships, such as the Projets Alimentaires Territoriaux in France, or, more generally, urban or territorial food policies that engage multiple actors (see Cape Town UFIL, Chapter 10, p. 189) linked to social enterprises and entrepreneurs who implement market-oriented activities that both look for profit and social impacts such as the aquaponic firm in Berlin or restaurants in Brasilia (see Chapter 8); and 2) a multi-actor collective process, emerging to respond to unsatisfied social needs by the public sector or by the market or to put into effect a desired change. This category includes the La Cagette cooperative supermarket in Montpellier (Valette et al., 2022).

SI was a key focus for the Urbal initiative from the outset. There was a deep commitment to exploring dimensions of social innovation across nearly all the UFILs. However, given the range of UFILs themes, it was not possible to uniformly apply or prioritize SI. Despite this constraint, social dimensions were highlighted wherever possible including as a key facet of sustainability. In practice, and as supported in the literature (Juan et al., 2020; Klein & Laville, 2014), the idea of social innovation varied significantly between UFILs as SI development and operations are context specific. As a result, contextual differentiation was crucial for understanding each social innovation's priorities, practices, organizational structures, and activities (Konstantatos et al., 2013). A methodological consequence is that it became clear that the Urbal approach can help identify relevant contextual elements to understand the conditions for the emergence and evolution of social innovations including elements that facilitate and constrain the activities or implementation of the innovation (Bonomelli, 2018).

2.2 Lessons and insights from UFIL research

There was significant theoretical development as we evolved the Urbal approach and, as early as in our pilot phase, participants found that engaging in the process of data gathering, impact pathway mapping, and workshop planning, participation, and facilitation helped build capacity and dialogues that strengthened organizations and networks, helped develop quick and easy impact assessments, and significantly contributed to theoretical development of the project. In addition, the UFILs provided living labs where we could test and develop the Urbal process and its application. This iterative approach helped to make a range of sustainability challenges more obvious. In practice, Urbal case studies were not just an academic exercise. They also helped the multiple UFILs identify and address hurdles and, in many cases, find new ways to deal with challenges and surface successes to build on and celebrate.

2.2.1 Sustainable food system dimensions

A systems lens offers an opportunity to grasp the kaleidoscopic shifts between people and the environment as food circles and moves from seed to table to waste (Hipel et al., 2010; Morgan et al., 2008). Urbal brought specificity to the impact pathway mapping approach in the context of sustainability and food systems combined by identifying how actual changes and impacts were the result of *sustainable* urban food system innovations. This was confirmed through the work in various UFILs. As researchers in the Cape Town UFIL observed about the impact pathway maps:

> [T]he interrelation, convergence, potential divergence between the various changes and pathways towards the different dimensions of sustainability, also build a systemic theory of change, emphasizing positive and negative feedback loops, unforeseen changes, and unforeseen contradictions between pathways, which we believe are particularly relevant to address the issue of the FSS [food system sustainability].
>
> (Chapter 10, p. 191)

Urbal helped to clarify the interconnectedness of sustainable food system dimensions as well as the need for careful assessment that helped avoid false assumptions (e.g., local equals more sustainable, Hinrichs, 2016; Born & Purcell, 2006). The combination of these two insights helped to generate realistic sustainability proposals for the future, an outcome that is of practical importance for many reasons. For example, researchers in the Milano Ristorazione (MiRi) UFIL (Chapter 6) explained that identifying logistical barriers and enablers with respect to the sustainability of the innovation allowed them to recommend concrete sustainability guidelines to be included in future contracts sent out for tender. In particular, the combination of sustainability and applying a systems lens helped them to clarify characteristics of sustainable food supply chains and how to determine ways to shorten the supply chain beyond simply geographical distance to include informational and relational proximity. Through the Urbal analysis, it was possible to identify ways logistics tenders could be used to enhance and/or monitor specific sustainability dimensions for the MiRi initiative using these three facets of sustainable food systems chains (distance, information, and relationships). These new sustainability considerations for tenders were specified as: 1) environmental, including alternative transportation options such as vehicle type; 2) food security, spelling out a commitment to regular and reliable food delivery; 3) improved social resilience through better working conditions; 4) more transparent accountability for delivery and carbon emissions; and 5) reduced inequity in the workplace. If taken up, these considerations could foster a more integrated and coherent approach to sustainable food systems.

In the Brasilia (Chapter 3) and Ma Cantine Autrement (Chapter 5) UFILs, this level of sustainability awareness focused the attention of participants on reducing food waste. In MCA, it raised the profile of reducing food waste in school canteens as part of environmental education. In Brasilia, this translated into a greater uptake of zero waste for restaurants as part of a circular economy. In the Mexico City UFIL (Chapter 4), the Urbal process helped to clarify the barriers that needed to be addressed to realize desired goals and impacts making the multiple impediments and levers more apparent and also pointed to the points in their process where intervention could be beneficial, and noted that "[t]hanks to the [Urbal] methodology, we realized that the impacts of the initiative were directed towards upstream activities rather than downstream" (Chapter 4, p. 72). Understanding how to best intervene to bring about change helped the participants in the Mexico City UFIL focus their efforts on the points in the supply chain where they could make a difference. This complemented insights into whose food security was being addressed through the innovation and the capacity to consider that producer food security was potentially being undermined as they are linked into bigger food supply chains where they have less control.

In the Cape Town UFIL (Chapter 10), Urbal helped to situate the innovations within existing policy and governance considerations making it clear that sustainability dimensions are 'co-dependent' and "contingent on societal justice, wellbeing, equity, and cohesion" (p. 189, this book) with governance mediating societal needs as they relate to ecological and consumption considerations. Using the Urbal approach in Berlin (Chapter 8) allowed for an increased understanding about the ECF Farm as a sustainable urban food system innovation and helped reveal existing and potential sustainability dimensions. In the case of Ma Cantine Autrement, the impact pathway analysis brought to light sustainability impacts for all five dimensions and allowed Ma Cantine Autrement to identify relevant, place-based sub-dimensions (see Chapter 1, Box 1.1 and Chapter 5). The impact pathway approach allowed participants to understand more about the impediments to sustainability and helped to determine ways forward including conditions to enable and multiply success. Key among these enablers were: 1) better information so people could act in an informed manner; 2) motivating and empowering staff to act in more sustainable directions; and 3) finding ways to adapt the Ma Cantine Autrement programme to scale up to the territorial level.

In the Hanoi UFIL (Chapter 7), sustainability was interpolated from the research results not only as an explicit goal, but also as a way to build trust through the creation of increasingly robust social networks. Practically, this resulted in more efficient capacity with direct phone and email links between consumers and farmers, in addition to intermittent online platforms. This in turn helped foster better working conditions as online and new on-the-ground markets provided economic support for local farmers. These new value chains also added more direct supply chains helping to build greener, more diverse and participative territorial food systems. Also, at the intersection of environmental and health considerations, these innovations helped to provide safer quality food as it was produced with fewer chemicals which also meant a lighter environmental impact due to reduced reliance on fossil fuel based chemical inputs. These results provide insights about how to reinforce local goals, for example, how to build institutional and interpersonal capacity.

The COVID-19 pandemic made many existing food system deficiencies more apparent (Blay-Palmer et al., 2020) and the experiences in some Urbal

UFILs were no exception. For example, in the Cape Town UFIL, COVID-19 led some actors to engage with and understand the multiple connections for both food and non-food, between governance and sustainability dimensions. The Urbal approach made connections between governance and food security far clearer, and the reports generated became key tools used by the enablers of Nourish to Flourish when trying to engage other departments to join the Nourish to Flourish process:

> The Urbal work also clearly demonstrated the intersections between the Nourish to Flourish strategy and elements of a sustainable food system… cross scale collaborations [between the province and CT] and mutual cooperation were clearly evident thanks to the Urbal approach… As a methodology, the Urbal process served as a unique tool to both capture these processes, while at the same time, provided great utility to the innovators themselves both as an external validation of their novel and arguably, high risk, work, but the methodology was also assimilated into their working processes to support their lobbying and consensus building process. Supporting the constant work of maintaining the authorising environment, the Urbal process of documenting, but not assessing or judging, offered a particularly powerful tool to capture unique processes, to allow innovators to expose themselves and their work without the risk of critique, and to co-produce an assessment of the innovation. In the contested and at times highly politicised areas of governance and food systems politics the ability afforded by the Urbal process enabled a robust but open assessment of the innovation. Documenting sustainable food systems is essential if others are to be able to replicate and the work of food system innovators. If this process can both document and deepen the innovation processes, this is of critical importance.
>
> (Chapter 10, p. 210)

As these examples make clear, applying a sustainable food systems lens provides a holistic entry point to understand more about the enablers and impediments to innovation. Urbal provides the guidelines to map and understand more about the related changes and impacts.

2.2.2 *Social inclusion*

Not unexpectedly given the focus on social innovation and participatory research, social inclusion was an important, common theme for UFILs. Actively engaging with social dimensions through the Urbal process-enabled several UFILs to clarify their goals, set priorities, and determine next steps. Urbal findings also contribute to the theory of socio-technical innovations by providing a more explicit consideration of social aspects helping to address one of the critiques of transition theory (Geels, 2019).

For example, in the case of Mexico City, the workshop enabled:

> learning for collective action in the context of smallholder market participation (Kruijssen et al., 2009). It helps the group to jointly defining problems, searching for and implementing solutions, and assessing the value of solutions for specific problems, in other words it participates to the social learning and allows to create a collective cognition (Koelen & Das, 2002).
>
> (Chapter 4, p. 60)

In the Brasilia UFIL (Chapter 3), Urbal helped to identify impediments including the identification of challenges faced by the chef network such as inconsistent supply from local producers and the difficulty this poses to planning and administration as chefs work to use local food in menus. The results of this uneven access to local food meant that only high-end restaurants were able to support these specialized local farmers making their inclusion in the broader food system challenging. In addition, high-end consumers seemed to prefer not to eat local, heritage foods. This further challenged chefs as they tried to educate people about sustainability through activist-oriented gastronomy.

In the Berlin UFIL (Chapter 8), they looked to increase their focus on social innovation by:

> explore [ing] how technical innovation in urban food systems can be expanded to include social dimensions in addition to environmental and economic considerations as part of a more holistic approach to sustainability. Given that the Urbal approach was designed to enable stakeholders to consider multiple sustainability dimensions concurrently, ECF helps to test and develop a more comprehensive sustainability assessment for urban food system innovations…as well as trying to understand how socio-cultural dimensions are being included by investigating the motivations and efforts provided by the ECF farm and evaluating additional steps to how these efforts could be further integrated into initiatives as part of sustainability framings.
>
> (Chapter 8, p. 144)

In the Hanoi UFIL (Chapter 7), Urbal enabled a better sense of existing obstacles and enablers which in turn helped to improve the innovations in an evidence-based way. In Ma Cantine Autrement (Chapter 5), the UFIL fostered multi-stakeholder interaction, as "[t]he workshop took place in good conditions, participants reported a good time and were unanimous on the importance of such multi-stakeholder arenas, previously non-existent, around school catering" (p. 144). This included a specific desire to develop a network between school canteens. In the Berlin UFIL (Chapter 8), the Urbal process supported a relationship between Technical University Berlin, a founding organization for ECF, and the Berlin Senate. And as discussed previously, in the Cape Town

UFIL, Urbal was taken up as an approach by the municipal and regional governments. These on-going relationships will help to embed Urbal findings and relationships as well as build capacity. As one Cape Town Respondent explained:

> An overarching philosophy behind the drafting process was a desire to not only arrive at a policy or strategy document, but to use the drafting process to build a community around what we ultimately wanted to implement.
>
> (Chapter 10, p. 199)

However, as the Cape Town UFIL notes, the Urbal approach also presented challenges in terms of social inclusion:

> This approach was not without its challenges. Unresolved dissonance remained. In the contested space that is food, opposing positions remained. Additionally, issues linked to food, but separate were frequently conflated with the food issue (such as land reform and water rights) by a number of attendees, particularly those without tenure or working in the informal sector. Additional care was taken to focus on positive actions and research that already existed, rather than re-doing the same work (R2, 2020).
>
> (Chapter 10, p. 198)

As the Urbal approach confirms, the complex and interconnected nature of food can make it challenging to determine opportunities for change that will include marginalized communities.

2.3 Challenges, opportunities, and future research

The Urbal project provides a tested approach to mapping sustainability outcomes, changes, and impacts from food systems innovation. It also results in timelines and network diagrams as well as a better sense of where the enablers and barriers exist on the path to increasing sustainability. Urbal is also easily tailored and adapted to various innovation initiatives. Combined, this offers a way to benchmark, create a vision for, plan, and even monitor change over time. As the chapter on Cape Town explains:

> The Urbal approach sought to map the impact of the Nourish to Flourish innovation and capture the emergent impact pathways. The Urbal process offered great utility as both an analytical tool in and of itself, and in the way in which outputs and outcomes of the methodology were used by research participants to give the work an afterlife… New work is emerging and the Nourish to Flourish plans are now being operationalised through explicit site level activities. This new work has been made

> easier as a result of the conversations and reflections enabled through the Urbal activities, and the utility of the Urbal approach in describing the innovation and its subsequent processes. The Nourish to Flourish document was seen as important and a small group of food system actors rallied around the strategy.
>
> (Chapter 10, p. 188)

As a multi-stakeholder participatory approach and convening tool, Urbal can help build links between otherwise siloed institutions, sectors, and actors and provide a neutral place from which to assess the progress of an innovation, as well as policies and programmes.

While the Urbal approach has many benefits, it also surfaces some questions about inclusion (Gibson et al., 2017; Gray et al., 2022). While place-based circumstances are foundational to how Urbal is interpreted and applied, the unique circumstances of each UFIL raise questions of cultural relevance. For example, in Vietnamese, the dominant language of Hanoi, there is no word for "sustainable". So, while it was possible to explore sustainability dimensions in the Hanoi UFIL (Chapter 7), the idea of sustainability as defined for this research was absent. The Hanoi chapter therefore takes on a reflexive perspective, questioning both the appropriateness of focusing on a concept as culturally specific as "sustainability", and the challenges raised by implementing a participatory approach in a strong state-driven context. As a result:

> Impact pathway maps designed during participatory workshops involving the main actors of those innovations reveal that economic efficiency, food safety, and trust are considered as the main dimensions of sustainability impacted by the e-commerce of quality food products. Those innovations do not target sustainability at large and explicitly. They rather emerge from an instrumental understanding of e-commerce as a way to improve the relationship between suppliers looking for market opportunities and consumers seeking convenient and reliable channels of provision. Environmental and ethical issues are rarely targeted *per se* by those innovations, although they might emerge as potential positive externalities. Most actors are concerned by issues pertaining to trust: the time and space lags between ordering, shipping and receiving the goods may result in poor appreciation of the products and in loss of quality; e-commerce is barely controlled by public authorities, which may allow for fraud and carelessness on both sides. Trust building is also a key issue in establishing reliable trading platforms, as shown by the Hanoi public-private platform which faced many obstacles and failures.
>
> (Chapter 7, p. 118)

While major concerns with food quality and safety exist, the key question that emerged in Hanoi was whether e-commerce could be deployed to address these concerns and if those solutions can deliver premium prices to farmers so their livelihoods were appropriately valued. The interviews and workshops revealed the difficulty in addressing food systems sustainability as a holistic and multi-dimensional concept with local actors and exposed gaps in Urbal's participatory development process. In the end, while Urbal was handed over for testing to UFILs with several key guiding foci, including the goal to address sustainability dimensions, the Hanoi UFIL makes it clear that Urbal's foundational concepts are not valid starting points in all cases.

While it is important to offer alternative approaches that future users of Urbal can draw on, each application of Urbal will be unique and so needs to develop its own approach. For example, the Ma Cantine Autrement UFIL findings point to the need to engage with stakeholders in appropriate ways:

> clearly informing the actors (children, parents, canteen staff) about the objectives and expected benefits of each activities implemented was identified as a main condition of success, what consequently underlined the key role of canteen staff—as key contacts for children and parents—in the success of the program. In the purpose of improving communication and information about the program, participants showed a strong interest for building a multi-actors committee gathering all stakeholders concerned by school canteens. The IP [impact pathway] analysis also highlighted the complementarity between different activities of [Ma Cantine Autrement], in particular for the cost of the program that was balanced by combining activities inducing higher cost with others allowing budget savings. Complementarity also stated in activities whose performance were mutually improved, or in negative effects balanced by positive effects within an activity, or between activities.
>
> (Chapter 5, p. 79)

Such a prescriptive approach would not have been useful in the governance focused UFILs such as the Agricultural Districts around Milan, or in Cape Town where creating safe discussion spaces for whatever was a key role for Urbal. Again, the importance of flexibility for the Urbal approach is apparent.

2.4 Concluding thoughts

As with the vast majority of current sustainability research, the looming question is, how can Urbal help accelerate transformation (Anderson et al., 2019; Tornaghi & Dehaene, 2020)? In the same way that a systems approach offers an integrative perspective for sustainability, such an approach can also help us understand dynamics between and across scales. Urbal provides insights into these cross-scalar transitional spaces (Bilali, 2020). As demonstrated in the Ma Cantine Autrement UFIL (Chapter 5), the Urbal approach provides insights on changes and impacts that uncover the process of food systems transformation directly addressing scaling issues. Urbal's focus on a multi-dimensional understanding of sustainability means that it can be applied at multiple scales so that "the systematic nature of interventions for the sustainability of the food system and thus, the fact that the area of impact are actually wider (sustainability dimensions of related activities are indirectly involved)" (Chapter 5, p. 79). Applying the Urbal approach also adds to what we understand about scaling as described by Moore and Riddell (2015) where: 1) *scaling up* is about impacting laws and policy; 2) *scaling out* occurs through duplication as the innovation spreads, evidence for which includes the replication or spreading of projects and programmes geographically and/or to greater numbers, or the dissemination of principles, knowledge, and experiences with adaptation to new territorial contexts; and 3) *scaling deep* is impacting cultural roots, and entails spreading cultural ideas by using stories and providing other evidence to shift norms and beliefs and can require significant investment in transformative learning and Communities of Practice. These three forms of scaling are not mutually exclusive and can help innovators shape hybrid strategies to think and act towards a wider change. The Urbal process supports the identification of the transformational opportunities that emerge from scaling including the modalities of change initiated by innovation activities as Urbal characterizes the enablers, conditions for success, impediments, and levers that make change and/or impact possible. This knowledge makes it possible to understand the diversity of the innovation impacts and helps to clarify the capacity to amplify these impacts as an opportunity to foster increased transformation.

Identifying these scaling opportunities is at the core of Urbal's focus on impact pathways, making various types of scaling more apparent. The ECF farm project in Berlin (Chapter 8) provides an example of scaling out and demonstrates how urban agriculture can be linked to its urban context and surrounding region, as well as how the ECF Farm's turnkey operations installed in other cities are connected to their communities, regions, and other places, and contribute to the dissemination of change. In the Hanoi UFIL (Chapter 7), scaling out was achieved through online platforms in various locations. In the Mexico City UFIL (Chapter 4), scaling deep occurred through the Urbal approach which raised questions about how to include actors and "raise the scope of food justice action" especially with respect to agency and power dynamics for farmers. Addressing this question is the main goal of Urbal Step 3 that offers a unique opportunity to go beyond the simple and limited assessment of the impact of isolated innovations and to reflect on the interconnections and possibilities for a wider impact on food system sustainability. Specifically, the Urbal approach can help stakeholders address questions such as how can innovations be more widely adopted, and ultimately lead to transformative impact? As such, whatever choices might be made regarding the specifics of an Urbal project, Step 3 can foster a reflexive exercise on the different forms of scaling.

Garnering the support of public authorities is a possible secondary impact of Urbal. As the case of Ma Cantine Autrement demonstrates,

> The exercise of cross-sectional analysis of Urbal results allows [us to] order and prioritise [Ma Cantine Autrement] activities according to their weight and influence on each other. This result can provide interesting knowledge for decision making for improving the sustainability trajectory that the project engenders.
>
> (Chapter 5, p. 79)

Ma Cantine Autrement sought to amplify the scope of the innovation by extending the measures taken by the programme and contributing to a spin-off via a cooperative initiative with neighbouring school canteens. This supported the goal to anchor change at the territorial scale, despite international trade agreements that limit their ability to procure local food.

In summary, Urbal enables innovators to: 1) identify multiple sustainability dimensions simultaneously across scales; 2) monitor short-, medium-, and long term indicators; and 3) develop a collective understanding of the innovation. As previously discussed, while it is challenging to include all the key actors, Urbal can result in a more balanced assessment as inclusive participation can raise both positive and negative considerations.

The results of Urbal thus invite us to think about the mechanisms, activities, and instruments, existing or to be created that can be used to ensure the short- and medium- term changes and long- impacts of innovation. The potential to use Urbal to monitor sustainability is also very promising for researchers, funders, and policymakers. As UFILs identify similar challenges, there is also the opportunity to build global Communities of Practice and create solidarity around sustainability action. Urbal can help expose spaces where change is needed and how this can happen, clarifying how innovation can contribute to the transition to more sustainable food systems.

References

Anderson, C.R., Bruil, J., Chappell, M.J., Kiss, C., & Pimbert, M.P. (2019). From transition to domains of transformation: Getting to sustainable and just food systems through agroecology. *Sustainability*, *11*(19), 5272.

Bilali, H. (2020). Transition heuristic frameworks in research on agro-food sustainability transitions. *Environment, development and sustainability*, *22*(3), 1693–1728.

Blay-Palmer, A., Carey, R., Valette, E., & Sanderson, M.R. (2020). Post COVID 19 and food pathways to sustainable transformation. *Agriculture and Human Values*, *37*(3), 517–519. https://doi.org/10.1007/s10460-020-10051-7

Bonomelli, V. (2018). Building a participative tool to map the impact pathway of urban driven innovations on food systems sustainability: How to consider specific features of social innovation? Master's thesis, Montpellier Supagro/Cirad.

Born, B., & Purcell, M. (2006). Avoiding the local trap: Scale and food systems in planning research. *Journal of Planning Education and Research*, *26*(2), 195–207.

Bouchard, M. J., Evers, A., & Fraisse, L. (2015). Concevoir l'innovation sociale: dans une perspective de transformation. *Sociologies Pratiques*, *31*(2), 9–14.

Bricas, N. (2017). Les enjeux de l'urbanisation pour la durabilité des systèmes alimentaires. In C. Brand et al. (coord.) *Construire des politiques alimentaires urbaines* (pp. 19–38). Editions Quae.

Ceasar, J., Peters-Lawrence, M.H., Mitchell, V., & Powell-Wiley, T.M. (2017). The communication, awareness, relationships and empowerment (CARE) model: An effective tool for engaging urban communities in community-based participatory research. *International Journal of Environmental Research and Public Health*, *14*(11), 1422.

Ciaccia, C., Di Pierro, M., Testani, E., Roccuzzo, G., Cutuli, M., & Ceccarelli, D. (2019). Participatory research towards food system redesign: Italian case study and perspectives. *Sustainability*, *11*(24), 7138.

Faure, G., Blundo-Canto, G., Devaux-Spatarakis, A., Le Guerroué, J.L., Mathé, S., Temple, L., Toillier, A., Triomphe, B., & Hainzelin, E. (2020). A participatory method to assess the contribution of agricultural research to societal changes in developing countries. *Research Evaluation*, *29*(2), 158–170.

Geels, F.W. (2019). Socio-technical transitions to sustainability: A review of criticisms and elaborations of the multi-level perspective. *Current opinion in environmental sustainability*, *39*, 187–201.

Gibson, S., Baskerville, D., Berry, A., Black, A., Norris, K., & Symeonidou, S. (2017). Including students as co-enquirers: Matters of identity, agency, language and labelling in an international participatory research study. *International Journal of Educational Research*, *81*, 108–118

Gray, B., Purdy, J., & Ansari, S. (2022). Confronting power asymmetries in partnerships to address grand challenges. *Organization Theory*, *3*(2), 26317877221098765.

Hinrichs, C. (2016). Fixing food with ideas of "local" and "place". *Journal of Environmental Studies and Sciences*, *6*(4), 759–764. https://doi.org/10.1007/s13412-015-0266-4

Hipel, K.W., Fang, L., & Heng, M. (2010). System of systems approach to policy development for global food security. *Journal of Systems Science and Systems Engineering*, 19, 1–21.

Juan, M., Laville, J.-L., & Subirats, J. (2020). Du social business à l'économie solidaire. Critique de l'innovation sociale. Erès.

Kirwan, J., Ilbery, B., Maye, D., & Carey, J. (2013). Grassroots social innovation and food localisation: An investigation of the local food programme in England. *Global Environmental Change*, *23*, 830–837.

Klein, J.L., & Laville, J.L. (2014). L'innovation sociale: Repères introductifs. In J.-L. Klein, J.L. Laville, & F. Moulaert (Éds.), *L'innovation sociale* (pp. 7–45). Eres.

Koelen, M.A., & Das, E. (2002). Social learning: A construction of reality. In C. Leeuwis, R. Pyburn, & N. Röling (Eds.), *Wheelbarrows full of frogs: Social learning in rural resource management: International research and reflections* (pp. 437–446). Van Gorcum.

Konstantatos, H., Siatitsa, D., & Vaiou, D. (2013). Chapter 20: Qualitative approaches for the study of socially innovative initiatives. In F. Moulaert, D. MacCallum, A. Mehmood, & A. Hamdouch (Eds.), *The international handbook on social innovation* (pp. 274–284). Edward Elgar Publishing. https://doi.org/10.4337/9781849809993.00036

Kruijssen, F., Keizer, M., & Giuliani, A. (2009). Collective action for small-scale producers of agricultural biodiversity products. *Elsevier*, *34*(1), 46–52.

Moore, M.L., & Riddell, D. (2015). Scaling out, scaling up, scaling deep: Advancing systemic social innovation and the learning processes to support it. *Journal of Corporate Citizenship*. https://doi.org/10.9774/GLEAF.4700.2015.ju.00009

Morgan, K., Marsden, T., & Murdoch, J. (2008). *Worlds of food: Place, power, and provenance in the food chain*. Oxford University Press on Demand.

Richez-Battesti, N., Petrella, F., & Vallade, D. (2012). L'innovation sociale, une notion aux usages pluriels: Quels enjeux et défis pour l'analyse? *Innovations*, *38*, 15–36. https://doi.org/10.3917/inno.038.0015

Tornaghi, C. & Dehaene, M. (2020). The prefigurative power of urban political agroecology: Rethinking the urbanisms of agroecological transitions for food system transformation. *Agroecology and Sustainable Food Systems*, *44*(5), 594–610.

Tribaldos, T.M., Oberlack, C., & Schneider, F. (2020). Impact through participatory research approaches: An archetype analysis. *Ecology and Society*, *25*(3): 15.

Valette, E., Lepiller, O., Bonomelli, V., & Pérignon, M. (2022). Des innovations à la transition des systèmes alimentaires: comment penser les conditions et les modalités de leur changement d'échelle? *Géocarrefour*, *96*(3): 21.

3 The role of chefs and gastronomy in transforming the Brasília food system

Jessica Pereira Garcia, Mauro G. M. Capelari, Stéphane Guéneau, Tainá Bacellar Zaneti and Janaína D. A. S. Diniz

3.1 Introduction

Contemporary gastronomy is an innovative field of sustainability practices in the food system (Pereira et al., 2019). Many chefs around the world choose ingredients noted for their sustainable attributes, whether they are local and organic ingredients or products that reflect regional culture and biodiversity (Pereira et al., 2019; Zaneti, 2017). Chefs supporting small-scale, local, agroecological production systems are particularly important in Brazil, where agribusiness is dominant and generates considerable social and environmental impacts (Sauer, 2018).

The link between gastronomy and sustainability refers to many issues concerning how dishes are prepared, where and how ingredients are produced, the environmental impact of restaurants, employment issues, and so on. Nevertheless, scholars have pointed out that the emergence of sustainable gastronomy is mainly due to the loss of value of food as a result of globalization, leading to the disempowerment of people in food preparation processes, including the stages of growing and cooking food (Sloan et al., 2015). "Sustainable Gastronomy Day", promoted by the Food and Agriculture Organization of the United Nations (FAO), defines the set of activities developed by these chefs to address the sustainability of gastronomy as "a cuisine that takes into account the ingredients—where they come from, how they are grown, how they reach our markets and, ultimately, our plates" (Sternadt et al., 2021, p. 2). In Brazil and other Latin American countries, the kitchen provides a space for introducing local native species that are little used and/or do not have a structured supply chain, thus demonstrating these foods' potential to (re)integrate the local food culture. Chefs concerned about socio-environmental issues promote actions to develop regional food through the use and dissemination of foods prepared with native plants that support family farming, strengthen ties between rural and urban areas, and reduce food waste (Barbosa, 2009; Niederle & Schubert, 2020; Pereira et al., 2019; Zaneti, 2017). For example, Teresa Corção, a renowned chef in Brazil, stands out for her use of native Brazilian ingredients in her gastronomic dishes and is known for her food activism (Franklin, 2012).

In Brasília, certain chefs have gained strong recognition for their efforts to create a gastronomic identity for the city. For a new city created just over 60 years

DOI: 10.4324/9781003285441-3

ago, Brasília's reputation as the third largest gastronomic hub in Brazil is striking (Congresso em Foco, 2017). Moreover, the population of the Federal District—the administrative area of which the city of Brasília is part—is about 3-million inhabitants (IBGE, 2022), and it is home to many civil servants and employees of international organizations who are endowed with a high financial and intellectual capital and are often concerned about sustainability issues. In the Federal District, one of the major sustainability concerns is the rapid deterioration of the Cerrado biome, which surrounds Brasília. The Cerrado biome is suffering from the expansion of agribusiness with high rates of deforestation and several forms of socio-environmental damage (Eloy et al., 2018).

Against this backdrop, some authors have sought to grasp the role of gastronomy in promoting regional products from the Cerrado biome and to analyse the process of developing markets for these products, which are often unknown to Brazilian consumers (Duarte et al., 2020; Guéneau et al., 2017; Zaneti & Balestro, 2015). Nevertheless, further research is still needed to better understand the relationship between gastronomy, the consumption of these products, and the impacts of the actions implemented by gastronomic actors on the transformation of food systems. Although gourmet chefs in Latin America present themselves as important actors in the development of alternative food systems (Zanella, 2020; Zaneti & Schneider, 2017), systematic studies of their roles and capacity to strengthen these systems are scarce.

This chapter analyses the sustainable practices of chefs working in Brasília and considers their potential to transform the food system of the Brazilian capital. In so doing, we seek to answer the following question: What are the ways in which chefs take action and what challenges do they face in the construction of sustainable food systems in the city of Brasília?

The chapter is divided into four sections. Section 3.2 presents the conceptual framework of the research. Based on a review of the literature on the concepts of food sustainability and gastronomy, we define the concept of "sustainable gastronomy", a new term used by international institutions such as the FAO but still little studied in the social science literature. This definition then serves as a baseline for our analysis of the changes resulting from the actions initiated by chefs in Brasília. Section 3.3 presents the methodological framework of the research, detailing the data collection process and the Urbal approach (Valette et al., 2019).

Section 3.4 outlines the results of the research in three subsections. The first subsection analyses the chefs' decision-making process surrounding sustainability, including the sustainability criteria they use in their activities and to what extent this may reflect a trend in Brasília's gastronomy. The second subsection considers the political dimension of chefs' work to build an alternative food system. Finally, the third subsection highlights the limitations of the chefs' practices and activism. Section 3.5 presents the conclusions of the research, setting out the main findings and reflecting on the future challenges facing the transformation of Brasília's food system.

3.2 Conceptual framework: Strengthening the relationship between food sustainability and gastronomy

Some strands of contemporary food culture are increasingly incorporating sustainability considerations into their approaches through movements aimed at reducing meat consumption, banishing food originating from monoculture production systems, promoting organic and agroecological products, and favouring food purchased directly from farmers (Portilho et al., 2011; Preiss et al., 2017).

Contemporary societies' rising interest in food sustainability also coincides with the growing importance given to aestheticization, taste appreciation, and pleasure in eating and cooking. This trend, which Barbosa (2009) describes as a process of gastronomization, has fostered an increasingly close relationship between gastronomy and rural areas, as the pleasure of cooking and eating combines a quest for better-quality ingredients and greater value given to products' origin, on the one hand, with the use of gastronomic techniques and sometimes traditional culinary knowledge on the other (Zaneti, 2017).

There is no consensus on the concept of gastronomy. Historically, it was shaped by the emergence of the first modern restaurants. It has sometimes been associated more closely with elite and taste, and at other times with social movements and markets. For the purposes of this study, we adopted the concept developed by Zaneti (2017), who defines gastronomy as:

> [A] socio-cultural process of interaction between, on the one hand, the trajectory of the ingredients—from their production to their distribution, their processing using culinary techniques, their consumption, and their disposal—and on the other hand the relationships established between the actors that make this trajectory possible—such as producers, distributors, chefs and/or cooks and consumers—mediated by knowledge, rituals, and symbolic and aesthetic representations along this path.
> (Zaneti, 2017, p. 47)

As a social phenomenon, gastronomy has also found its way into the political arena. Some authors, such as Franklin (2012), Barber (2015), and Niederle and Schubert (2020), argue that chefs play a social and political role surrounding food. This role can be described as gastronomic activism in the sense that, in using specific products in their kitchens and justifying these choices, chefs may influence and educate their consumers towards sustainable gastronomy.

Moreover, owing to their fame, gourmet chefs are also claim-makers who can act as policy entrepreneurs (Kingdon, 1995). As Sloan et al. (2015) note, "chefs have the power to change opinions and have highly influential roles to play in shaping the gastronomic desires of society to a more sustainable future" (p. xvi). Because of their institutional position, famous chefs have a certain legitimacy regarding food issues and are in a position to defend a cause and propose solutions to policymakers.

Krause and Bahls (2013) and Sloan et al. (2015) outline a number of characteristics that can make gastronomy a sustainable activity. These include in particular:

1) the creation of sustainable menus, "in connection not only with new gastronomic trends, but also with a rational and sensible method for using our resources" (Krause & Bahls, 2013, p. 439) based on seasonality, organic and local products, and cultural factors;
2) the choice of ingredients, informed by packaging and storage, transportation, locality/authenticity, and biodiversity considerations;
3) environmental education, with education and training of the sector's workforce on this subject, so that they can incorporate the tenets of sustainability into their work and everyday practices.

It is interesting to note that although many renowned avant-garde restaurants do not use the term sustainable gastronomy to define their establishments, a significant number of these practices have been adopted by contemporary gastronomy chefs. Moreover, these practices are identified as the basic ethos of restaurants recognized for serving creative haute cuisine (Zaneti, 2017). Renowned chefs, especially the stars of gastronomic guides and rankings, routinely incorporate certified and traceable organic foods into their cooking because these ingredients are produced on a small scale, often by groups of traditional peoples and communities and are endemic to a specific region. Beyond these ingredients' sensory attributes—qualities that may help define a chef's creative signature—chefs often choose local and traditional products for ideological reasons (Azevedo, 2015). In this sense, there appears to have been a shift in the very concept of gastronomy, which has emerged from its technical and elitist bubble built around the French school[1] (Pulici, 2012) and which, as Zaneti (2017) argues, is expanding both horizontally in the world of cuisine and vertically to incorporate less elitist cuisines. These cuisines both offer dishes that are more affordable while still being produced using elaborate techniques and, above all, place sustainability criteria at the centre of meal production.

Guided by this shift, several movements are driving contemporary sustainable gastronomy, including: a) the Slow Food movement, created in 1989 in Italy to promote good, clean, and fair food based on a cooperative relationship between farmers, cooks, and other consumers (considered as co-farmers) (Petrini, 2015); b) the Locavore movement, created by Californian chef Alice Waters in 1971, which advocates consuming local products as a way to boost the economy and local development by bringing farmers and consumers together (Azevedo, 2015); and c) the Farm to Fork movement, created by New York chef Dan Barber, which commits participating chefs to not buying products from more than 100 km away (Barber, 2015).

Within these movements, it is worth highlighting the work of certain chefs at the forefront of innovative gastronomic practices striving to incorporate elements of sustainability, namely: René Redzepi, from the now closed restaurant Noma in Denmark, who initiated an itinerant school to improve local actors' gastronomic techniques in order to enable them to cook with local ingredients (Leleux & van der Kaaij, 2019); Virgilio Martinez, from Restaurant Central in Lima, Peru, who applies modern cooking techniques to indigenous Peruvian ingredients and embraces approaches that respect Andean ecosystems (Barandiarán, 2018); and chefs Ray Adriansyah and Eelke Plasmeijer, from the restaurant Locavore in Bali, Indonesia, where 95% of the kitchen's ingredients are Indonesian (Sgarbi, 2019).

Such projects have also developed in Brazil, where several factors have converged to foster sustainable food initiatives. In this country, the agricultural sector is mainly characterized by large-scale monoculture farming and the promotion of commodity exports that contribute to separating society from nature and rendering food issues invisible (Cruz et al., 2016). However, since 1990, debates on the theme of food sustainability have been taking over the policy agenda as well as scientific research and development in Brazil (Monteiro et al., 2015; Portilho et al., 2011). Food activists are eager to better understand and communicate where food comes from, how it is produced, and why it is consumed (Darolt et al., 2016; Martinelli & Cavalli, 2019).

Among the Brazilian representatives of a contemporary gastronomy that promotes sustainable food initiatives, chefs Tainá Marajoara and Teresa Corção in particular are worth mentioning. Together with her companion Carlos Ruffeil, Tainá Marajoara created the food culture centre 'Iacitatá' in the Amazonian metropolis of Belém.

> Iacitatá' promotes the same values and forms of dissidence against the dominant food systems by criticizing the exploitative relations brought about by the industrialization of food production and the attending standardization, reduced varietal diversity, loss of flavours and culinary knowledge, and seed control.
>
> (Granchamp, 2019, p. 13)

Teresa Corção founded the Maniva Institute which aims to restore traditional food knowledge.

Based on a review of the literature exploring how the issue of sustainability has percolated into the concept of gastronomy, and how social actors themselves are implementing innovations to transform gastronomy, the concept of sustainable gastronomy can be understood as an approach whereby ingredients are chosen according to their social, environmental, and health-related characteristics (factoring in dimensions such as proximity, authenticity, fairness, nutritional quality, modes of production, packaging, transport, and distribution). Furthermore, the way these ingredients are combined is informed not only by specific culinary techniques to obtain refined dishes with gustatory and aesthetic qualities but also by the goal of making optimal use of available ingredients in order to preserve the environment and avoid food waste. Beyond the confines of the restaurant, sustainable gastronomy strives to influence consumption choices and wider policy processes to transform the food system as a whole so that it can become more inclusive and sustainable.

3.3 Tailoring the Urbal approach to the analysis of the pathways of food system transformation induced by Brasília chefs

In order to analyse the sustainable practices adopted by chefs working in Brasília, a qualitative research methodology was implemented in two stages. The first stage included interviews with key actors.

Between 2018 and 2019, 26 semi-structured interviews were conducted: 16 with chefs and restaurant owners in Brasília; 1 with a food cooperative; 6 with food producers (including 3 Community Supported Agriculture (CSA) farmers and 3 farmers from traditional communities); 2 with commercial intermediaries; and 1 with the person managing a gastronomic programme that operates in partnership with the Federal District Education Secretariat. All interviews were recorded and transcribed, and a content analysis guided by the research question was performed to identify and categorize the actions associated with sustainable gastronomy and the challenges that the chefs face in implementing them.

Restaurants were chosen on the basis of their own statements about their willingness to engage in sustainability and according to criteria set out in the literature on sustainable gastronomy. We searched for these "sustainability-oriented" establishments using the snowball technique (Vinuto, 2014), until the number of chefs selected and interviewed satisfied the principle of saturation (Glaser & Strauss, 2006).

Several interview guides were produced for the different types of actors interviewed. With restaurants, the questions focused primarily on how the chefs conceive of their restaurants, what differentiates them from other establishments, and the history and trajectory of the restaurants' creation. A series of questions then explored each chef's practices: the types of products used; the product selection criteria; the supply chain for the ingredients used in the restaurant; the restaurant's waste policy; the chef's relationships with suppliers, customers, and other restaurants; and the innovations implemented specifically to make their establishment or the city's food system more sustainable. The guides for interviews with the other actors focused on the sustainability of the actors' practices (for farmers, cooperatives, and intermediaries) or their programmes and actions to advance sustainability in food systems (for the public sector), and on the nature of their relationship with the restaurants of Brasília. The aim was particularly to investigate the type of partnership built with the restaurants and the way in which this partnership was able to change these other actors' practices or actions.

The second stage of the research consisted of a participatory workshop organized in Brasília in June 2019. The workshop allowed the researchers to analyse the actions, identified through the interviews, which contribute to the transformation of the food system, using a methodology developed within the framework of the Urbal Project (Valette et al., 2019). Rather than measuring the impact of the innovative actions implemented by the chefs, the Urbal approach aims to identify the sustainability changes produced by these innovations as well as the pathways that led to the changes. A simple participatory method was applied, so as to be able to use the words of the main actors involved, based on the impact pathways pre-identified during the interviews.

The workshop brought together several actors of interest for this research: two chefs; two family farmers; two representatives of traditional peoples and communities; two representatives of cooperatives in the Cerrado product supply chain; two representatives of the government; and two researchers. It also included an audience of university students and professionals in the fields of education, nutrition, health and gastronomy, public servants, farmers, and representatives of traditional peoples and communities.[2] Although they speak and understand Portuguese, some of the participants from traditional populations express themselves more easily in their own languages. For this reason, guiding questions were pre-established by the researchers and organized into four impact pathways: social inclusion, economic justice, nutrition, and the environment. In order to ensure full engagement by all participants, the food system actors were invited to answer questions orally and to interact with others in the workshop. Video and audio recordings were collected to produce a summary video, and the audio recordings were transcribed for content analysis.

3.4 Sustainability and gastronomy practices, innovations and challenges in Brasília

3.4.1 Characterization of sustainable gastronomy practices

This subsection first characterizes chefs' diverse range of sustainability practices, mainly identified through the interviews, to produce a typology. Second, we highlight our findings regarding the impact pathways towards sustainability induced by these practices, based on the indications provided by the stakeholders during the participatory workshop.

The sustainable gastronomy practices implemented by the group of chefs involved at least five characteristic actions. The sustainable practice most frequently identified among the establishments surveyed was the inclusion of foods from local producers in the menu. This practice was mentioned in almost all the interviews, evidencing a connection between chefs and family farmers from the region surrounding Brasília. The goal of this close relationship with farmers is not only to supply restaurants with local products which chefs deem to have better taste and freshness attributes but also to foster the social inclusion of a category of farmers who are often marginalized.

Unsurprisingly, the second sustainable practice most frequently identified in the interviews was the use of organic products, which highlights a strong interest, among the chefs, in the environmental and health impacts of food. The use of organic products is clearly a political act to oppose the overuse of chemicals in industrial agriculture in the Cerrado. Yet some of the restaurants justify their practices by emphasizing the nutritional benefits and impacts on consumer health rather than environmental impacts. Providing healthy food was the main objective of most of the vegan restaurants surveyed.

Some restaurants, however, both purchase food from local farmers and use organic products in their culinary practices. The relationship with local agroecological farmers is the product of the chefs themselves seeking out this type of supplier. They first make contact by visiting local open fresh markets, where farmers and consumers can come together. The chefs can also draw on the support of the Technical Assistance and Rural Extension Company of the Federal District (Emater-DF) which, in addition to promoting an exclusive open fresh market for family farmers, provides contact details and fosters dialogue between chefs and producers upon request. This is highlighted by Zaneti (2017), who notes that the relationship between chefs and farmers influences both the menu of restaurants and the selection of ingredients grown by the farmers.

Another practice which the actors interviewed saw as innovative and sustainable was the commitment to systematically using Cerrado fruits in the composition of the dishes of the establishments surveyed. Apart from a few fruit varieties that are part of the regional culinary heritage, such as the pequi fruit (*Caryocar brasiliense*), most fruits native to the Cerrado biome are consumed very little in Brazilian cities and are even unknown to most Brazilian consumers (Garcia, 2017). For instance, baru (*Dipteryx alata*), now known as the Cerrado nut, was hardly consumed a few years ago, even by traditional peoples. The inclusion of Cerrado fruits in the dishes of the establishments surveyed appears to evidence that for chefs, sustainable gastronomy involves not only an appreciation of products from the region where the restaurant is established but also chefs playing a key role in preserving local biodiversity through the use of specific local foods in fine dishes. Choosing foods based on both their environmental qualities and their origin, be it produce from local farmers or products that are typical of specific regions, is a defining feature of sustainable gastronomy in Brasília. Other studies also identify these approaches as guiding principles for establishing more sustainable kitchens (Zanella, 2020). However, the use of Cerrado fruits by chefs does not guarantee that the fruit is grown sustainably (Guéneau et al., 2020). For this reason, some chefs seek to combine their local supply of Cerrado fruit with a direct relationship with the farmers, which enables them to visit the farms and observe the sustainability of the farming systems.

The fourth important innovative practice witnessed among chefs in Brasília is the use of Non-Conventional Food Plants (NCFP).[3] These edible wild plants usually grow spontaneously and are classified as "weeds". They are consumed on a small scale or are no longer used by most of the population, who are not aware of the plants' nutritional and economic value and potential uses. More than half of the interviewees confirmed that their menus featured NCFP, such as ora-pro-nóbis (*Pereskia aculeate*)—common English names for which include Barbados gooseberry leaves and leaf cactus—and taioba (*Xanthosoma sagittifolium*), known as arrowleaf elephant ear in English. The frequent use of these plants demonstrates strong adherence to a movement driven by the publication of the NCFP guide (Kinupp & Lorenzi, 2014), which seeks to revive the consumption of neglected wild plants in Brazil, in clear opposition to the dominant species grown in industrial agriculture.

The fifth most frequent sustainability-oriented practice identified among chefs and their establishments concerned waste generation. The chefs consistently stressed the importance of properly disposing of what has been discarded in restaurants. This illustrates that for the interviewees, the sustainability of gastronomy is not restricted to the production of dishes and food in general, but also extends to the actions that establishments take or can take to protect the environment. Moreover, the interviewees showed concern about producing less waste and not just disposing of it properly. The establishments thus reflect on practices they can adopt to better manage their waste, as well as actions to reduce the quantity of waste they generate.

The interviews also revealed other less frequently mentioned sustainable practices of the establishments surveyed. For instance, a few interviewees mentioned having a seasonal menu and selling food produced by family farms in the restaurant, but these actions do not appear to be consistently carried out or of immediate interest to chefs and their restaurants. Surprisingly, only a few restaurants have close relationships with Community Support Agriculture (CSAs) initiatives, even though the latter are one of the main channels for bringing urban consumers closer to the rural world in Brasília. As of 2020, 36 CSAs were registered in Brasília, the largest concentration of this type of initiative in the country's major cities.

Based on the interview data we analysed, we organized the 16 sustainably-oriented restaurants into three categories according to each establishment's adherence to the criteria of sustainable gastronomy:

1) **Conventional**: these restaurants are primarily focused on the nutritional dimension of sustainability, with menus informed by functionality considerations and which prioritize generic foods that appeal to most customers. Generally, these menus consist of salads, types of rice, beans, pasta, dishes with white and red meat, and desserts. The choice of ingredients is based on cost/benefit attributes and objective qualities relating to food safety and nutritional balance.
2) **Gastronomic**: these establishments are led by a chef, who interacts with the diverse segments of the gastronomic world, for instance at events, in social networks, and in the media.[4] This type of restaurant is based on classic and French cuisine, but brings in contemporary elements such as techniques, ingredients, and presentation styles. The choice of ingredients is based on

both objective qualities (free of contaminants) and subjective qualities (artisanal, seasonal, regional, sensory, terroir), informed by sensory as well as authenticity considerations.

3) **Alternative Gastronomic**: these establishments are led by a cook or chef who establishes kitchen practices informed by a political or ideological position that they share with their audience. This is also coupled with other sustainability practices, such as composting and serving organic and/or agroecological food. The choice of ingredients is primarily guided by the cook's ideology (grown by family farmers and/or traditional groups; agrochemical free; free of certain types of ingredients such as soy and wheat), but also takes into account the ingredients' objective and subjective qualities, as the gastronomic restaurants do. These establishments use culinary techniques from both classic cuisines and politicized cuisine movements, such as veganism and live cooking.

The impacts of sustainable gastronomy practices are very different depending on the type of restaurant concerned, as we can observe in Table 3.1 regarding the use of native products (Cerrado fruits) and NCFP. These impacts vary

Table 3.1 Use of native Cerrado fruits according to the types of restaurants surveyed

	Name	*Type of establishment*	*Category*	*Use of Cerrado fruits and/or NCFP*
1	Aquavit	Gourmet	Gastronomic	Yes
2	Atelier café	Gourmet coffee shop	Gastronomic	Yes
3	Authoral	Gourmet	Gastronomic	Yes
4	Baco Pizzaria	Pizzeria	Gastronomic	Rarely
5	Buriti Zen	Vegan alternative restaurant	Alternative Gastronomic	Yes
6	Daniel Briand	Gourmet confectionery	Gastronomic	No
7	Ernesto Cafés Especiais	Gourmet coffee shop	Gastronomic	No
8	Faz Bem	Vegan restaurant	Alternative Gastronomic	No
9	Finatec	Company restaurant	Conventional	No
10	Girassol	Vegan restaurant	Alternative Gastronomic	Yes
11	Mysth	Organic/vegetarian restaurant	Alternative Gastronomic	No
12	Piauíndia	Fusion restaurant	Alternative Gastronomic	Yes
13	Sallva	Gourmet restaurant	Gastronomic	No
14	Mesa pra Doze	Gastronomic project	Alternative Gastronomic	Yes
15	Olivier	Gourmet restaurant	Gastronomic	Rarely
16	Rubato Chocolates	Chocolate & coffee shop	Gastronomic	Yes

from cases where only the nutritional dimension is taken into consideration, in conventional restaurants, to practices focusing on the socio-cultural identity of foods with limited sustainability impact (mainly promoting local products from family farms) in the case of gastronomic restaurants, to more pronounced impacts on several dimensions of sustainability in the case of alternative gastronomic restaurants. The latter impacts consist of economic benefits and the social inclusion of local communities (through direct relationships in geographical proximity), the sustainable use of neglected native species of the Cerrado biome, the non-use of chemical or monoculture products, recycling, food waste reduction, nutritional education, and diet improvement (diversifying the range of food products in the meals).

3.4.2 Food activism to make food systems more sustainable

The actions taken by Brasília chefs to transform the food system are not limited to the sustainable gastronomy practices implemented in their establishments. They are also involved in social movements defending specific causes. Many actors consider this activism to be far more impactful than the gastronomic practices alone, as mentioned by a representative of the Central do Cerrado, the main cooperative that supplies restaurants with Cerrado products:

> These types of restaurants do not have the capacity to absorb these Cerrado products in large volumes. … In terms of consumption, it does not generate much direct impact. … Making a dish with Kalunga monkey pepper,[5] the chef will buy 1 kg from me every 6 months. … But the moment she or he features in an article in the Correio Braziliense[6] and talks about monkey pepper, this generates a lot of indirect sales.
>
> (Interviewee 17, 2019)

The Central do Cerrado, created in 2004, brings together several community organizations involved in developing farming activities through the sustainable use of the biodiversity from the Cerrado biome, with a view to promoting and introducing community products on regional, national and international markets. Various chefs in Brasília support the cooperative, not only through direct purchases, but also through various activities implemented in partnership with the Central do Cerrado and other actors promoting sustainable food systems. For instance, together the chefs and the cooperative managers take part in training sessions, cooking workshops and even policy events on sustainability issues related to food production and consumption.

Another form of political activism observed, though not directly focused on food sustainability, is the development of a coalition of chefs to build a food identity for the city of Brasília. This movement seeks to ground Brasília's cuisine in local ingredients that are characteristic of the region and to ensure that it is recognized among peers and consumers across the country. An important action supporting this activism was the launch of the Panela Candanga (Brasília Pan) initiative, which celebrates the foods and culinary traditions of the citizens of Brasília, known as Candangos. The purpose of the movement is to:

> provide a different culinary experience. It is to present, through gastronomy, a Brasília that its people still do not know. It is to bring the history of its ingredients to each dish. It is to offer new ways of understanding food and identifying each mouthful with our own culture. It is to be able to meet and feel part of this panela candanga.
>
> (Panela Candanga, 2021)

As a strategy for action, the Panela Candanga project launched a biannual fair that is now in its fifth edition, as well as a website and a blog to share information, tips and recipes for using the fruits and products of the Cerrado biome.

Another important movement is Slow Food Cerrado. With a social network of almost 5,000 followers, this movement created in 2004 promotes a "greater connection with and appreciation of the rich biome of the Cerrado. And nothing could be more pleasurable than to do so through ecogastronomy" (Slow Food Cerrado, 2019). Slow Food Cerrado organizes courses, lectures, festivals, parties, fairs, celebrations, tastings, meetings between producers and consumers, and countless other activities around the overarching theme of the protection of the Cerrado biome and ecogastronomy, an approach that combines respect for and interest in gastronomic culture with support for those fighting to defend food and agricultural biodiversity around the world (Slow Food Cerrado, 2019).

A network of chefs in Brasília is also working to implement circular economy initiatives, in order to foster practices, within and across restaurants, to reduce, reuse, share, and recycle products. As mentioned earlier, there is concern about restaurants properly disposing of their waste, while implementing practices to help reduce the amount of resources used and of waste to landfill. In 2018, a group of chefs created a civil society organization called Instituto Ecozinha (Ecokitchen Institute) which operates in Brasília, collecting the waste generated by participating establishments and supporting a network of zero-waste restaurants (Instituto Ecozinha, 2021). This initiative is particularly important, as the Brasília region was previously home to the largest open-air landfill in South America (the second largest in the world). Although this landfill was closed in 2018, without viable large-scale waste treatment solutions for residues such as glass and plastic in the Federal District, another place has been designated in the area for a new, equally polluting landfill. According to the chefs interviewed, Ecozinha is an initiative that shows the authorities of Brasília that waste collection and recycling are possible. With more than 80 participating establishments, the Institute collects and sends over 100 tons of waste per month to specialized recycling units located in São Paulo, thus diverting it from the public landfill of the Federal District and preventing thousands of tons of greenhouse gas emissions per year. These actions make the Institute one of the most significant waste treatment organizations in the Federal District.

3.4.3 Challenges to and limitations of sustainable gastronomy

The perspectives shared by the group interviewed suggest that the first challenge faced by the chefs and other actors of sustainable gastronomy in Brasília is local farmers' limited supply capacity. This is due to the fact that the large restaurants of Brasília require a guaranteed supply of specific products on a regular basis, but also to the expansion of sustainable gastronomy in the region. According to the interviewees, many of the family farming businesses are small and informal, which hinders the development of strong partnerships with restaurants. This precarious supply structure among family farmers entails legal and contractual difficulties, as many farmers cannot issue invoices and restaurants have to fragment their purchases, adding on greater fiscal complexity for the establishments. An account by one of the interviewees exemplifies this situation:

> A huge difficulty in working with family farming is that, in my view, it is still a group that has not organized itself very well, and our weekly purchase is gigantic, and I have already faced several difficulties in getting hold of the farmer and saying "man, can you supply me with 200 kilos of tomatoes?" and he said "no, I can offer you 40" and I said "and next week?" and he said "next week I can't offer you anything, because 40 is my whole production." The trickle of contact is very difficult, because nowadays you go to Ceasa,[7] you can find a giant wholesaler, or three giant wholesalers that can supply an entire restaurant [on their own], and it's difficult to work with family farming like this.
>
> (Interviewee 15, 2019)

This type of situation, brought on by local producers' limited supply capacity, tends to favour restaurants that adapt their menus to the available food supply, creating dishes from what the farmers can provide. These restaurants generally have a clientele that can adapt to the offer: consumers who come not to taste a specific dish, but rather because they adhere to a set of principles upheld by the restaurant while also appreciating the overall quality of the dishes offered. These customers normally spend a greater amount on purchases. In this sense, referring to our typology of restaurants engaged in sustainable gastronomy in Brasília, it appears that "alternative gastronomic" restaurants are generally restricted to small establishments that serve a higher social class (see Table 3.1).

Although the use of fruits from the Cerrado was a practice mentioned by more than half of the chefs interviewed, these fruits generally feature in small quantities and often on an irregular basis, for instance on special occasions such as gastronomic festivals dedicated to the Cerrado, with the exception of a few restaurants in the alternative gastronomic category (Duarte et al., 2021). A second challenge for sustainable gastronomy in Brasília is thus the inclusion of larger quantities of Cerrado fruits in establishments' dishes, on a more regular basis. Two important factors help to understand this challenge.

The first is the chefs' lack of commitment to including Cerrado fruits in their cuisine. This may be linked to the trend already identified by Zaneti and Balestro (2015), who point to a gap between the chefs' rhetoric on the protection of the biome and their actual commitment to changing their culinary practices. According to the authors, this trend can be due either to operational considerations by the restaurants (associated with the difficulty of working with a changing menu, or the purchasing relationship with farmers), or to consumers choosing these restaurants for the refinement of their dishes rather than to preserve the Cerrado biome. Furthermore, the lack of specialized staff who understand the importance of following the guidelines of sustainable gastronomy can make it difficult to turn discourse into reality (Krause & Bahls, 2013), ultimately leading to the maintenance of the status quo.

The second factor that explains the low quantity of Cerrado fruits in the everyday menus of Brasília's restaurants relates to chefs constantly sensing their customers' reluctance to try these specific fruits. Many of them reported that when they offer their customers the choice between two dishes, the one containing Cerrado fruits and the other without these fruits, the customers consistently choose the option without Cerrado fruits. The following interview excerpt clearly illustrates this situation:

> I think people here are not very comfortable leaving their comfort zone, trying something new, trying something different. I see it a lot here in Brasília, it seems that other people have to test it and say that it is good for it to be accepted. We have a lot of cases like that, when I get called to a table to suggest it and the person says "no, I want the steak with risotto".
>
> (Restaurant 15, 2019)

This account indicates that the clients of gastronomic restaurants are not willing to change their consumption habits and have a very conservative gastronomic profile. Many of Brasília's upper-class residents still see meals made from Cerrado products as popular dishes, as in the case of the traditional "rice with pequi", which would remove them from their elitist bubble. In this sense, the more consistent inclusion of Cerrado fruit is hampered by a market rationality that is not yet socially constructed (Guéneau et al., 2017). The following account illustrates this problem:

> A restaurant that serves dinner and that wants to sell something sophisticated ... ends up creating a cycle where you need to have commercial dishes to be able to pay the rent, and this ends up diluting the concept with standard options, because that's what people buy. And so the restaurant ends up selling, I don't know, risotto with fillet steak to be able to pay the rent.
>
> (Restaurant 14, 2019)

Some collective initiatives involving chefs are striving to change this representation among consumers. The publication of gastronomic recipe books and the organization of gastronomy festivals and culinary events hosted by groups of chefs—private banquets of sorts dedicated to Cerrado gastronomy, the entrance fee for which necessarily limits participation to the upper classes—are examples of such initiatives by the abovementioned activist movements. These events communicate the need to support the gastronomy based on Cerrado products in order to protect this threatened biome.

The issues described above point to the third challenge to and limitation of sustainable gastronomy in Brasília, which is the need for social inclusion or, in other words, the need to expand gastronomic sustainability to less privileged customers who have a lower per capita income. Brasília has the highest per capita income in Brazil (IBGE, 2021), and this income is concentrated within a small group of residents of the capital—usually civil servants and their families—who live in more centralized and upmarket areas of the city. This is also where the researched establishments with a sustainability profile are located. Based on our findings, it is clear that the city of Brasília promotes sustainable gastronomic actions for a more affluent social class. These are the actors who seek, consume in and sustain this gastronomic circuit striving to develop sustainable practices. Even so, there are exceptions, especially in the case of chefs linked to local universities, which are working to establish university extension practices in less affluent areas, such as schools on the outskirts of the city. However, this is not the dominant pattern of sustainable gastronomy observed in the capital of Brazil. On the contrary, the prevailing approach is elitist and restricted to more affluent social classes, thus raising questions about future challenges for socially inclusive sustainable practices and the extent to which such practices, even though they exist on a small scale in the capital[8] (IESB, 2016), can serve as an instrument for improving the diet of Brasília residents.

3.5 Conclusion

This chapter analysed the role of Brasília chefs in transforming the local food system, and the challenges they face in this endeavour. Our findings shed light on an activist profile shared by the chefs surveyed that steers their actions towards:

- Improving the quality of the food served, using organic, neglected, and native species, and sourcing their supply from local family farmers, thereby generating support for local small-scale producers and cooperatives such as the Central do Cerrado.
- A set of activities that promote a sustainable gastronomy based on products from the Cerrado biome, which suggests the beginnings of building a food identity for the region of the Federal District, based on sustainability principles and supported by movements that seek to give the Cerrado political visibility, such as Slow food Cerrado and Panela Candanga.
- Attentiveness to the waste generated by their establishments, which has encouraged the search for self-organized alternatives for the adequate collection and treatment of waste with the innovative organization Ecozinha, the largest zero-waste restaurant initiative in Brazil.

This set of innovative actions, arising from coordinated engagement by a specific group of chefs in the city of Brasília, demonstrates the potential for food systems transformation towards more sustainable practices. This transformation has not happened yet in Brasília. Innovative actions are still restricted to higher-income consumers, even though they increasingly include rural communities in Brasília and the surrounding area. It can also be said that this higher-class audience, which embraces a European ideal of gastronomy, shares a somewhat romanticized understanding of sustainability. Despite chefs' environmental concerns, regarding modes of production and the conservation of biodiversity for instance, economic considerations often limit new action, in addition to such action having little social impact, with a large part of the local population still excluded.

Chefs' very limited adoption of some of the most relevant sustainable practices, such as making full use of the ingredients, serving seasonal menus, and fostering links with CSAs, reflects the significant gap between their discourses and their practices. Moreover, it reveals the shortcomings of public policies dedicated to the transformation of food systems, with a lack of technical assistance and rural extension services, for instance, to support innovative chefs in their efforts to build sustainable food markets and help farmers and traditional communities to access these emerging markets.

Gastronomy provides a space for the creation of new markets and new products. In various places around the world, it has come to encompass solidarity restaurants, participatory canteens, and 100%-bulk or zero-waste restaurants, which can increasingly be found in working-class neighbourhoods. The initiatives that have emerged in Brasília are still in their early stages, but could draw inspiration from these innovations to transform the city's food system.

Notes

1 Pulici conducted surveys among members of the Brazilian elite and analysed gastronomic reviews published in the Paulist Press between 2005 and 2009. She showed how the Brazilian elite created a gastronomic universe, guided by French professional gastronomy in the 2000s, in order to distinguish itself from the working class. Classical or professional gastronomy takes the French school as its frame of reference, as the discipline was born in the post-French Revolution era when the ex-cooks of the fallen nobility started to open restaurants for the emerging bourgeoisie.
2 The Brazilian term "traditional peoples and communities", as defined in the Brazilian Constitution (Decree 6.040 of 07/02/2007), includes native, Afro-descendant, and multi-racial populations.
3 In Portuguese *Plantas Alimentícias Não Convencionais* (PANC).
4 Social media has become an extension of the restaurant as well as the chef. Both the chef's persona and the restaurant's image are constructed through their media presence. The media are used as a space for marketing, nurturing a relationship with the public and, most of all, gastronomic branding.
5 A species native to the Cerrado, *Xylopia aromática.*
6 A very popular local newspaper.
7 Ceasa (Centrais de abastecimento) are the main supply centres of metropolitan areas in Brazil, bringing together most food wholesalers in the same location.

8 The Bandeneón social project developed by chef Sebastian Parasole is one of the few examples of sustainable gastronomy in Brasília catering to the lower classes. The project provides itinerant education for vulnerable people, and works towards solidarity and sustainability around the theme of food. Information about this project is available at https://www.sebastianparasole.com/bandoneon

References

Azevedo, E. (2015). Food activism: The locavorism perspective. *Ambiente & Sociedade, 18*(3), 81–98. https://doi.org/10.1590/1809-4422ASOC740V1832015

Barandiarán, J. (2018). *Science and environment in chile: The politics of expert advice in a neoliberal democracy*. MIT Press.

Barber, D. (2015). *O terceiro prato. Observações sobre o futuro da comida*. Rocco.

Barbosa, L. (2009). Tendências da alimentação contemporânea. In M.L. Pinto & J.K. Pacheco (Eds.), *Juventude, consumo e educação* (pp. 15–64). ESPM.

Congresso em Foco. (2017). Terceiro polo gastronômico, Brasília atrai restaurantes consagrados do eixo SP-Rio. https://congressoemfoco.uol.com.br/opiniao/colunas/terceiro-polo-gastronomico-Brasília-atrai-restaurantes-consagrados-do-eixo-sp-rio/

Cruz, F.T., Matte, A., & Schneider, S. (2016). *Produção, consumo e abastecimento: desafios e novas estratégias*. Editora da UFRGS.

Darolt, M.R., Lamine, C., Brandenburg, A., Alencar, M.D.C.F., & Abreu, L.S. (2016). Alternative food networks and new producer-consumer relations in France and in Brazil. *Ambiente & Sociedade, 19*(2), 1–22. https://doi.org/10.1590/1809-4422ASOC121132V1922016

Duarte, L.M.G., Guéneau, S., Diniz, J.D.A.S., & Passos, C. J. S. (2020). Sistemas agroalimentares alternativos, construção social de mercados e gastronomização de produtos agroextrativistas do Cerrado brasileiro. In S. Guéneau, J.D.A.S. Diniz, & C.J.S. Passos (Eds.), *Alternativas para o bioma Cerrado: agroextrativismo e uso sustentável da sociobiodiversidade* (pp. 405–446). Mil Folhas.

Duarte, L.M.G., Guéneau, S., Diniz, J.D.A.S., & Passos, C.J.S. (2021). Valorización de los patrimonios alimentarios y productos agroextractivistas del Cerrado brasileño en la gastronomía: un estudio sobre el Festival Gastronómico Cerrado Week. In N. Rebaï, A.G. Bilhaut, C.E. de Suremain, E. Esther, & M. Paredes (Eds.), *Patrimonios alimentarios en América Latina: recursos locales, actores y globalización* (pp. 109–136). IRD-IFEA. https://doi.org/10.4000/books.irdeditions.42804

Eloy, L., Guéneau, S., Nogueira, M.C.R., Diniz, J.D.A.S., Leme, A., & Passos, C.J.S. (2018). Alternatives durables pour le biome Cerrado: occupations et usages des territoires par les producteurs agroextractivistes. *Problèmes d'Amérique Latine, 4*(111), 85–100. https://doi.org/10.3917/pal.111.0085

Franklin, S.B. (2012). Manioc: A Brazilian chef claims her roots. *Gastronomica, 12*(3), 40–45. https://doi.org/10.1525/GFC.2012.12.3.40

Garcia, J.P. (2017). Valorização de produtos agroextrativistas do Cerrado: comercialização e construção dos mercados da sociobiodiversidade. [Masters Thesis, Universidade de Brasília]. UnB Repository. https://repositorio.unb.br/handle/10482/24443

Glaser, B.G., & Strauss, A.L. (2006). *The discovery of grounded theory: Strategies for qualitative research*. Aldine Transaction.

Granchamp, L. (2019). Penser l'alimentation d'un point de vue décolonial. *Revue des Sciences Sociales, 61*, 132–141. https://doi.org/10.4000/revss.3611

Guéneau, S., Diniz, J.D.A., Mendonça, S.D., & Garcia, J.P. (2017). Construção social dos mercados de frutos do cerrado: entre sociobiodiversidade e alta gastronomia. Século XXI, *Revista de Ciências Sociais*, *7*(1), 130–156. https://doi.org/10.5902/2236672528133

Guéneau, S., Diniz, J.D.A.S., Bispo, T.W., & Mendonça, S.D. (2020). Cadeias de produtos da sociobiodiversidade como opção de desenvolvimento sustentável no cerrado: o desafio da comercialização. In S. Guéneau, J.D.A.S. Diniz, & C.J.S. Passos (Eds.), *Alternativas para o bioma Cerrado: agroextrativismo e uso sustentável da sociobiodiversidade* (pp. 329–367). Mil Folhas.

IBGE. (2021). Rendimento nominal mensal domiciliar per capita da população residente. https://cidades.ibge.gov.br/brasil/df/pesquisa/48/48986?tipo=ranking&indicador=48986

IBGE. (2022). Cidades e Estados. Brasília. Retrieved 20 May 2020, from https://www.ibge.gov.br/cidades-e-estados/df/Brasília.html

IESB. (2016). Conheça a Iniciativa Bandoneón de Gastronomia. Retrieved 23 March 2020, from https://www.iesb.br/noticias/conheca-a-iniciativa-bandoneon-de-gastronomia/

Instituto Ecozinha. (2021). Restaurantes sustentáveis. Retrieved 26 October 2021, from https://www.institutoecozinha.org.br/

Kingdon, J. (1995). *Agendas, alternatives and public policies* (2nd ed.). Harper Collins. https://doi.org/10.3886/ICPSR28024.v1

Kinupp, V.F., & Lorenzi, H. (2014). Plantas alimentícias não convencionais (PANC) no Brasil: guia de identificação, aspectos nutricionais e receitas ilustradas. Instituto Plantarum de Estudos da Flora.

Krause, R.W., & Bahls, A.D.S.M. (2013). Orientações gerais para uma gastronomia sustentável. *Turismo – Visão e Ação*, *15*(3), 434–450. https://doi.org/10.11606/issn.1984-4867.v26i3p668-694

Leleux, B., & van der Kaaij, J. (2019). Stellar performance from sustainability teams. In B. Leleux & J. van der Kaaij (Eds.), *Winning sustainability strategies* (pp. 243–261). Palgrave Macmillan. https://doi.org/10.1007/978-3-319-97445-3_12

Martinelli, S. S., & Cavalli, S. B. (2019). Alimentação saudável e sustentável: uma revisão narrativa sobre desafios e perspectivas. *Ciencia & Saude Coletiva*, *24*(11), 4251–4262. https://doi.org/10.1590/1413-812320182411.30572017

Monteiro, C.A., Cannon, G., Moubarac, J.C., Martins, A.P., Martins, C.A., Garzillo, J., … Jaime, P.C. (2015). Dietary guidelines to nourish humanity and the planet in the twenty-first century. A blueprint from Brazil. *Public Health Nutrition*, *18*(13), 2311–2322. https://doi.org/10.1017/s1368980015002165

Niederle, P., & Schubert, M.N. (2020). How does veganism contribute to shape sustainable food systems? Practices, meanings and identities of vegan restaurants in Porto Alegre, Brazil. *Journal of Rural Studies*, *78*, 304–313. https://doi.org/10.1016/j.jrurstud.2020.06.021

Panela Candanga. (2021). Um movimento, uma celebração da cozinha de Brasília. Retrieved 14 November 2021, from http://panelacandanga.com.br/

Pereira, L.M., Calderón-Contreras, R., Norström, A.V., Espinosa, D., Willis, J., Guerrero Lara, L., … Pérez Amaya, O. (2019). Chefs as change-makers from the kitchen: Indigenous knowledge and traditional food as sustainability innovations. *Global Sustainability*, *2*, e16. https://doi.org/10.1017/S2059479819000139

Petrini, C. (2015). *Food & freedom: How the slow food movement is changing the world through gastronomy*. Rizzoli Publications.

Portilho, F., Castañeda, M., & de Castro, I.R.R. (2011). Food in the contemporary context: Consumption, political action and sustainability. *Ciencia & Saude Coletiva, 16*(1), 99–106. https://doi.org/10.1590/S1413-81232011000100014

Preiss, P., Charão-Marques, F., & Wiskerke, J.S. (2017). Fostering sustainable urban-rural linkages through local food supply: A transnational analysis of collaborative food alliances. *Sustainability, 9*(7), 1155. https://doi.org/10.3390/su9071155

Pulici, C. (2012). Le solennel et le parcimonieux dans l'alimentation. Les pratiques gastronomiques comme source de distinction des élites brésiliennes. IdeAs. *Idées d'Amériques, 3*. https://doi.org/10.4000/ideas.441

Sauer, S. (2018). Soy expansion into the agricultural frontiers of the Brazilian Amazon: The agribusiness economy and its social and environmental conflicts. *Land Use Policy, 79*, 326–338. https://doi.org/10.1016/j.landusepol.2018.08.030

Sgarbi, G. (2019). Sustainability: "This is just the beginning". In conversation with the Locavore chefs. William Reed Ltd. Retrieved 12 March 2020, from https://www.theworlds50best.com/stories/News/eelke-plasmeijer-locavore-sustainable-restaurant-award-just-getting-started.html

Sloan, P., Legrand, W., & Hindley, C. (2015). *The Routledge handbook of sustainable food and gastronomy*. Routledge.

Slow Food Cerrado. (2019). Slow food cerrado: Sobre. Retrieved 18 March 2019, from https://www.facebook.com/SlowFoodCerrado/

Sternadt, D., Mellado, J., Rivas-Mariño, G., & Moyano, D. (2021). Tasty and waste-free food – The alternative to improve the use of public resources in School Feeding Programmes in Latin America and the Caribbean: Case studies in three countries. FAO. https://doi.org/10.4060/cb4910en

Valette, E., Schreiber, K., Conaré, D., Bonomelli, V., Blay-Palmer, A., Bricas, N., & Lepiller, O. (2019). An emerging user-led participatory methodology. Mapping impact pathways of urban food system sustainability innovations. In A. Blay-Palmer, D. Conaré, K. Meter, A. Di Battista, & C. Johnston (Eds.), *Sustainable food system assessment: Lessons from global practice* (pp. 19–41). Routledge.

Vinuto, J. (2014). A amostragem em bola de neve na pesquisa qualitativa: um debate em aberto. *Temáticas, 22*(44), 203–220. https://doi.org/10.20396/tematicas.v22i44.10977

Zanella, M.A. (2020). On the challenges of making a sustainable kitchen: Experimenting with sustainable food principles for restaurants. *Research in Hospitality Management, 10*(1), 29–41. https://doi.org/10.1080/22243534.2020.1790207

Zaneti, T.B. (2017). Cozinha de raiz: as relações entre chefs, produtores e consumidores a partir do uso de produtos agroalimentares singulares na gastronomia contemporânea [PhD thesis, Universidade Federal do Rio Grande do Sul]. UFRGS LUME Digital Repository. https://www.lume.ufrgs.br/handle/10183/164708

Zaneti, T.B., & Balestro, M.V. (2015). Valoração de produtos tradicionais no circuito gastronômico: lições do Cerrado. *Sustentabilidade em Debate, 6*(1), 22–36. https://doi.org/10.18472/SustDeb.v6n1.2015.10709

Zaneti, T.B., & Schneider, S. (2017). Muito além de ingredientes: A contribuição da gastronomia para o fortalecimento da agricultura familiar - o caso da relação entre chefs, agricultores e consumidores do Instituto Maniva, no Rio de Janeiro. In CLAEH & GEPAD (Eds.), *Experiências inovadoras na agricultura familiar brasileira: atores, práticas e processos para o desenvolvimento rural* (pp. 1–92). Departamento de Publicaciones del CLAEH.

4 Traditional tortillas in Mexico

Opportunities and challenges for producers and consumers

Héloïse Leloup and Julie Le Gall

4.1 Introduction

This chapter presents the application of the Urbal approach (see Chapter 1) in the Mexican context of the company Maizajo, which is working to set up an alternative distribution network for tortillas made from native maize, processed through nixtamalization. This process involves cooking the maize kernels in an alkaline solution, usually limewater. The maize is then milled after soaking overnight to obtain a wet dough (masa) used to make tortillas and other maize products (Briones et al., 2000).

The company's premises consist of a production unit, a mill located on the outskirts of Mexico City, which processes native maize harvested directly by local farmers. The products obtained, mainly tortillas, are sold to restaurants in Mexico City. The background of the two partners behind the project, who both trained in gastronomy, facilitates access to this outlet.

Maizajo is an urban-based initiative. More importantly, it is a market-chain innovation. The company was born out of the observation that the quality of the tortillas sold in the capital was deteriorating, which was seen as unfair to consumers who were unable to obtain quality tortillas. The quality of tortillas and their preparation methods have evolved considerably over time as production has had to adapt to extremely high demand, especially in Mexico City. At present, the tortilla market in Mexico is largely controlled by major food companies (Maseca and Minsa, the main suppliers of maize flour) (De Ita, 2007). This industrial configuration emerged in the 1950s and has lastingly disrupted the tortilla trade.[1] Unlike nixtamalized tortillas, tortillas sold by these companies are made from maize flour. There are also many tortillas on the market in the capital that are dyed with artificial colouring. These processes are used to mimic the colours of tortillas made from native maize—which can range in colour from pink to blue depending on the variety—when most tortillas are made from selected hybrid seeds. The number of processing mills has drastically reduced, making more room for industrial tortillas (Cerra, 2020; Rubio & Rubio, 2013) and intensifying the competition between the food companies and the processing mills offering fresh dough (Sánchez, 2017). Thus, the

DOI: 10.4324/9781003285441-4

initiators of the project have positioned themselves on a very competitive market, seeking to revive processing and distribution activities that were losing ground. Maizajo is also driven by the desire to foster better collaboration between the market and farmers and to build relationships of trust between the different partners.

The vision of the initiative, or its narrative (Devaux et al., 2009), is to offer a new way to improve the prospects of small farmers on agricultural markets (Shepherd, 2007), while responding to urban demand for higher quality foods that meet increasingly stringent safety standards and contributing to the renewal of food processing models. The initiative's model of collective action tends to involve not only small farmers, but other stakeholders as well. Here, the intermediary is a food processing industry player, a type of actor that does not tend to be found in collective action, or in initiatives guided by a participatory market chain approach (Devaux et al., 2009). Unlike grassroots innovations, Maizajo is a market-based innovation, and it is not striving to change values in the system (Gernert et al., 2018). Rather, it aims to generate more benefits for small farmers as well as other market chain actors.

According to classic definitions, innovation—the introduction of something new into an economic and social organization—is more than ever a factor that drives the competitiveness of companies. Innovation allows for reducing costs, improving productivity or product quality, and creating new markets in a context of globalized competition (Porter & Heppelmann, 2014). For Maizajo, innovation means positioning itself competitively on an already saturated market, standing out with the quality of the products it offers.

In using a traditional transformation process, Maizajo is endeavouring to connect the past with the present. Nixtamalization predates the Spanish conquest, yet it is intertwined with contemporary knowledge, technologies, and questions (e.g., concerns about the hygiene of the process). During this process, dry maize kernels are boiled in an alkaline solution and then rinsed. The method softens the kernels and forms a paste, the "nixtamal", which is then used to cook tortillas. Nixtamalization has particularly interesting nutritional benefits, as it releases niacin, an amino acid that is lacking in maize. A niacin deficiency can cause pellagra, a disease involving skin, digestive, and nerve problems. Beyond tortillas, nixtamal is the core ingredient of many other products derived from maize, including pozole (a traditional soup made from nixtamalized maize grains), atole (a drink made by boiling and diluting the paste in water, possibly flavoured with ground fruit or chocolate), and tamales.

With this method, Maizajo has the particularity of being a retro-innovation, a term generally denoting the deliberate revival of historical practices, ideas, and/or technologies (Zagata et al., 2020). In this process, old (retro-)elements become drivers for new (innovative) ideas. According to Rogers (1962), what matters is not whether an idea is objectively new, but how people perceive the idea: "If the idea seems new to the individual, it is an innovation" (Rogers, 2010, p. 11).

This concept is relatively central to contemporary discussions on rural development and agricultural transition (Zagata et al., 2020). Often, retro-innovation opposes modernist agricultural practices and generates specific knowledge systems that represent a "starting point of transition" (Stuiver, 2006). Stuiver demonstrated early on that retro-innovation is a practice that has been developed to counter problematic trends in the agricultural sector. A very similar dynamic can be witnessed in the context of food processing. The rise of nixtamalization is a response to the generalized industrialization of tortillas. Maizajo's idea was born out of the lack of quality tortillas accessible to all on the capital city's market and grounded in discontent with the present regime (Stuiver, 2006). Developing and disseminating nixtamalization appears to constitute a critical practice, "an active effort to counter prevailing modernisation trajectories in the agri-food sector" (Zagata et al., 2020, p. 643). This criticism of the current system represents the trigger for change in Maizajo's practices (Sutherland et al., 2012). The Maizajo Urbal Food Innovation Lab (UFIL) has positioned itself within a specific gap in the market: a demand for products that are non-industrialized but also meet the agroindustry's strict hygiene and quality standards.

The basic attributes of retro-innovation are also consistent with territorial strategies for rural development (Zagata et al., 2020). Maizajo's vision aligns with this dimension of the concept, as it claims to work to empower the rural sector on the fringes of the capital.

The UFIL is currently largely positioned on a niche market, selling its tortillas to restaurateurs in Mexico City. However, the project leaders' ambition is to extend their model and contribute to a profound change in the eating habits of the inhabitants of the Mexican capital. Geels and Schot's (2007) work shows how initiatives can emerge in niches that allow them to mature or be eliminated and can then grow, spread in their original form or in a new form, and ultimately change the dominant sociotechnical regimes. With the Urbal approach, we endeavoured to highlight the factors crucial to achieving the objectives of the initiative, allowing it to become self-sustaining. We also borrow from Geels to identify other factors that support the maintenance and growth of an innovation, such as "politics and power", "cultural discourse and framing struggles", and "policy analysis" (Geels, 2019, p. 187). The analysis of these factors was made possible by the methodology chosen, which considers all the actors of the supply chain, as well as external factors that can foster or hinder the innovation's development.

This chapter considers all the characteristics of the UFIL (an innovation that revives old processes, with food processing at the core of the initiative) to highlight the impacts of the innovation on producers and consumers, as well as observed or potential barriers. In Section 1, we first reflect on the particularities of the product (maize and nixtamalized paste) and the company (as a processor, a category of actors often forgotten in studies on food systems). Before analysing the results of our research, we outline the different stages of the

Urbal process in Section 2. As the UFIL and its expectations are central to the method, we also explore the perspectives shared by the researchers and the project leaders, which guided the formulation of exercises tailored to Maizajo.

We then present the results of the first stage of the methodology, the diagnosis in Section 3, explaining how this led us to focus on producers and their relationship with the UFIL. The last section discusses the results of the impact pathways. These reveal the most significant activities for Maizajo and its network. We focus on the network that makes up the innovation and its intermediary steps which are fundamental to stimulating interaction, facilitating negotiations, mobilizing resources, generating or rediscovering novelties, and capitalizing on experience (Klerkx et al., 2010). In particular, we illustrate how the configuration of networks is continuously changing during innovation processes, fostering the creation of new links while causing others to disappear (Faure et al., 2018).

The last step of the methodology could not be carried out due to the COVID-19 pandemic. However, this crisis revealed and emphasized asymmetries in the relationship between Maizajo and the producers, which we discuss in the last section of this chapter.

4.2 Investigating the link with production: An innovation based on maize, the symbol of Mexican gastronomy

Maize, sometimes presented as a "Mesoamerican gift to the world" (Vargas, 2014), has a special place in Mexico at all levels of the food system. The protection of native seeds is central to issues surrounding both cultural and biological heritage (Boege, 2008; Xolocotzi, 1985). This chapter does not revisit the ambiguities surrounding the conflation of environmental preservation with the protection of indigenous peoples, an issue many authors have already addressed (Conklin & Graham, 1995; Demeulenaere, 2014; Foyer & Ellison, 2018). However, it is important to acknowledge that maize cultivation can potentially impact sustainability in multiple ways and concerns a range of stakeholders with conflicting interests. The special place of maize in Mexican culture and society significantly facilitated the recruitment of experts from the field to take part in the workshops.

Geels stresses that "positive salient discourses can enhance the cultural appeal and social acceptance of niche-innovations" (Geels, 2019, p. 193). Maize and its conservation have a particularly positive image in Mexico as a food symbol of the national heritage. The emergence of innovation based on this product benefits from very positive frames of representation and storylines, which also encourage the development of policies for stronger support (Rosenbloom et al., 2016).

Despite the green revolution that took place in Mexico in the 1940s, native seeds have retained a central place in maize cultivation, since almost 75% of the area planted with maize is thought to be planted with local native varieties (Perales & Golicher, 2014). Maizajo is taking on the issue of seeds by sourcing only native varieties for the production of its tortillas. Unlike many tortillas sold in Mexico City, which are artificially coloured, the colours of the UFIL's products come from the various varieties of maize used. Maizajo hopes to eventually source untreated maize. Production monitoring is currently insufficient. The Urbal diagnosis confirmed that only native seeds were used (instead of hybrids), although this does not preclude the application of fertilizers, fungicides, and insecticides by some farmers for crop protection.

At the same time, nixtamalization is a particularly time-consuming process. The preparation of tortilla involves several stages: the maize is cooked in lime water, rinsed, ground, shaped, and baked (Vargas, 2014). If done entirely by hand, this work can take one person up to four hours. Nowadays, the kernels are often ground in mills. Increasingly, nixtamal is substituted with nixtamalized flour in the tortilla making process. Flour-based tortillas have replaced tortillas made with nixtamal in household consumption, as they have the benefit of considerably reducing the manufacturing time.

The nixtamal used by Maizajo is the product of a series of tests carried out by its team in order to find the quantities of lime needed for each type of maize. The company develops empirical methods to find the right dosage for each variety in order to standardize the process and align it with the expectations of the current food market. The UFIL's founders do more than use an "old" recipe: they must ensure that their process is compatible with the current sociotechnological structures of their environment (Zagata et al., 2020).

The characteristics of the seeds depend not only on their variety but also on the treatments they undergo while growing and at the post-harvest stage. Thus, Maizajo develops a testing protocol for each supply. The relationship with the growers is therefore crucial, and Maizajo has every interest in maintaining a long-term partnership with them. The company's discourse, particularly in its work to raise funds and secure institutional support, gives centre stage to farmers and supports the rural sector on the outskirts of the capital.

4.3 The methodology used to implement the Urbal approach: Focusing on the role of the stakeholders

4.3.1 Phase 1: The diagnosis

During our diagnostic work, we met with eight farmers. We were able to have regular interviews with three of the interviewees throughout the implementation of the methodology. Even before starting the interviews with the farmers, the promoters of the initiative had signalled a high turnover of suppliers and the difficulty of maintaining a lasting relationship with producers.

One of the objectives of the collaboration between Urbal and Maizajo was to pinpoint the root causes of the barriers to strong relationships between producers and processors. We therefore steered our research in this direction. Very quickly, with Maizajo's suppliers we were able to identify a number of barriers that prevented the business relationship from continuing.

4.3.2 Phase 2: A workshop co-constructed building on the diagnosis

The format of the workshop aimed to facilitate learning in support of collective action in the context of smallholder market participation (Kruijssen et al., 2009) to help the group of participants jointly define problems, search for and implement solutions, and assess the value of particular solutions for specific problems. In other words, it contributed to social learning and fostered collective cognition (Koelen & Das, 2002). The design of this workshop prioritized joint activities, following the Urbal process.

At the end of the diagnosis stage, the research team inventoried the activities conducted by the company as exhaustively as possible. We split these activities into four categories: supply, production, distribution, and other ancillary activities (dissemination of the model, corporate social responsibility activities, and promotion). We then detailed the activities within each category.

At this stage, it was crucial to consult with the promoters of the initiative, so that they could tell us which themes they felt were most important to analyse in depth. Together we selected three activities that would be discussed during the workshop: 1) the nixtamalization process; 2) the purchase of native maize; and 3) the introduction of native maize in gastronomy. Strictly speaking, this selection of activities exceeded the initial scope of the diagnosis, which focused on analysing the relations between producers and the initiative. In so doing, we sought to open the debate to take into account other dimensions of the initiative, in particular food processing.

The workshop was ultimately attended by 12 participants: four UFIL members (the two project leaders and two employees), two producers, two consumer representatives (Maizajo customers), and four experts (a member of a trade association for tortilla, a member of a consumer group, an academic, and a researcher at the CIMMYT[2]). We formed three heterogeneous groups, each comprised of one Maizajo member (project leader or employee), one producer representative, one consumer representative, and one "expert". A member of the Urbal team was assigned to each group to facilitate the activities and lead the discussions.

The first exercise followed a classic Urbal approach as we wanted to highlight the impacts of the Maizajo initiative. To this end, we asked the participants to list the short-, mid-, and long-term effects of the three activities selected ahead of the workshop with the agreement of the founders of the initiative. The goal was to distinguish between what we called "real effects", which can already be observed, and "potential effects", which are the expected impacts that can occur if an activity follows its course as expected. Each group started on one activity and then completed the work started by the two other groups.

Once all the groups had listed the effects of each of the three activities, the second exercise began with each group selecting two of the effects (both real and potential) identified in the previous exercise. The groups then had to break down the steps of the path leading from the activity to the impact and detail the associated levers and barriers. The value of working on both real and potential impacts is that it forced participants to anticipate possible barriers to achieving impact at the end of pathway. This exercise provided the founders of

Maizajo with visibility on areas to which they would need to be attentive in order to reach their objectives. It also gave them an idea of potential levers.

The last exercise focused on the stakeholders taking part in Maizajo and on their activities. The aim of this exercise was to get the participants to consider which actors played an important role in the continuation of the initiative. We also wished to focus on actors who could play a potential role in the project but were not yet involved, actors who were left out and how to involve them, and actors who may have an interest in joining the initiative in the future. To this end, we drew up a table (Table 4.1) for participants to fill out in the third and final exercise of the workshop.

Agricultural innovation is not just about new technology; it is also about institutional change (Klerkx et al., 2010). It requires alternative forms of organization, for instance of markets, labour, land tenure, and the distribution of benefits (Leeuwis et al., 2003). In this sense, we consider Maizajo and its

Table 4.1 Table showing the roles of the players in the "Formalising the transformation (through invoicing)" activity

	Name of the actors	*What is the actor doing? What could he/she do?*	*How is he/she doing it?*	*What hinders or prevents its involvement?*
Actors directly involved	Maizajo. Producers.	Declaration of purchases/ sales to the "Tax Adminis-tation Service"	Reinforcing farmers selection criteria.	Over-regulation
Actors indirectly involved	Final consumers: - Restaurants - Everyone consuming maize	Enhancing the value of products resulting from formalisation.		Lack of financial resources: "we buy what we can". Lack of education.
Actors potentially interested (not involved yet)	Nixtamalisation mills			
Actors that can potentially support the activity	Governement. "Tax adminis-tration service". Civil society. Universities. Farmers' children.	Support with procedures	Documenting procedures, including in native languages. Support procedures. Differentiated political recognition.	Lack of transparency of information.
Actors left out	Small farmers. Small consumers.			Lack of appeal.

effects as a complex system, resulting from the interaction of heterogeneous actors. During the workshop, we wished to shed light on the diverse range of actors involved in the company's activities, and those who could be involved in the future. These actors may contribute to food system innovation in a range of capacities (e.g., technological development, institutional change, supply chain reorganization, market development, fostering social acceptance).

Identifying these different actors provided a way to establish the drivers of success, which can be influenced by various factors such as consumer preferences, government policies, and market factors at several levels (regional, national, global) (Blay-Palmer, 2005).

4.4 The results of the diagnosis: The ambivalent relationship between Maizajo and its producers

Initial discussions with the promoters of the initiative clearly revealed a lack of knowledge about the players in the supply chain, especially in the farming sector. Well before we arrived, they had identified pain points relating to the producers. They were concerned about securing a regular maize supply and stressed the difficulty of maintaining long-term relationships with producers.

By mutual agreement between the founders of the initiative and the research team, the diagnosis focused on the producers, their perceptions of their collaboration with Maizajo, the opportunities this opened up, and the potential barriers to pursuing the relationship. If we consider Maizajo only from its own perspective, the agreement between the company and the producers seems to be advantageous for the latter. They are offered prices higher than market rate, as well as support in the formalization of sales. With the Maizajo team's agreement, we wished to understand the relationship between the initiative and the producers from the latter's point of view. This line of study had so far received little attention within the Urbal project and allowed us to introduce a complementary perspective on urban food systems: that of the producers.

4.4.1 Profile of the producers

Maizajo works with a limited number of producers. In total, around 20 farmers have supplied the company over its lifetime, but fewer than 10 maintain regular relations with Maizajo. Most of the producers we were able to meet shared several common features that seem to align them with the company's expectations and requirements. They were highly educated and often had several sources of income. They had almost all completed secondary school, and most of them had a university degree in agriculture, biology, or business. This high level of education helps producers to respond to Maizajo's demands. Invoicing is a crucial issue for both the producers and the company. For legal reasons, Maizajo requires the issuing of invoices. For many small-scale producers, this process is not straightforward, in fact, it is a minority practice. The producers we interviewed told us about the difficulties of setting up invoicing. Travelling to the appropriate authorities, understanding which documents need to be provided, and the time spent on these procedures are all barriers to formalizing their farming activity. Moreover, producers told us that billing, which automatically entails paying taxes, was not financially beneficial for them. Several actors stressed their lack of trust in the authorities and were reluctant to declare their activity to them. Many persisting factors underlie the refusal to formalize the commercialization of agricultural produce on Mexican farms, and issuing invoices for crop represents a distinct change in practices for producers. The choice to maintain an informal system is also explained by farmers' greater familiarity with the associated practices and networks (a familiarity that reduces their risks), which can ultimately "lock in" development pathways (Haydu, 1998; McGuire, 2008). Maizajo's billing practices disrupt the path dependency of producers (Sutherland et al., 2012) and can thus foster mistrust.

The above reasons explain why producers with several sources of income more easily subscribe to the Maizajo approach. Among the most regular suppliers of the initiative are producers who also have another profession, including a mechanical engineer, a young biology graduate, a chef, and an agricultural engineer employed by the Ministry of Agriculture. These professions are characterized by a certain autonomy with regard to legal protocols. One of the suppliers we met, who had only sold to Maizajo once, explained to us the difficulties he faced in declaring his sales. He was supported in these steps, on an ad hoc basis, by an association for the protection of native maize. Without this support, the relationship could not continue.

4.4.2 *Storage: Who should be in charge?*

One of the problems recurringly mentioned by producers and Maizajo representatives was crop storage. The company does not have premises to store maize while it awaits processing, so they must buy maize weekly, which adds to the company's logistical burden.

Typically, Maizajo agrees with the producers on the amount of maize it will purchase, to be collected by the company as and when it needs it. The burden of storage therefore falls on the producers, who do not always have the necessary infrastructure to protect their crops from potential losses (e.g., rotting, pests). A promise of purchase is made, but no compensation is provided in case of loss. Producers prefer to sell their entire crop so that they do not have to worry about storage. In many cases, this deferred purchase is a disincentive for farmers, despite the attractive prices offered. Actors with several sources of income are at an advantage here: they do not depend solely on resources from farming to sustain their activity. Maizajo is aware of this problem and is looking to set up storage support. Research has been undertaken to provide producers with low-cost solutions, but to date this has not been successful.

Although the project emphasizes its capacity to bolster rural areas, we noted a persistent gap between production, on the one hand, and processing and distribution on the other. As an example, visits to suppliers are very rare and contact is largely digital. More significantly, the producers informed us that they had never tasted Maizajo's tortillas made from their maize. The interviews with producers particularly showed that the buyer's requirements did not align with the constraints of production. To meet the expectations of the company's founders, we broadened the reflection carried out as part of the Urbal framework to consider the production-related dimension of the initiative's activities.

4.5 Results from the impact pathways: Shedding light on the core of the initiative

This section highlights how the Urbal approach, through the collective identification of impact pathways, can draw attention to specific aspects of the initiative and ultimately reveal the core of the food system innovation. According to Devaux et al. (2009), a number of factors can influence the performance of innovation systems, such as the external environment, the range of actors involved, the values and attitudes of the key actors, institutional arrangements, and patterns of interaction. Different factors can also trigger the innovation, such as changes in policy, markets, and technology. The aim of the Urbal workshop was to identify and explore these factors collectively. Any innovation process goes through periods of acceleration, slowdown, and crisis, and not all innovations are viable—a selection process occurs (Nelson, 1993). The workshop strove to develop awareness, within the UFIL network, of its position in the institutional environment, using interactive learning and a monitoring approach (Schuetz et al., 2009). It shed light on the resources and competences available to the UFIL to foster innovation, including institutional features such as actors' norms and rules (Edwards, 2000). Section 4.5.2 presents some of the main results of the workshop.

Maizajo takes part in the food system by promoting a specific marketing circuit, and therefore has several potential and expected impacts on sustainability. Most significantly, the initiative reduces the number of intermediaries between maize producers and the buyer, with positive repercussions on the economic dimension of sustainability. As a food distributor, it must play a role in food security. At the same time, Maizajo tends to communicate on the nutritional value of its product, especially the nutritional value derived from the use of nixtamalization to process the maize kernels.

The project also has potential impacts on the sociocultural and environmental dimensions of sustainability. The product is central to Mexican gastronomy and its history. The nixtamalization process is a distinctive characteristic of Mesoamerican cooking that has survived to this day (Fernández Suárez et al., 2013). Maizajo is contributing to spreading the nixtamalization process so as to promote traditional Mexican expertise.

4.5.1 An innovation that addresses food security… for whom?

The impact pathway analysis shows that Maizajo's activities can affect several dimensions of sustainability (Figure 4.1). Among them, food security is the one that was mentioned most often, in connection with both opportunities and risks, for the producers as well as consumers. We define food security based on the five A's of food security identified by Cecilia Rocha: food availability, accessibility, adequacy, acceptability, and agency (Chappell & LaValle, 2011; Rocha, 2007).[3] Furthermore, Hammelman and Hayes-Conroy (2015) have suggested

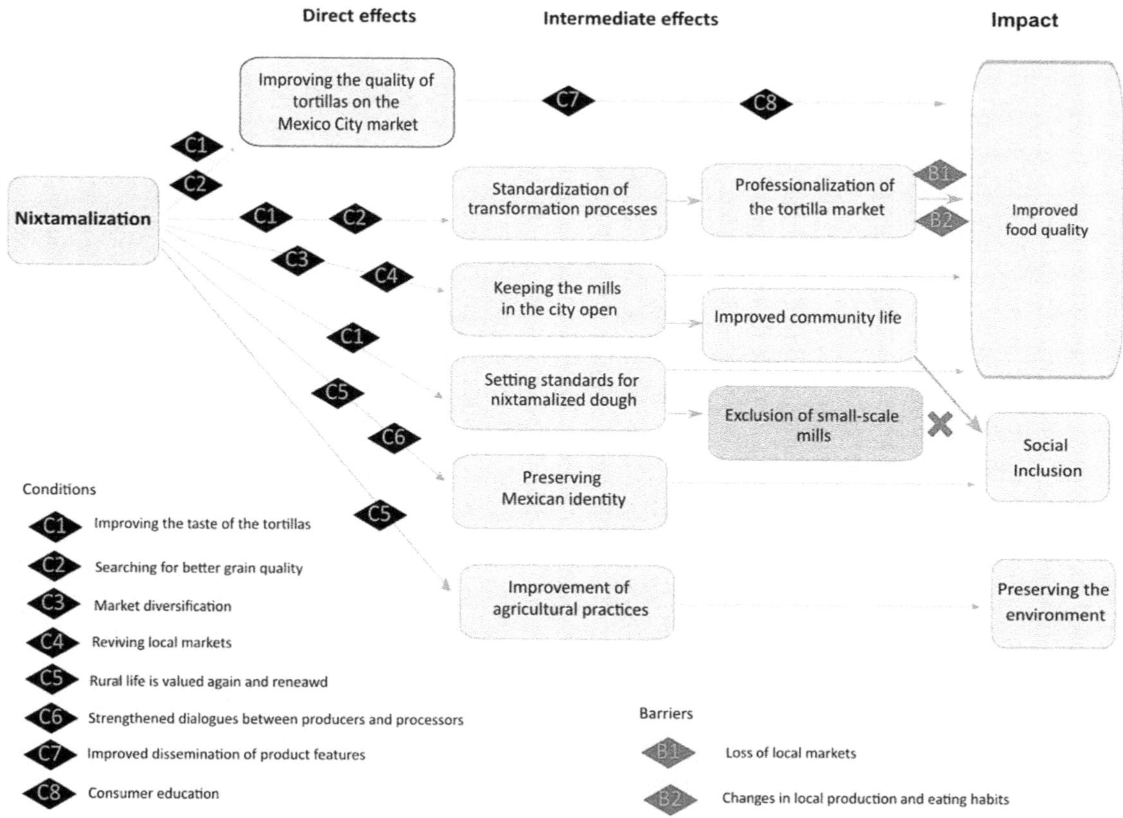

Figure 4.1 Impact pathway for the activity "Nixtamalization" based on the results of the first exercise in the workshop. It shows the different stages leading to impacts, as well as the conditions and obstacles along the way.

adopting a more comprehensive understanding of cultural acceptability in the context of food security, informed by "human rights-based approaches, cultural values evident in production and consumption processes, the importance of interweaving multiple knowledges, and challenging decision-making powers in today's corporate food regime" (p. 43).

Spreading better quality tortillas, a staple of the national diet, seems to logically lead to an improved diet. However, this spread is subject to many constraints and requires adjustments and support in order to break out of the niche market in which Maizajo is currently positioned. In particular, the group discussions highlighted the importance of education on the taste, texture, and storage of nixtamalized tortillas compared to flour tortillas. It is also necessary to support consumers in re-learning to recognize the taste of a nixtamalized tortilla. A similar observation applies to cooks, as well as suppliers of prepared food in the broadest sense—from the person in charge of a household's food supply to the chef at a restaurant to the street vendors who abound in Mexico City. It is necessary to facilitate these food actors' integration of nixtamalized tortillas in their preparations and teach them how to handle them properly so as to reduce the risk of losses (see the map of actors in Figure 4.3 to understand the significant role played by actors from different sectors in the development of Maizajo's activities). It is important to note that the discussions focused on the place of food system actors who typically receive little attention: the food processors, especially the local mills. These mills, once central to the distribution of tortillas, are now disappearing in the capital (Cerra, 2020). In order to achieve the impact of "improving food security" for the inhabitants of the capital, Maizajo cannot act alone. Its goal is to share its model with other processors. However, this dissemination must go hand in hand with political support in order to restore these establishments' central role. This is not a recent concern: as early as 2017, the processors' trade associations turned to the Mexican authorities to be better taken into account in the aid schemes for alternative industries.

In terms of risks, Maizajo's activities may have several unintended adverse effects on food security. For example, the attractive prices offered by Maizajo may cause farmers to sell their entire crop, without saving any seeds for their own consumption. Producers, who are suppliers of quality grains, could be forced to buy flour tortillas from classic market chains, which are of a lower quality and less nutritious. The introduction of a staple food in a specialised market channels has already been highlighted as a risk factor for producers in the case of quinoa in Bolivia (Jacobsen, 2011). The representative of a consumer association present at the workshop also pointed to the example of the sale of Mexican coffee to agroindustry, which had the effect of impoverishing producers and weakening the country's food sovereignty. Similarly, the creation of new opportunities for native maize may lead to increased demand for this crop, at the expense of other crops for household consumption, and even to the detriment of milpa.[4]

Another risk concerns not the producers, but the processors. To make nixtamalized tortillas widely available, Maizajo is striving to make them meet a number of sanitary standards regarding the traceability of the seeds' origin and the control of production systems (see Figure 4.2). These standards have

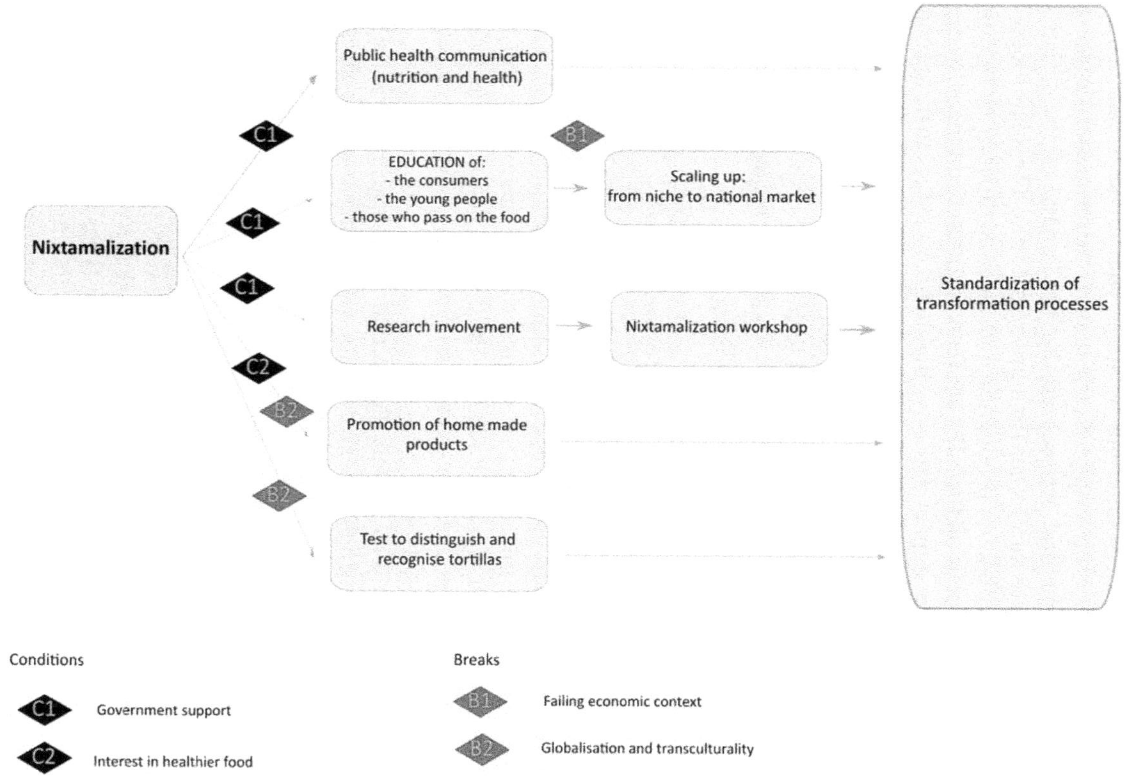

Figure 4.2 Detailed pathway leading to an intermediate effect (standardization of transformation processes) based on the results of the second exercise in the workshop. It details a specific pathway from the activity to the intermediate effect chosen by the participants. More specifically, it sheds light on the multiple barriers and levers at play.

also been identified as a condition for the success of impact pathways. At the same time, they represent a barrier for many small-scale processing mills, which do not have the necessary means to adopt and meet these standards.

This example of the contradictory effects associated with the implementation of regulatory standards highlights one of the roles of the group discussions, where ambivalent effects have been pointed out by actors with different perspectives. This shows the importance of involving a diverse range of actors in social learning.

Thanks to the Urbal method, we realized that the impacts of the initiative related to downstream activities rather than upstream ones. The steps focused more on grain processing than on production and the modalities of collection. While we had wished to focus on the links between producers and the initiative, the process of defining the impact pathways highlighted the fact that this concern was secondary in the conduct of Maizajo's activities. Surprisingly, this interest in downstream activities was shared not only by the managers of the initiative but also by the other actors involved. Maizajo's innovation lies above all in grain processing and the nixtamalization technique. Furthermore, generalizing nixtamalized tortillas is more of a priority for the project's promoters than ensuring fairer incomes for local producers.

4.5.2 Results derived from the perspectives shared by stakeholders

Given the nature of the innovation, the workshop participants' attention was directed to the overall supply chain capacity—not just the producers—and the degree to which the chain in its entirety can compete/enter the market. Since our methodology focused on actors, we wanted to take this opportunity to create an ad hoc stakeholder forum to identify the current and potential future roles of all the actors across the supply chain, including those who were absent from the workshop (see Figure 4.3).

The aim was particularly to prepare the second workshop included in the Urbal approach by shedding light on the institutional and macroeconomic environments.[5] These play a role through the rules, norms, and values that support the dominant trajectory or allow niche innovations to flourish (Faure et al., 2018). The importance of involving a diverse range of actors has been highlighted by a large number of studies on collective action. As Devaux and colleagues point out, innovation is stimulated by the interaction of individuals and groups with different backgrounds, interests, and perspectives (Devaux et al., 2009).

Figure 4.3 shows all the actors mentioned during the exercise concerning stakeholders and distinguishes between the different types of actors most frequently mentioned in relation to the conduct of activities. We organized the actors into six categories. The producer/processor/consumer triptych is the most significant. A particular feature of the innovation is the increased presence of processing actors, who are rarely mentioned in food system innovations. As Maizajo is a processing actor, this finding is not surprising. However, this category encompasses a wide variety of actors, present on many different scales and markets (from street vendors to chefs at upmarket restaurants). The

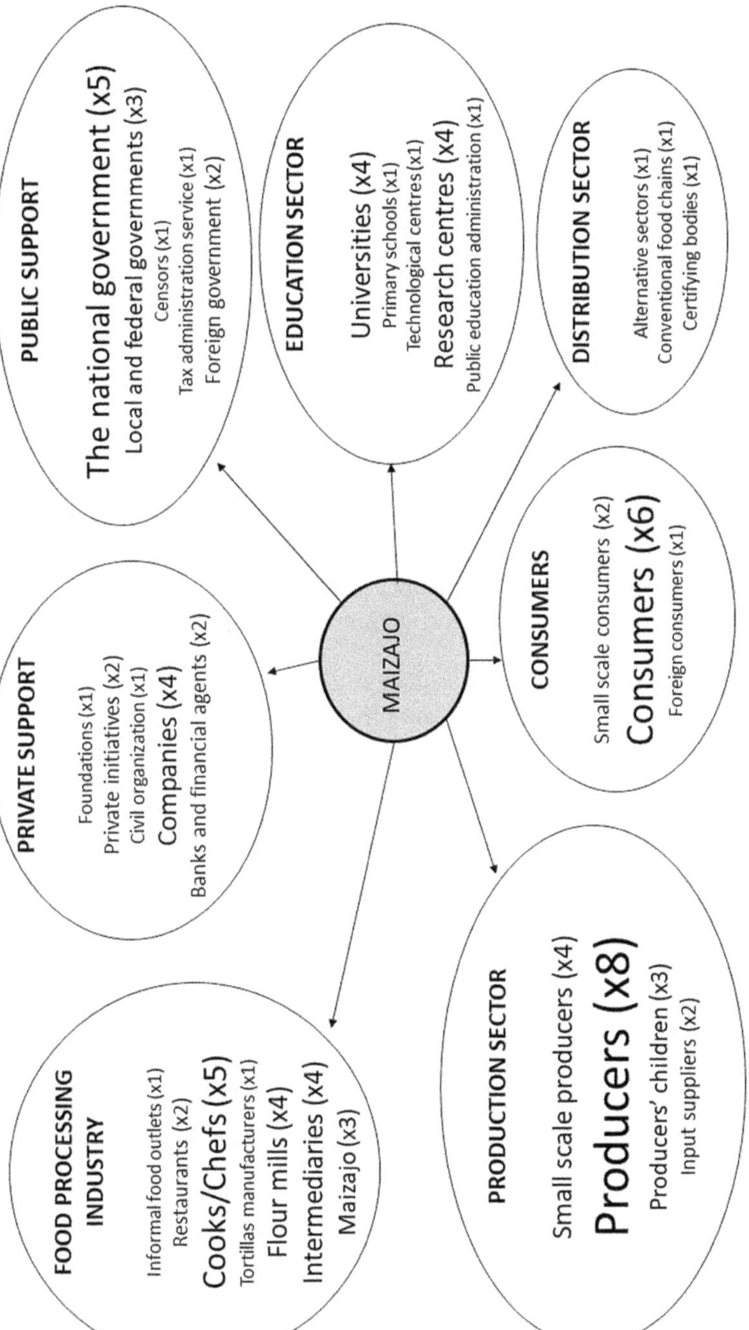

Figure 4.3 Map of actors.

workshop exercise regarding actors (mentioned above) illustrated processing actors' importance in the food system and the value of including them in food innovations.

However, Figure 4.3 also highlights the role of the education sector, particularly in research and support for innovation. Participants stressed the role of universities not only in supporting alternative market initiatives but also in conducting research on native seeds and providing technical guidance. According to the literature on governance, policymakers should play a key role in facilitating the interaction, discussions, learning processes, and information sharing surrounding an innovation (Smith et al., 2005). There are therefore high expectations of government support, particularly in the form of standards for native seeds and nixtamalized dough. Governments and policymakers can provide long-term direction and formulate specific policy targets, which enable action and accountability (Kattel & Mazzucato, 2018).

Depending on the composition of each group, the actors identified varied. The group that included a UNAM[6] researcher thus placed greater emphasis on the role of universities in the dissemination of more sustainable food models. Likewise, the group that included a member of an association for the protection of native maize seeds pointed to the importance of certification bodies or policies for the public dissemination of information about the characteristics of native seeds.

This exercise provided an opportunity to think about the population left out and their possible integration: not only the marginalized population but also powerful actors that could possibly intervene to support the project and its scaling. This in turn raised the question of how to reach and involve these actors, and how to broaden the scope of action for food justice.

Experts present at the workshop suggested a variety of potential developments. The CIMMYT representative pointed to the possibility of extending the process to hybrid, selected seeds, which could provide security for producers, while members of Mexican maize protection associations stressed the importance of keeping native seeds at the heart of the process. Meanwhile, the food systems researcher discussed possible ways of marketing the tortillas to move away from systematically involving restaurant owners. This diverse range of actors allowed for different kinds of issues to emerge, which the UFIL leaders can reflect on in order to enhance their decision-making regarding the initiative.

4.5.3 The effects of the COVID-19 health crisis on the company's market orientation

The COVID-19 crisis forced Maizajo to reduce its native maize supply. For the producers, this has meant fewer orders from the company. Contrary to expectations, producers were not so concerned about losing this buyer, or even about the direct consequences of the recession (Leloup & Le Gall, 2020). The feedback from the producers revealed continuity mechanisms more than clear sudden changes in their organization (e.g., production factors such as rainfall, access to inputs, and government support remained primary concerns). The continuation of the producers' activities and the continuity of their concerns, despite the loss of a buyer that positions itself as an agent of fairer trade, demonstrate the relatively low impact of such an enterprise on the territories where the maize is grown. Market outlets are not a factor limiting their activity. While Maizajo's prices are certainly attractive, other opportunities are available to the producers. What matters to them is selling their produce; the profits afforded by a higher price are secondary. The health crisis has highlighted the fractious relationship between the producers and the initiative, but there were warning signs. The relationship with producers is central to the vision of the initiative and it is part of the discourse and symbolism developed by Maizajo (Plowman et al., 2007). This has remained the case throughout the innovation process, as partners had left and joined the network. In the case of Maizajo, the narrative has remained the same, although the activity has changed radically. The company continues to project the image of locally grown maize and remuneration for local producers, even if this is not core to its current activity. Its focus has shifted downstream, while it continues to sell itself thanks to its upstream activities.

4.6 Conclusion: Upstream and downstream challenges

The company's vision is to impact all segments of the marketing chain, from improving the living conditions of producers to enhancing the Mexico City population's food supply. The methodology proposed by the Urbal approach shed light on the impact pathways of the UFIL's activities to promote sustainability, as well as the accelerators, conditions, and obstacles along the way.

During the workshop, by exploring the levers for and barriers to conducting an activity, and thanks to the presence of a range of actors (some of whom were sceptical of the initiative), we were able to identify many points of caution. While the UFIL can have positive impacts on consumer nutrition (health dimension of sustainability) and on the preservation of seed diversity (social dimension, environmental dimension), stakeholders are also aware of the potential negative effects of Maizajo's activities. For instance, this chapter provided an in-depth discussion of the impacts of "retro-innovation". The analysis of impact pathways enabled us to highlight some of the dangers of this type of innovation. By reviving old processes in urban neighbourhoods, which are still used in rural areas of Mexico, the company is at risk of causing a trend towards the gentrification of nixtamalized tortillas. The modernization of this process and its adaptation to align with sanitary and legal requirements, including stringent hygiene and administrative standards, may push out the actors contributing to maintaining the process in the first place (e.g., local mills, informal tortillerias). In this case, the impact of the UFIL could negatively affect the economic wellbeing of different stakeholders, from small food processors to low-income consumers.

Beyond the impact pathways, the Urbal methodology highlighted Maizajo's main priorities, with processing as its core business. The company's initial concern regarding the weakness of its relationship with producers was confirmed during the diagnosis and the workshop. This is one of the main contributions of this UFIL: it shed light on the difficulties, for the productive sector, of integrating appropriate food innovations arising from urban areas. There are still many barriers to the widespread adoption of the innovation by producers. Many producer profiles remain excluded from the marketing circuit proposed by Maizajo.

While the initiative highlights the continuity of relations with producers as a guarantee of the quality of the final product, this aspect of Maizajo's activities is probably the most uncertain. The fragility of the relationship between the processor and the producers reflects the risks raised by this kind of initiative surrounding the economic dimension of sustainability, such as the fragility of outlets for producers and poor resilience of the relationship in case of crises, as the health crisis of 2020 confirmed.

Box 4.1 On the role of chefs in food system sustainability

Maizajo is an innovation that was envisioned by chefs. As outlined in Chapter 3 (Brazilian case) of this book, chefs contribute to creating a gastronomic identity and can play an influential role in shaping a more sustainable food system for the future. While Maizajo's initiators have a keen understanding of the possible outlets and potential of a nixtamalized tortilla on the capital's market, they are less familiar with the realities of the productive sector. This discrepancy was confirmed during the diagnostic phase and in their response to the health crisis as the project leaders naturally turned to the sale of prepared meals to eat at home. The two leaders had expertise in cooking and pastry making.

Given this context, what role can chefs play in supporting sustainable food initiatives?

Klerkx et al. (2010) highlight the role of "boundary spanning actors" in "enhancing adaptive management capacity for effective reformism". Chefs, and gastronomy in general, can be influential and powerful actors who help create a conducive institutional environment when the latter is not supportive of change (Klerkx et al., 2010). In the case studied, the food craze in Mexico represents an opportunity to develop innovations around food systems. Chefs can showcase producers' know-how and become ambassadors of a country's food heritage (Matta, 2015). In this context, chefs, although they are disconnected from the realities of production, can create an environment favourable to the development of innovations that promote better production conditions. In food sustainability, gastronomy can play the role of an "innovation broker".

Notes

1 Our interviews with trade associations for tortilla and producers as well as the UFIL itself revealed a telling figure: around 90% of the tortillas sold in Mexico City are manufactured by these companies. However, we were not able to corroborate these statements with official figures.
2 Centro International de Mejoramiento de Maiz y Trigo—International Maize and Wheat Improvement Center.
3 From Chappell and LaValle (2011, p. 36): "Availability refers to the sufficiency of a food supply to meet people's needs; Accessibility refers to people's economic and physical ability to acquire food; Acceptability addresses the cultural and nutritional suitability of the available food; Appropriateness evaluates the ecological sustainability and the safety of a food supply; Agency is the 'right to knowledge, and knowledge of rights' – access to accurate information on food supply, quality, and safety in order to make informed market choices, rights to such information and to the other aspects of food security, and a competent sociopolitical system to guarantee these rights".
4 An agricultural technique which consists in combining complementary crops, usually squash, beans, and maize. The word has come to be used in Mexico to refer to a small agricultural plot on which this technique is practised.
5 Due to the COVID19 health crisis that occurred in 2020, we were not able to implement the 2nd workshop included in the Urbal methodology. Indeed, we were not in position to guarantee the necessary safety distances for a public event. Our results are therefore based on the results of the diagnostic phase and the first workshop.
6 Universidad Nacional Autonoma de Mexico—National Autonomous University of Mexico.

References

Blay-Palmer, A. (2005). Growing innovation policy: The case of organic agriculture in Ontario, Canada. *Environment and Planning C: Government and Policy*, *23*(4), 557–581. https://doi.org/10.1068/c17r

Boege, E. (2008). El patrimonio biocultural de los pueblos indígenas de México: Hacia la conservación in situ de la biodiversidad y agrodiversidad en los territorios indígenas.

Briones, F. C., Iribarren, A., Peña, J. L., Rodriguez, R. C., & Oliva, A. I. (2000). Recent advances on the understanding of the nixtamalization process. *Superficies y vacío*, *10*, 20–24.

Cerra, D. (2020, January 12). Sobre los casi extintos molinos de nixtamal (y por qué comprarles masa). local.mx. https://local.mx/ciudad-de-mexico/molinos-nixtamal/

Chappell, M. J., & LaValle, L. A. (2011). Food security and biodiversity: Can we have both? An agroecological analysis. *Agriculture and Human Values*, *28*(1), 3–26. https://doi.org/10.1007/s10460-009-9251-4

Conklin, B. A., & Graham, L. R. (1995). The shifting middle ground: Amazonian Indians and eco-politics. *American Anthropologist*, *97*(4), 695–710. https://doi.org/10.1525/aa.1995.97.4.02a00120

De Ita, A. (2007). Catorce años de TLCAN y la crisis de la tortilla. *Programa de las Américas, Reporte Especial.*

Demeulenaere, E. (2014). A political ontology of seeds: The transformative frictions of a farmers' movement in Europe. *Focaal*, *2014*(69), 45–61. https://doi.org/10.3167/fcl.2014.690104

Devaux, A., Horton, D., Velasco, C., Thiele, G., López, G., Bernet, T., Reinoso, I., & Ordinola, M. (2009). Collective action for market chain innovation in the Andes. *Food Policy*, *34*(1), 31–38. https://doi.org/10.1016/j.foodpol.2008.10.007

Edwards, T. (2000). Innovation and organizational change: Developments towards an interactive process perspective. *Technology Analysis & Strategic Management*, *12*(4), 445–464. https://doi.org/10.1080/713698496

Faure, G., Chiffoleau, Y., Goulet, F., Temple, L., & Touzard, J.-M. (2018). Introduction: Renouveler les regards sur l'innovation dans les systèmes agricoles et alimentaires. In *Innovation et développement dans les systèmes agricoles et alimentaires* (Quae, pp. 19–37).

Fernández Suárez, R., Morales Chávez, L. A., & Gálvez Mariscal, A. (2013). Importancia de los maíces nativos de México en la dieta nacional : Una revisión indispensable. *Revista fitotecnia mexicana*, *36*, 275–283.

Foyer, J., & Ellison, N. (2018). Conserver les maïs mexicains. *Etudes rurales*, *202*(2), 120–139.

Geels, F. W. (2019). Socio-technical transitions to sustainability: A review of criticisms and elaborations of the Multi-Level Perspective. *Current Opinion in Environmental Sustainability*, *39*, 187–201. https://doi.org/10.1016/j.cosust.2019.06.009

Geels, F. W., & Schot, J. (2007). Typology of sociotechnical transition pathways. *Research Policy*, *36*(3), 399–417. https://doi.org/10.1016/j.respol.2007.01.003

Gernert, M., El Bilali, H., & Strassner, C. (2018). Grassroots initiatives as sustainability transition pioneers: Implications and lessons for urban food systems. *Urban Science*, *2*(1), 1. https://doi.org/10.3390/urbansci2010023

Hammelman, C., & Hayes-Conroy, A. (2015). Understanding cultural acceptability for urban food policy. *Journal of Planning Literature*, *30*(1), 37–48. https://doi.org/10.1177/0885412214555433

Haydu, J. (1998). Making use of the past: Time periods as cases to compare and as sequences of problem solving. *American Journal of Sociology*, *104*(2), 339–371. https://doi.org/10.1086/210041

Jacobsen, S.-E. (2011). The Situation for Quinoa and Its Production in Southern Bolivia: From Economic Success to Environmental Disaster. *Journal of Agronomy and Crop Science*, *197*(5), 390–399. https://doi.org/10.1111/j.1439-037X.2011.00475.x

Kattel, R., & Mazzucato, M. (2018). Mission-oriented innovation policy and dynamic capabilities in the public sector. *Industrial and Corporate Change*, *27*(5), 787–801. https://doi.org/10.1093/icc/dty032

Klerkx, L., Aarts, N., & Leeuwis, C. (2010). Adaptive management in agricultural innovation systems: The interactions between innovation networks and their environment. *Agricultural Systems*, *103*(6), 390–400. https://doi.org/10.1016/j.agsy.2010.03.012

Koelen, M., & Das, E. (2002). Social learning. In C. Leeuwis & R. Pyburn (Eds.), *Wheelbarrows full of frogs: Social learning in rural resource management: International research and reflections* (pp. 437–446). Koninklijke Van Gorcum.

Kruijssen, F., Keizer, M., & Giuliani, A. (2009). Collective action for small-scale producers of agricultural biodiversity products. *Food Policy*, *34*(1), 46–52. https://doi.org/10.1016/j.foodpol.2008.10.008

Leeuwis, C., Leeuwis, C., & Ban, A.W. van den. (2003). *Communication for rural innovation: Rethinking agricultural extension* (3rd ed.). Blackwell Science, Iowa State Press, for CTA.

Leloup, H., & Le Gall, J. (2020). Une petite entreprise agro-alimentaire mexicaine face à la Covid-19 : Maizajo, productrice de tortillas nixtamalisées, au devant de la continuité. Cahier des UMIFRE.

Matta, R. (2015). *Conocimiento y poder. Prácticas alimentarias y patrimonialización cultural. Alimentos, cocinas e intercambios culinarios. Confrontaciones culturales, identidades, resignificaciones* (pp. 205–220). Guadalajara: Universidad de Guadalajara.

McGuire, S. J. (2008). Path-dependency in plant breeding: Challenges facing participatory reforms in the Ethiopian sorghum improvement program. *Agricultural Systems, 96*(1–3), 139–149. https://doi.org/10.1016/j.agsy.2007.07.003

Nelson, R. R. (1993). *National innovation systems: A comparative analysis*. Oxford University Press.

Perales, H., & Golicher, D. (2014). Mapping the diversity of maize races in Mexico. *PLoS ONE, 9*(12), e114657. https://doi.org/10.1371/journal.pone.0114657

Plowman, D. A., Baker, L. T., Beck, T. E., Kulkarni, M., Solansky, S. T., & Travis, D. V. (2007). Radical change accidentally: The emergence and amplification of small change. *Academy of Management Journal, 50*(3), 515–543. https://doi.org/10.5465/amj.2007.25525647

Porter, M. E., & Heppelmann, J. E. (2014). How smart, connected products are transforming competition. *Harvard Business Review, 92*(11), 64–88.

Rocha, C. (2007). Food insecurity as market failure: A contribution from economics. *Journal of Hunger & Environmental Nutrition, 1*(4), 5–22. https://doi.org/10.1300/J477v01n04_02

Rogers, E. M. (1962). *Diffusion of innovations*. New York: Free Press of Glencoe.

Rogers, E. M. (2010). *Diffusion of innovations*, (4th ed.). Simon and Schuster.

Rosenbloom, D., Berton, H., & Meadowcroft, J. (2016). Framing the sun: A discursive approach to understanding multi-dimensional interactions within socio-technical transitions through the case of solar electricity in Ontario, Canada. *Research Policy, 45*(6), 1275–1290. https://doi.org/10.1016/j.respol.2016.03.012

Rubio, B., & Rubio, B. (Eds.). (2013). La crisis alimentaria mundial : Impacto sobre el campo mexicano (Primera edición). Universidad Nacional Autónoma de México, Instituto de Investigaciones Sociales : Miguel Ángel Porrúa.

Sánchez, G. V. (2017). El mercado de harina de maíz en México. Una interpretación microeconómica. *Economía Informa, 405*, 4–29. https://doi.org/10.1016/j.ecin.2017.07.001

Schuetz, T., Boru Douthwaite, C., & Alvarez, C. S. (2009). *Participatory impact pathways analysis (PIPA)*. Ghana: International Water Management Institute.

Shepherd, A. (2007). *Approaches to linking producers to markets* (Vol. 13). Food & Agriculture Org.

Smith, A., Stirling, A., & Berkhout, F. (2005). The governance of sustainable socio-technical transitions. *Research Policy, 34*(10), 1491–1510. https://doi.org/10.1016/j.respol.2005.07.005

Stuiver, M. (2006). Highlighting the retro side of innovation and its potential for regime change in agriculture. *Research in Rural Sociology and Development, 12*, 147–173. https://doi.org/10.1016/S1057-1922(06)12007-7

Sutherland, L.-A., Burton, R. J. F., Ingram, J., Blackstock, K., Slee, B., & Gotts, N. (2012). Triggering change: Towards a conceptualisation of major change processes in farm decision-making. *Journal of Environmental Management, 104*, 142–151. https://doi.org/10.1016/j.jenvman.2012.03.013

Vargas, L. A. (2014). El maíz, viajero sin equipaje11Trabajo modificado a partir de su presentación en el simposio "Somos de maíz : Principio y destino", con motivo del vigésimo quinto aniversario de la revista Cuadernos de Nutrición, en el Instituto Nacional de Ciencias Médicas y Nutrición "Salvador Zubirán", 24 de julio de 2007. *Anales de Antropología, 48*(1), 123–137. https://doi.org/10.1016/S0185-1225(14)70492-8

Xolocotzi, E. H. (1985). Maize and man in the Greater Southwest. *Economic Botany*, *39*(4), 416–430. https://doi.org/10.1007/BF02858749

Zagata, L., Sutherland, L., Hrabák, J., & Lostak, M. (2020). Mobilising the past: Towards a conceptualisation of retro-innovation. *Sociologia Ruralis*, *60*(3), 639–660. https://doi.org/10.1111/soru.12310

5 The role of school canteens in building more sustainable food systems

The impact pathways of the "Ma Cantine Autrement" programme in Montpellier

Marlène Perignon, Olivier Lepiller, Beatrice Intoppa, Élodie Valette, Ophélie Roudelle and Amélie Wood

5.1 Introduction

5.1.1 The multiple roles of school canteens

Global estimates suggest that one in every two school children, or 388 million children, receive school meals every day (WFP, 2020). Aside from increasing school enrolment, the main purpose of school feeding programmes is to help improve children's nutritional status by giving them access to school meals that meet nutritional recommendations (CNA, 2017). By providing low-cost healthy school meals to all and particularly children from low-income families, school canteens play a crucial role in the reduction of social inequalities in health. In this respect, in order to be effective, measures to improve school canteens cannot overlook the social inclusion challenges surrounding the way in which they are received by different groups and social categories. Beyond public health issues, school catering addresses many other challenges relating to education, economic development, and environmental issues (CNA, 2017; FAO, 2017). Its educational role involves social dimensions, for instance in teaching civility and good manners during school meals. Canteens are a space for socializing and the meals are a time for sharing and social interaction, but also for food education to encourage healthy eating habits, taste education to help the children discover and enjoy new foods, and education about the food system—where the food comes from, how it is produced, and by whom. Furthermore, school canteens are a place to raise children's awareness of the impact of their food choices on the environment and can thus help teach children to adopt dietary behaviours with a lesser environmental impact and to minimize food waste. Finally, school canteens recently took on an additional role, in the reterritorialization of food and local economic development. The large quantities of food required for school meals make public catering

DOI: 10.4324/9781003285441-5

establishments a major stakeholder on the food market, and their food procurement strategies provide a key lever for supporting territorial agricultural economies.

5.1.2 The French context

In France, public school catering is embedded in the public school system, an institution that has been secular, free, and compulsory since 1881. In a way, public service is thus core to its mission. Paradoxically, however, public school catering was long not run as a public service: it depended on the involvement, at local levels, of the municipalities, parents, social organizations, or teachers and therefore took on various forms, when it existed at all. Only after the Second World War did school meals become widespread (Comoretto et al., 2020).

In France, nearly 70% of children aged 3 to 17 have lunch at school at least three times a week (ANSES, 2017), making school canteens a real lever for promoting sustainable dietary behaviours. The nutritional quality of school meals is structured by several laws and recommendations. Nutritional guidelines were developed in 2001 and updated in 2007, 2011, and 2015 by the Groupe d'Etude des Marchés de Restauration Collective et Nutrition (GEM-RCN, task force on the institutional catering and nutrition markets) (GEM-RCN, 2007, 2011, 2015). French regulation provides that school meals must necessarily include four or five components (a starter and/or a dessert, a main dish, a side dish, a dairy product). Furthermore, frequency standards that are set by the GEM-RCN for 15 type of dish (e.g., any dish that qualifies as a "starter containing more than 15% fat" must be served no more than four times in a series of 20 consecutive meals) became mandatory across all schools in 2011 (République Française, 2011a, 2011b).

Since 2017, all children in France have been entitled to register for school meals. As of 2019, the EGalim law (République Française, 2018) to achieve a balance in trade relations in the agricultural sector and a healthy, sustainable, and accessible diet for all requires school catering services to offer at least one vegetarian meal (without meat or fish) per week. The EGalim law also provides that as of 2022, public catering establishments must include 50% sustainable and quality-certified products with a minimum of 20% organic products (as a share of total purchase value excluding VAT). Additionally, this law extended the obligation to implement a framework to combat food waste—estimated at 115g per meal and per child in school canteens (AMORCE-ADEME, 2019)—to all institutional catering actors in both the public and private sectors. Moreover, school catering establishments preparing more than 3,000 meals per day must enter into a food surplus donation agreement with an authorized nonprofit. The French legal framework thus upholds the principle of equal access to food that meets quality standards defined according to nutritional quality and sustainability criteria (Chiaverina et al., 2022; Sanz Sanz et al., 2022). However, it is hampered by social differentiation in canteen attendance, with pupils from disadvantaged backgrounds eating at school less often than those from more privileged backgrounds (Caillavet et al., 2021; Poinsot, 2021).

Concerning the food supply, as in all European countries, French public catering is subject to the public procurement code that requires school canteen supply contracts above an authorized threshold to go through a tendering process. With regard to the inclusion of local products in school meals, it is worth noting that the public procurement code makes it difficult to include geographical criteria in calls for tenders, since they could be considered as discriminatory according to free European market exchanges rules. Nevertheless, these restrictions were recently relaxed. As of 2015, social and environmental clauses can be introduced in calls for tenders in order to facilitate local procurement. Prior to this, the restrictions could be circumvented by requiring short delivery times, for example. Specific attributes, such as organic certification, can also legally be mentioned in calls for tenders.

For some years now, the policy and regulatory context has thus been evolving to provide better conditions for developing more sustainable school catering. Such improvement has also been encouraged by the introduction of food policies at local level, with a stronger commitment from regional and municipal institutions as well as the emergence of Territorial Food Projects (*projets alimentaires territoriaux*, PAT), an institutional framework defined by French law in 2014 (Guillot & Blatrix, 2021; Lamine et al., 2019). Local institutions can set up PATs to obtain funding from the French State in order to relocalize the food system within their territories.

5.1.3 The "Ma Cantine Autrement" programme in Montpellier

The city of Montpellier is actively committed to this evolution towards more sustainable and relocalized food systems. It has been a signatory city of the Milan Urban Food Policy Pact since the pact's launch in 2015. The city self-manages the production and distribution of 14,600 meals a day for its 89 primary school restaurants and 42 recreation centres for children aged 3 to 11, with 22,000 families making use of the city's school catering. Meals are prepared in the city's central production unit (CPU) and distributed to schools in refrigerated trucks. In 2016, following a food waste diagnosis in its school canteens, the Food Policy Department (FPD) of the city of Montpellier launched a programme to optimize its school catering system, with a view to reducing food waste and promoting sustainable diets for children. This programme, called "Ma Cantine Autrement" (MCA), was designed as an interactive framework of 23 actions organized into four main pillars: 1) food procurement policy; 2) production management; 3) meal distribution; and 4) sustainability awareness.

This chapter describes how the Urbal participatory approach was applied to identify the impact pathways (IPs) of the MCA programme on the different dimensions of a sustainable food system and discusses the lessons learned from this analysis. The application of the Urbal approach was the result of a relationship between CIRAD and the city of Montpellier that predates the project. Even before the Urbal project was launched, Montpellier's FPD was seeking a tool to evaluate and monitor its innovative actions. The MCA case study was one of the first identified to test the Urbal approach. The participatory approach aimed to shed light on the IPs by taking into account the perspectives of diverse stakeholders concerned by the programme to provide insights on what impacts should be expected and how/why they could be achieved.

5.2 Methodology

The MCA case study was carried out in three steps, guided by the Urbal methodological framework. First, a study characterized and provided a better understanding of the MCA programme, its innovative activities, timeline, and stakeholders. The research team then carried out a multi-stakeholder participatory workshop to collectively identify the main impacts and IPs of a set of innovative activities. Faced with the legal and practical difficulty of directly involving school children in the workshop, the research team decided to conduct a separate study to collect their views. The research team analysed all the data collected to develop a more detailed and explicit understanding of the IPs of activities and produce a synthetic map showing barriers to and levers of the impacts. Finally, the research team organized a second workshop, during which this analysis was presented and informed a discussion about strategies to scale out an innovation such as the MCA programme.

5.2.1 Characterization of the programme (activities and stakeholders)

The study was carried out from mid-January to early May 2019, drawing on a range of sources. The Urbal project research team benefited from the direct support of the Montpellier Food Policy Director, who is also the Montpellier School Catering Director and the main MCA designer. The Food Policy Director helped to provide access to documents, made himself available to answer questions, and connected the Urbal intern in charge of carrying out this first stage of the research with an intern at the FPD. The initial data sent by the FPD comprised of documents in various formats (PowerPoint presentations, internship reports, documentary notes, maps, teaching scenarios) and of different kinds, such as urban food policy benchmarks, food waste management documentation, action plans, decisions made by the MCA steering committee, engagement letters from the Mayor, progress reports and evaluations of the measures' implementation, press releases, etc. These documents were organized and categorized. Interviews with the Food Policy Director completed this data. This material was used to produce three main documents:

1. A timeline of the different measures implemented as part of the MCA programme from 2014, when the first food waste measurement operations were launched, to the end of 2019
2. A list of the activities carried out as part of the MCA programme from 2016 to 2020 (see Table 5.1)
3. A map representing the main actors and categories of actors involved in the MCA programme (see Table 5.2)

Table 5.1 Complete list and description of the MCA programme activities

Axes	*Activities*
Pillar 1: Food procurement policy	1. **More targeted allotment by product or family of products**: the size of the batches ordered is reduced and products are unbundled to encourage smaller local producers to respond to calls for tenders 2. **Specification of higher quality standards for public contracts**: this activity allows for the integration of quality criteria such as organic certification and other quality labels 3. **Working group on local outlets**: these multi-stakeholder groups, which include farmers, meet regularly to structure and facilitate the local response to calls for tenders 4. **Administrative services cooperative supporting local producers**: this service offer aims to strengthen local farmers' capacity to respond to public calls for tenders
Pillar 2: Production management	5. **Creation of fruit and vegetable processing stations**: this production tool makes it possible to use a greater number of first-range products (raw agricultural produce that has not yet been processed) in the production of meals 6. **Improvement of recipes and portion weights**: these adjustments are made dish by dish, guided by preliminary studies of the meal leftovers, to minimize food waste 7. **Reorganization of the booking system**: an online platform is set up to allow parents to book meals for a shorter period than before (6 weeks) 8. **Seasonal menu cycles**: this menu design aims to promote local and seasonal products and is supported by communication targeting the parents and children 9. **Four-component meals (replacing the usual five-component meals)**: this simplification of the meal structure was informed by a study of meal leftovers to minimize waste 10. **Food donation agreement with charities**: this agreement with local charities facilitates the recycling of production surpluses through food aid
Pillar 3: Meal distribution	11. **Nutrition training for staff**: these training courses are accessible to kitchen and facilitation staff and provide them with nutritional knowledge and skills 12. **Hospitality and service training for staff**: these training courses are accessible to kitchen and facilitator staff and provide them with hospitality knowledge and skills 13. **Cutting kit**: this set of tools is designed to facilitate the work of kitchen staff and allows for cutting fruit directly at the table 14. **Limiting cutting work to one task per meal**: this action aims to facilitate the work of kitchen staff 15. **Experiment with self-service restaurants**: this experiment aims to minimize waste by allowing children to choose dishes according to their taste preferences

(*Continued*)

Table 5.1 (Continued)

Axes	*Activities*
Pillar 4: Sustainability awareness	16. **Eco-citizen meal (without any animal-based food)**: this menu, which was initially served monthly, is coupled with communication on limiting environmental impacts and on nutritional quality 17. **Bio-compostable food containers**: these plant-based containers, which hold portions for an entire table, replace plastic containers 18. **Generalization of waste sorting and biowaste recovery**: this action is aimed at better sorting the different types of waste while involving the children 19. **Sorting table with an integrated scale**: this device makes the quantities of waste generated by meals visible to all 20. **Educational booklet and interactive map**: these communication tools are designed to raise parents' and children's awareness of MCA actions and can be used as a teaching device during school time 21. **Educational theatre play "Opération Brocoli"**: this recreational play aims to raise the children's awareness of the sustainability issues and challenges surrounding food 22. **Teaching activity on taste run by dietitians**: this activity strives to expand the children's palate by enabling them to open up to new tastes 23. **Communication sent to parents with proposed evening menus**: this communication tool suggests menu and recipe ideas for dinner meals at home

5.2.2 *Identification of impact pathways by the stakeholders*

Based on the set of activities identified in the first stage of the study, the research team organized a participatory workshop, but decided to focus on just 12 activities, spanning all four MCA pillars and from among those with the most potential for impact. This allowed the participatory exercise to be conducted during a few hours' workshop covering a limited but comprehensive range of activities.

5.2.2.1 *Participatory workshop*

We organized the participatory workshop on Wednesday 26 June 2019, in a large classroom designed to accommodate 50 people, from 5: 00pm to 8: 00pm (in other words after the end of the workday, but not too late). The chosen location was on the campus of the agronomic school of Montpellier, close to the city centre and easily accessible. We informed the participants that drinks and snacks would be provided during the workshop and that a friendly, more informal chat would follow.

The invitation mentioned the event's title: "What are the impacts of 'Ma Cantine Autrement'?" Based on the inventory of relevant actors carried out in the previous stage, we wished to bring together a diverse range of protagonists: the Director of Food Policy and School Catering; people working in

Table 5.2 Main groups of actors involved in the MCA programme

Institutional actors
Actors whose decisions and support have direct effects (mayor, elected representatives, municipal service departments, etc.) or indirect effects (local chamber of agriculture, Regional Department of Food and Agriculture, Environmental and Energy Management Agency, etc.) on the implementation of the MCA programme.

Field actors
Actors that are directly involved in running school catering and the MCA programme on a daily basis (FPD, cooking staff, facilitators of extracurricular activities and school support staff, dietitians, composting centre, waste treatment plant, Montpellier Market of National Interest, National Centre for Local Civil Service, etc.).

Economic/industrial actors
Actors that are directly involved in the production of meals (suppliers, CPU, etc.).

Financial actors
Actors that fund the MCA programme (municipality, Regional Department of Food and Agriculture, Environmental and Energy Management Agency, etc.).

Non-profit/foundation actors
Social organizations that are partners of the MCA programme (charities, local farming organizations, etc.).

Social actors
Children, parents, parent associations, voters, etc.

Research actors
The Urbal research team, researchers from the MoISA research unit, the French Agricultural Research Centre for International Development, the National Research Institute for Agriculture, Food and Environment, and the UNESCO Chair in World Food Systems.

Network actors
Actors involved in structuring the local sustainable food network.

production at the CPU; a dietitian from the FPD; farmers/producers supplying the CPU; a person working at Montpellier's Market of National Interest (Montpellier wholesale market); a person from the Chamber of Agriculture; representatives of non-profits interested in MCA (organizations that can benefit from the production surpluses, such as Saint Vincent de Paul, or that are working to improve the sustainability of school catering, such as Greenpeace); parents, including some involved in a non-profit promoting the use of organic and local food in Montpellier's canteens (named Collectif Cantines); organizers of extracurricular activity (managers and facilitators); maintenance staff (school operations managers, maintenance, and catering staff); and expert researchers of sociology, economy, nutrition, and agronomy. In order to run the workshop efficiently, we chose to limit participation to 20 people.

We faced difficulties in inviting facilitators of extracurricular activities, actors who play a crucial role in canteens since they are in charge of facilitating mealtimes. They are employed by the municipality, more precisely by the

Department of Education, which was not willing to let them take part in the workshop for fear that they might voice criticism. This may have had to do with the fact that an election was coming up—which also explained the Department of Education's lack of involvement in the MCA programme—and with the power asymmetry between the FPD and the Department of Education, a much bigger branch of the municipal services. We ultimately decided to conduct separate interviews with extracurricular activity facilitators to collect their views about the activities' impact pathways. Some of the statements collected were quoted during the workshop.

In order to reach the target of 20 workshop participants, we sent an invitation to about 40 people. Thirteen people attended the workshop. Although this was fewer than expected, it was enough to organize the workshop following the desired structure, that is, with plenary sessions at the start and end of the workshop, and with working group sessions.

In practice, the workshop was structured as follows:

1. First, we held a plenary session to present the Urbal approach, the IP concept, the dimensions of sustainability, and the set of 12 innovative MCA activities.
2. We then split the participants into groups—the core stage of the workshop. We had three groups of three participants, and one group of four participants. Each group worked on three activities and had its own table, with one facilitator per table, and moved to a different table once, in order to produce cumulative views about another set of three activities (Table 1: (a) more targeted allotment by product or family of products, (b) more organic and local products, and (c) alternative eco-citizen meal (without any animal-based food); Table 2: (a) four-component meal, (b) improvement of recipes and portion weights, and (c) reorganization of the booking system; Table 3: (a) staff training, (b) cutting kit, and (c) bio-compostable food containers; Table 4: (a) generalization of waste sorting and biowaste recovery, (b) sorting table with an integrated scale, and (c) educational booklet and interactive map). We endeavoured to have diverse groups, with one expert, one person directly involved in MCA, and one parent or non-profit member per group. Each group spent 45 minutes discussing the first set of three activities before rotating and spending 30 minutes on the second set of activities, which had been discussed by a previous group. Each group thus worked on six activities in total. After the rotation, each group arrived at a new table was briefed on what had been said by the previous group. We used paperboards to summarize and transcribe the discussions in real time, making sure that all participants agreed on the formulation. The facilitator at each table was in charge of facilitating, audio-recording and transcribing the discussion.
3. Finally, the third stage brought all the participants together again in a plenary session. While the aim was initially to collectively discuss the synergies between the activities, this time essentially allowed the participants to share their thoughts on the workshop, their surprises regarding certain impacts, their learnings, or their assumptions that had been confirmed.

The workshop ran smoothly, and participants shared positive feedback about the event and were unanimous on the importance of such multi-stakeholder spaces—which previously did not exist—surrounding school catering.

5.2.2.2 Interviews with children and observational work

Before organizing this workshop, we had to make a decision regarding a sensitive question: should school children be invited to the workshop? While school children could indeed be considered as the main actors impacted, it seemed very difficult to involve them directly, due to legal considerations and the difference in language used. We therefore decided to conduct a separate study with school children before the workshop, so as to be able to share some of their statements during the workshop and to aggregate their views on the activities' impact during the analysis stage following the workshop. We conducted a qualitative study with children at several schools in Montpellier. With the support of facilitation staff, eight group discussions with five to eight children, each lasting about 30 minutes, were carried out "to talk about the canteen", as was announced to the children. We were also able to take part in three sessions of the children's municipal council, with time dedicated to discussing what the children knew and thought about the MCA activities. Each session brought together the elected representatives of the children from four different schools. Eight children took part in the first session, five in the second session, and 12 in the last one. This study was completed by *in situ* observations and by discussions with about 45 different children in total, while sharing meals with them at their canteens, around tables of six to eight children. While we did quote some of these field data during the workshop, their analysis took place largely after the workshop.

5.2.3 Synthesis/mapping of the impact pathways and identification of barriers and levers by the research team

Based on the material produced in the workshop, the separate fieldwork with school children and the additional interviews, the research team worked on drawing the IP maps of each of the 12 activities. The raw data from the workshop, namely 12 paperboards showing an activity at their centre and boxes listing the effects associated with this activity, could be hardly called "IP maps". They could better be described as "effects maps": for the most part, the intermediate effects leading to the long-term effect or impact, in other words the concrete pathways from the activity to its impacts, were not made explicit.

The research team analysed the raw material, listening to the audio recordings when the notes taken during the workshop or the interviews were not sufficiently clear. In order to arrive at readable impact pathways, the research team often had to reformulate the impacts in a clearer, more precise way and state the intermediate effects that were not explicitly mentioned by the workshop participants. In some cases, the research team also added some obvious impacts that had not been identified during the workshops but were documented in the scientific literature. This analytical step amounted to a translation process, balancing two distinct requirements: to capture all the information provided by the participants and remain true to what they meant, while also producing significant and precisely defined IPs that could be understood unambiguously. This analytical step also involved situating barriers, levers, and possible bifurcations as milestones on the pathways from activities to their impacts. Some of these levers, barriers, and bifurcations had been identified by the participants during the workshop, but were mainly identified and formulated by the research team based on the scientific literature and the raw data. In fine-tuning the formulation and identification of hypothetical or documented barriers, levers, and bifurcations, we made the choice to essentially strike a balance between the participatory spirit of Urbal and the value added by the knowledge in the literature. This balance was informed by the availability and allocation of time and human resources to the workshop, on the one hand, and to the analysis by the research team on the other. The result of this analytical step consisted of 12 IP maps—one for each activity—and a global map synthetizing the overall impacts of these 12 activities (the IP maps of two activities are shown further in this chapter). Each identified impact was assigned to one or several of the five different dimensions of sustainability addressed in the MCA case study: environmental, health, socio-cultural, governance, and economic.

5.2.4 Identification of strategies to support the programme's effectiveness, and conditions for its scaling out

Based on this synthetic IP mapping and working in close collaboration with the FPD, the research team decided to collectively further the discussion on the conditions of success and on the issues involved in scaling out the MCA programme, that is, in transferring the concept and methods of MCA to implement the programme in other territories or communities. At the time of the project, the MCA programme implemented in the city of Montpellier was starting to be seen as an inspiring proof of concept for other French cities, and several communities asked the FPD to share its experience. The municipality's commitment to improving school catering in support of greater sustainability, which began in 2016, anticipated and in several ways even exceeded the recommendations of the 2018 EGalim Law. The FPD expressed the need to reflect on how the programme could be efficiently transferred to other contexts. The decision was thus made to explore the question of scalability collectively, as part of the Urbal study.

To this end, the research team organized a second workshop on Tuesday 3 December 2019, from 5:00 pm to 8:00 pm. It invited 74 people: the attendees from the previous workshop (N = 13); the people who had been invited but had not participated (N = 26); and other people whose presence had been identified as relevant given their involvement in programmes similar to MCA or activities associated with the programme (N = 35). A total of 24 people attended this workshop, spanning a diverse range of positions and forms of involvement with school catering and the MCA programme. It is worth noting that we were once again unable to secure the attendance of teachers from the schools involved and that two children were present with a parent. The event's objective was twofold:

1) To share and discuss the results of the previous workshop; and
2) To organize a debate around two major crosscutting questions that had emerged from the IP mapping: (a) how to foster the involvement of all stakeholders and ensure the success of the programme "Ma Cantine Autrement" for a more sustainable food system; and (b) what are the major barriers to and conditions of transferability of the MCA programme?

The workshop was organized in three stages. First, a plenary session was held, in which the research team presented Urbal and the MCA programme and summarized the findings from the previous workshop, stressing the issues that appeared to be common to several MCA activities (see Section 5.4.2). The second stage of the workshop was dedicated to discussing the major crosscutting questions around involvement and transferability. The participants were split into two diverse groups of 11 and 12 people respectively, each at a separate table. For 45 minutes, one group worked on Question (a) while the other worked on Question (b). The two groups then swapped tables to spend 25 minutes discussing the other question, so that the discussion was cumulative. Each table had a facilitator moderating the discussion and another research team member taking notes on a paperboard. The third and final stage consisted of a plenary session to summarize the discussions and collect the participants' feedback about the workshop. We concluded with more informal discussions over refreshments.

After the workshop, the research team analysed the results and synthesized them in a 10-page document that was sent to all the participants and published as a working paper on the MoISA research unit's website.

5.3 Results and discussion

5.3.1 What are the impacts of MCA? Who do they affect and how/where do they materialize?

The IP analysis (Douthwaite et al., 2007) highlighted the inputs, outputs, outcomes, and impacts of each of the 12 MCA activities studied. Inputs refer to the resources (material, financial, etc.) used to implement an activity; outputs refer to the immediate effects produced by the activity; outcomes refer to the changes or intermediate effects resulting from the outputs; and impacts refer to the long-term effects generated by the activity (Barret et al., 2018; Walker et al., 2008). Figure 5.1 provides an example of the raw data from the workshop. This sheet summarizes the discussion on one of the MCA activities (the implementation of four-component meals). It was completed by audio recordings. Figure 5.2 shows the final version of the IP map for this same activity.

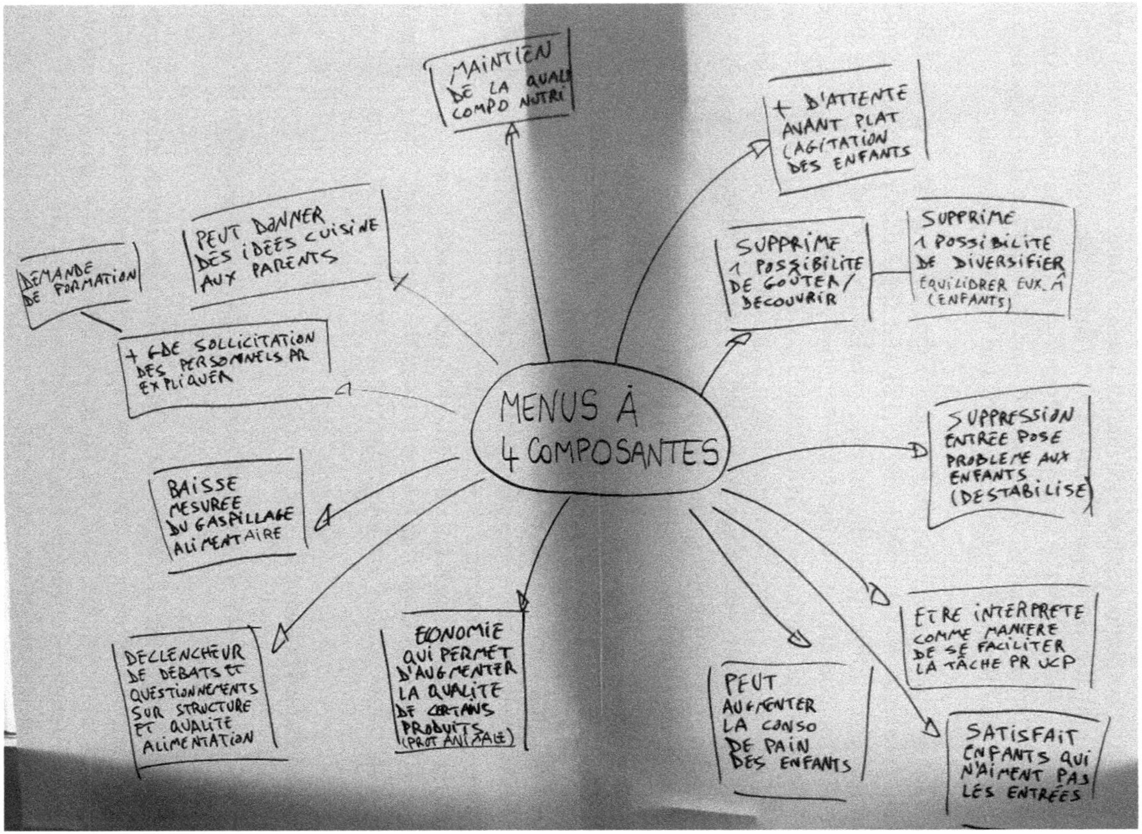

Figure 5.1 Sheet summarizing the workshop discussion on the activity “Implementation of four-component meals”.

Source: Roudelle, 2019.

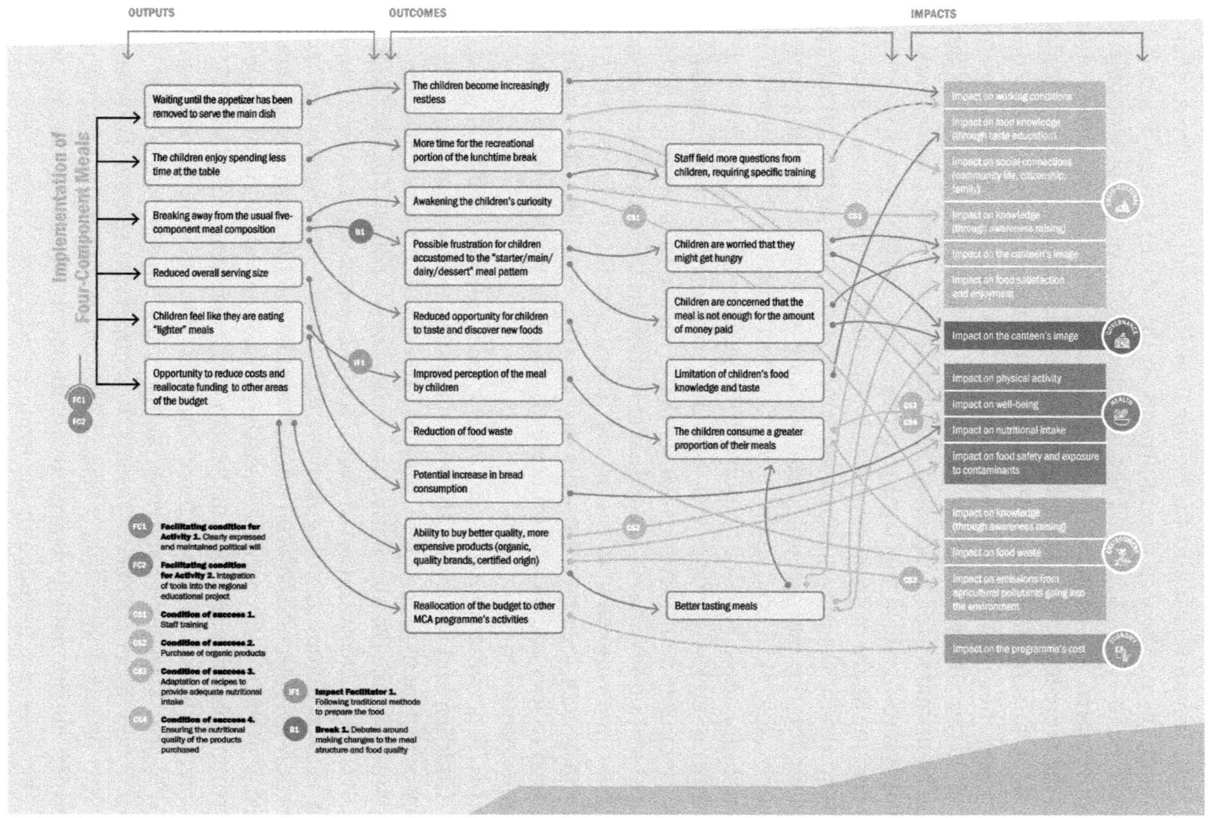

Figure 5.2 Impact pathway map of the MCA activity "Implementation of four-component meals".

Different types of *inputs* were identified: *context-related, material, and organizational inputs*. Moreover, these inputs could be either *conditions of implementation* (i.e., necessarily required to implement the activity), or *implementation facilitators* (i.e., not required but increasing the likelihood of implementation). Inputs relating to the national or international context, such as the EGalim law or the city's commitment to the Milan Urban Food Policy Pact, were factors that facilitated the implementation of the programme, but were not required. By contrast, inputs associated with the territorial context, such as the presence of local farmers to supply the school canteens with local food products, were required. A diagnosis of the food supply available on the territory was thus identified as a key step to carry out prior to the implementation of actions that fell under the "Food procurement policy" pillar of MCA. The primary food processing unit available at Montpellier's Market of National Interest,[1] which was used to process raw vegetables, was also needed to increase the share of local products in the food supply. Some inputs were assets required for the programme's implementation, such as the software program used for the new school meal booking system, the cutting kits, the bio-compostable meal containers, and the educational tools. Financial input was needed for some activities requiring the purchase of equipment (e.g., the waste-sorting tables, cutting kits and bio-compostable meal containers). Finally, organizational factors such as the existence of a working group to structure local supply chains, the management of the training session schedule to work around canteen staff's working hours, and the FPD receiving feedback from school facilitators on the dishes liked or disliked by children to adjust meal recipes and quantities, were also conditions required for the activities' implementation.

The MCA activities' *outputs (or direct effects)* affected different groups of actors. Children and canteen staff were the most directly impacted—the children by seven activities (more organic and local products; cutting kits; four-component meals; alternative eco-citizen meal; educational booklet and interactive map; generalization of waste sorting; waste-sorting tables) and the staff by eight activities (training sessions; cutting kits; improvement of recipes and portion weights; educational booklet and interactive map; bio-compostable meal containers; alternative eco-citizen meal; generalization of waste sorting; sorting table with an integrated scale). Farmers, dietitians, and CPU staff were directly affected by two to three activities. Parents were the least directly affected by MCA: of the 12 activities studied, only the new school meal booking system had direct effects on parents. It is important to note, however, that MCA also included an action whereby recommendations for evening meals and recipes, nutritionally balanced to complement the school lunches served during the week, are included in the menu schedules sent to parents. Though this activity was not selected for the IP analysis since it had only just started at the time of the study, it is expected to have a direct impact on the parents.

While most of the MCA outputs were classified as positive/beneficial, the analysis did identify some negative outputs, such as a workload increase for different types of actors (canteen staff, dietitians). The IP analysis found that, provided the conditions for success were met, the outputs led or could lead to *outcomes (or intermediate effects)*. The outcomes allowed for the activities' spread to a wider pool of actors than the direct outputs: they affected the children and parents across all 12 activities. However, these outcomes' ability to extend to the parents was subject to certain conditions being met, including, in most cases, the children communicating about the activities to their parents. This involves the children having a good understanding of the activity objectives, a requirement that is indirectly dependent on the canteen staff or teaching team.

Moreover, the IP analysis revealed that *negative outcomes* could occur instead of or in addition to the expected positive effects. *Two types of negative outcomes were identified: avoidable negative outcomes*, that is, outcomes that occur if certain conditions are not met, *and unavoidable outcomes* that necessarily arise with the implementation of the activity and should be alleviated or accepted. For instance, the introduction of four-component meals (substituting the usual five-component meals) led to an avoidable negative outcome. Some children thought that the fifth component (starter or dessert) had been removed due to a problem with the preparation of the dish that had prevented it from being served, or as a way for the FPD to save money at their parents' expense. Such misunderstandings could then spread to the parents and discredit the school canteen. This highlighted the crucial role of canteen staff in explaining the MCA activities, so that children could properly understand the activities' objectives and be reassured if they had any concerns and could then communicate the right information to their parents. On the other hand, the workload increases indirectly induced by the implementation of MCA activities, for instance with canteen staff having to cover for their colleagues attending training sessions, could be considered as an unavoidable negative outcome that should be offset by other means.

The IP analysis identified *potential impacts on five dimensions of a sustainable food system* (environmental, health, socio-cultural, governance, and economical) and highlighted *sub-dimensions impacted by the activities under each pillar*. Not all dimensions were equally affected. The IP analysis confirmed that every MCA activity had an environmental impact. This was to be expected since the objective of the programme was initially geared towards reducing food waste and promoting a sustainable diet. Regarding the environmental dimension, the programme could have an impact on food waste reduction, greenhouse gas emissions reduction, the reduction of non-renewable resource use, and the promotion of organic farming. The IP analysis also revealed that the socio-cultural dimension of sustainability was highly affected by the programme: each activity had an impact on this dimension and did so by affecting a range of different sub-dimensions. The socio-cultural dimension involved the greatest number of sub-dimensions, indicating multiple ways to make an impact. The sub-dimensions identified were working conditions/quality of life at work, social cohesion/social ties, empowerment through knowledge, taste education, and the reduction of social inequality (in health and access to a sustainable diet). The health dimension was also impacted by most activities. Impacts on this dimension could relate to the fulfilment of children's nutritional needs, well-being, physical activity, and exposure to food contaminants (e.g., pesticides, endocrine disruptors). The governance component could be impacted through sub-dimensions such as trust in the school canteen system among parents, children, and canteen staff, and awareness raising on each actor's role and contribution to the system. The analysis revealed that several of the negative impacts classified as "avoidable" pertained to the governance dimension and could arise as a result of activities not being properly explained to children, parents, or canteen staff, leading to dissatisfaction or loss of confidence in the quality of the food supplied by the canteen. Regarding the financial dimension, the main impact that could occur would affect the economic structure of the territory, through support to local farmers. Moreover, activities either induced a higher cost for the municipality or, on the contrary, afforded budget savings and thus room for manoeuvre to invest in another action of the programme.

5.3.2 *What are the factors hindering or enabling the achievement of sustainability goals?*

Mapping out the IPs helped to visualize the processes whereby activities' outputs turn into outcomes and then impacts and shed light on the *barriers and enablers observed in this process*. Several factors that could either facilitate or hinder impact were identified and categorized as: 1) *conditions for success* (required to reach the expected impact); 2) *impact facilitators* (not necessary to reach the impact but conducive to its achievement); and 3) *barriers* (i.e., factors that limit the efficacy/performance of the programme).

A major condition for success that became apparent in the IP of several activities (e.g., four-component meals, alternative eco-citizen meal, reorganization of the booking system, etc.) was ensuring that the actors, particularly the children, canteen staff, and parents, had a good understanding of the purpose, benefits, and constraints associated with the activity. Without this, outputs could end up not having any impact, or even result in negative impacts (see Section 5.3.1) if the activity was misunderstood. This condition mainly relies on canteen staff and the teaching team, who are key points of contact for children and parents who have questions regarding canteen meals, meaning they themselves need to be trained/informed. Communicating and informing actors, in particular parents, about MCA activities proved to be a major condition of success to achieve greater sustainability, since impact in the field of governance was mainly contingent on communicating the objectives and benefits of MCA activities to the parents. Another important condition of success was ensuring that the activities' implementation did not affect the nutritional adequacy of the meals. This condition is entirely dependent on the FPD's dietitians, who are key to the programme's sustainability goals since nutrition is a core dimension of a sustainable diet. Regarding activities in the area of food procurement policy, maintaining a multi-stakeholder working group to structure local supply chains was identified as an important condition of success.

Motivation among the actors involved in the implementation of activities was identified as a facilitating factor for several activities of the programme. For instance, the effectiveness of the waste-sorting tables and of educational tools would be enhanced by higher motivation to engage with them among canteen staff and children. Additionally, continuing to serve traditional dishes was also mentioned as a factor to facilitate the acceptability of certain activities. Some activities were considered to play a facilitating role in synergy, that is, they mutually supported their respective outputs. For instance, the educational tools implemented to raise children's awareness regarding food waste and sustainable diet could increase their motivation to use the waste-sorting tables in school canteens or help them better understand the benefits of introducing four-component meals or reducing the amount of animal products in school meals. Moreover, since some activities involve higher costs (introducing more organic products, using bio-compostable meal containers, etc.) and others afford cost savings (four-component meals, alternative eco-citizen meal), their simultaneous implementation is synergetic, as it allows the programme to be carried out at no additional cost.

Barriers appeared to relate either to the programme's context or to its implementation. For instance, at the time of the study the waste-sorting tables could not be set up in four schools due to structural reasons, which resulted in unequal access and limited the sustainability of the action. Another example of a context-related barrier pertained to the staff training sessions. The staff in charge of the children during mealtimes generally have a background in education/facilitation techniques but do not necessarily have knowledge or skills surrounding nutrition or children's mealtime needs. Since such skills are not included in current professional training, all staff involved had to attend the training sessions provided as part of the MCA programme. As a result, it took several years to achieve equal access to the benefits of this activity. Some barriers directly related to the programme's implementation: they included the workload increase for the dietitians (e.g., to provide training sessions), canteen staff (e.g., to sort waste) and farmers (the administrative burden of applying for calls for tenders), and the greater constraints placed on the parents with the new meal booking system. The cost and lack of availability of some food products on the territory were also identified as hindrances limiting the growth of local and/or organic food supplies.

5.3.3 *Suggestions of actions to limit the barriers identified and/or to promote levers, and the conditions required or desirable for the deployment of the programme in other communities/territories (scaling out)*

The barriers and conditions of success that emerged from the analysis of the IP maps were discussed with the different stakeholders during the second participatory workshop. The actors suggested different actions to limit the barriers identified and/or to foster the conditions required for success, which could be split into two categories: *1) actions to improve communication and better inform the actors* (children, parents, canteen staff) about the MCA activities' objectives and benefits; and *2) actions to stimulate actors' motivation and involvement in the programme despite the additional workload.* To improve communication, the participants suggested using different media like posters to be displayed in the canteen and in front of the school, or a short movie that could be shown to children by the teaching team and sent to the staff and parents. They also suggested mobilizing and involving the teachers, as well dedicating teaching time to helping the children understand MCA. They recommended minimizing the disconnect between teaching time and after-school time and argued that school meals could provide a valuable teaching tool to address environmental issues and the concept of sustainability. Another suggestion was to organize a school trip to visit local suppliers, the CPU and the Montpellier Market of National Interest (MIN), and to encourage parents to go on such visits, so as to foster transparency/full disclosure and trust. Regarding actions to stimulate the actors' motivation and involvement, the participants showed a strong interest in building a multi-actor committee to bring together all school canteen stakeholders. They advocated widening the existing working group focused on the structuring of supply chains to include other actors (parents, teachers, and children in particular). The participants suggested organizing a school canteen commission for each of the eight districts of Montpellier and highlighted the need to continue carrying out multi-actor workshops.

Participants were also invited to share their perspectives on the conditions required or desirable for the deployment of the MCA programme to other territories (scaling out). The availability of inputs, such as a primary processing facility or human resources, was mentioned as a condition required in order to replicate the programme. The participants thus recommended a strategy of expansion with adaptation to the territorial context rather than replication per se. The MCA programme's systemic approach, with actions across the four pillars—food procurement policy, production management, meal distribution, and sustainability awareness—ought to be maintained, while the activities to implement could be selected/prioritized based on available inputs. Participants suggested creating a charter or a brand defining a common set of priority actions that could be implemented in any context, and a list of additional activities to be selected according to the territorial context. Finally, they stressed that scaling out the programme would require training on the MCA approach and concepts and pointed to the role of groups comprised of different stakeholders or municipalities in providing inspiration and ideas to promote more sustainable food systems.

5.3.4 MCA's social inclusion challenges highlighted by the Urbal approach

The application of Urbal to the MCA programme shed light on several issues relating to social inclusion. One example is the different ways in which MCA actions can be interpreted. While only serving organic bread and offering meals free of animal-based foods are spontaneously welcome as positive developments among certain social groups, for others this is not so straightforward. Suspicions and even criticisms regarding these two actions were shared with us (Lepiller & Valette, 2021). Some parents and children criticized the cost of the organic bread measure, considering that price reduction should be a higher priority. Others perceived the introduction of animal-free menus as a strategy to cut costs at the expense of end users or saw it as depriving the children of animal protein. Collecting these observations was particularly made possible by including children in the Urbal process. Bringing the various social groups concerned together to co-develop actions and better communication, for example to demonstrate that the actions carried out are cost-neutral, appeared to constitute possible solutions to address the differences in interpretations. The Urbal process also highlighted the importance of progressive social pricing as a tool to ensure that efforts to improve food quality can benefit all audiences, including the less affluent. This progressive pricing, which is already practised in Montpellier, has been further developed since the implementation of Urbal. Moreover, the study of the IPs of the alternative eco-citizen meal raised a point of caution: in certain highly socially disadvantaged groups, school catering plays a more important role in ensuring children's access to meat and its nutrients of interest (in particular iron) than in other communities. More precise nutritional studies should therefore be carried out to assess the relevance of that action for these groups.

5.4 Conclusion and prospects

5.4.1 Learnings to improve the implementation of the Urbal approach

The MCA case study offers numerous learnings for the Urbal process. Two categories of learnings stand out, namely regarding the composition of the workshops and their preparation.

5.4.1.1 Learnings about the composition of the workshops

By bringing together a diverse range of actors and points of view, the participatory approach of the Urbal framework allowed for building collective and, significantly, shared knowledge on the IPs of MCA activities. The confrontation of points of view during the workshops enabled us to collect the perspectives of the widest possible range of actors involved in and/or impacted by the activities, all at once and in a same place. Such an approach ensures collective control of what is said, as the format of the workshop involves speaking publicly, while also avoiding illegitimate spokes-personship effects. The public nature of the situation, as well as the cumulative process of the consecutive group discussions, likewise encourages impact assessments that are collectively balanced. For instance, when a group arrived at a table at which mostly negative impacts had been identified, they tended to think about more positive ones.

In the MCA workshops, the research team failed to fully apply these principles, as no child was present in the first workshop, and no teacher attended either of the workshops. The workshop facilitation method could have been adapted so as to directly involve children, and a solution could have been found to reach teachers and motivate them to attend. Teachers' attendance was difficult to secure due to the strong separation between extracurricular activities and school, in terms of both the times of days when they take place and the administrations governing them. Ultimately, the research team was constrained by this limitation and was unable to overcome it. Yet some teachers are very interested in food and are even involved in educational projects on the topic. If they took part in the MCA programme and the city of Montpellier's food policy, they could play an active role in this innovation towards more sustainable food.

5.4.1.2 Learnings about the preparation of the workshops

The preparation of the workshops could have been improved to facilitate the participants' contribution to the mapping, and consequently facilitate the analysis work performed by the research team. It appears crucial to very precisely define the different activities discussed during the workshops, so as to be able to easily explain them to the participants and avoid any ambiguity in the formulation of the impacts. Moreover, as mentioned above, the first workshop produced raw material that could not really be considered as IP maps, but only maps of impacts, without intermediate effects or causality chains.

To focus the discussion more directly on IPs, or even the barriers, levers, and conditions of success, and thus make better use of the workshop time, it would be more beneficial to prepare the IPs upstream, perhaps with the MCA programme designer, and to have them discussed and validated collectively during the workshop. The participants could thus be shown IP maps—at least the most obvious ones. Finally, a phrasing rule could also facilitate the post-workshop analysis significantly, namely asking the participant to systematically define the impacts following this simple formula: *who/what does what to who/what?*

Both the FPD and the research team saw the second Urbal workshop as a good opportunity to collectively explore the conditions required to scale out the programme. It is important to note, however, that this was optional and that other topics could be explored, depending on the context in which the innovation is deployed.

5.4.1.3 Summary of the methodological and conceptual recommendations to facilitate the mapping of impact pathways

The IP analysis highlights the inputs, outputs, outcomes, and impacts of an action. To facilitate the IP analysis, we recommend categorizing *inputs* as either *conditions of implementation* (i.e., necessarily required to implement the activity) or *implementation facilitators* (i.e., not required but conducive to implementation), and to identify whether they are *context-related, material, or organizational inputs*. For the *outputs and outcomes step*, we recommend specifying which group of actors they affect, and categorizing them as either *positive or negative effects*. In addition to this, negative effects should be categorized as either *avoidable or unavoidable effects*, in order to subsequently identify how the former could be avoided, and how the latter could be alleviated. As a *last step in the analysis of impacts*, we recommend *identifying the sub-dimensions* that could be affected by the activities targeting each sustainability dimension. As much as possible, the set of sub-dimensions identified should be standardized across the different activities studied, to make the maps easier to read. Finally, we recommend identifying the *barriers and enablers associated with each IP* and categorizing them as 1) *conditions of success* (required to reach the expected impact), 2) *impact facilitators* (not necessary to reach the impact but conducive to achieving it), or 3) *barriers* (i.e., factors that limit the efficacy/performance of the programme).

5.4.2 *Learnings and prospects for the MCA stakeholders*

5.4.2.1 *Learnings on the impact pathways of the MCA programme*

The Urbal approach allowed the research team to identify the different groups of actors directly or indirectly impacted by the MCA actions. While children and canteen staff were the most directly affected by the programme, intermediate effects and impacts reached a wider pool of actors, in particular parents. The programme has the potential to have an effect on the five dimensions of sustainability, especially the environmental and social dimensions. The analysis highlighted that most negative impacts categorized as "avoidable" pertain to the governance dimension, and mainly involve a loss of confidence in the school canteen quality caused by a lack of understanding of the activities implemented. Clearly informing the actors (children, parents, canteen staff) about the objectives and expected benefits of each activity implemented was thus identified as a major condition of success. This in turn underscored the decisive role of canteen staff—as key points of contact for children and parents—in ensuring the programme's success. When discussing ways of improving communication and the information on the programme, participants showed a strong interest in forming a multi-actor committee bringing together all school canteen stakeholders. The IP analysis also highlighted the complementarity of different MCA activities, which particularly allowed for balancing the cost of the programme by combining activities involving higher costs with ones that afford budget savings. Furthermore, complementarity was found to mutually enhance the results of different activities, or to offset negative effects with positive effects, either within a same activity or across several activities.

5.4.2.2 *After the impact pathway mapping: Identifying indicators for a quantitative assessment of impact*

For stakeholders requiring a quantitative evaluation system, the in-depth and nuanced analysis, using collective intelligence, of the processes of change induced by a programme (IPs) can play an important role in the preparation or improvement of quantitative sustainability assessments (Chapter 10). The development of a standardized quantitative evaluation framework to document and monitor the impacts of MCA, and if necessary adjust actions, was requested by the FPD. Quantified indicators carry great weight in the evaluation of public policies. But the core question remains: what should be measured and how? The Urbal qualitative approach helps to answer this question by identifying socially relevant indicators. Focusing on the processes of change rather than on the results, and building on multi-stakeholder dialogue, the Urbal approach can guide the choice of indicators by prioritizing certain key elements that support or hamper the achievement of sustainability objectives, and by taking into account the context and the views of stakeholders.

The FPD already had a basic set of indicators to assess the results of the MCA programme, and intended to demonstrate the implemented actions' alignment with and contribution to the multi-scale normative frameworks on food sustainability to which it has committed, including the agri-food policy of Montpellier (called P2A, "*politique agroécologique et alimentaire*"), the French Food law (EGalim), and the Milan Urban Food Policy Pact.

To meet the FPD's needs, it therefore seemed valuable to test the usefulness of the knowledge acquired through the application of the Urbal approach by refining a set of existing MCA indicators, so as to enhance their relevance and better align them with the three abovementioned normative frameworks. The last chapter (Chapter 11) of this book discusses the study of the use of Urbal results to guide the development of relevant indicators, and the experiment conducted around Ma Cantine Autrement.

Acknowlegment

The authors thank Luc Lignon, Director of the Food Policy Department of the city of Montpellier, France, for his contribution to the content of this chapter.

Note

1 The Markets of National Interest ("*Marchés d'intérêt national*", MINs) are wholesale markets located near major cities. There are about 20 such markets in France. The MIN status, created in 1953, is a public service status. The management of MINs can be carried out directly by a public authority, or it can be delegated to a public or private actor. The best-known MIN is that of Rungis, which supplies Paris and the Ile-de-France region. The Montpellier MIN was created in 1965.

References

AMORCE-ADEME. (2019). Réduire le gaspillage alimentaire en restauration collective Recommandations et bonnes pratiques pour ajuster les grammages des portions [Brochure]. https://librairie.ademe.fr/dechets-economie-circulaire/769-reduire-le-gaspillage-alimentaire-en-restauration-collective-recommandations-et-bonnes-pratiques-pour-ajuster-les-grammages-des-portions.html

ANSES. (2017). Étude Individuelle Nationale des Consommations Alimentaires 3 (INCA 3) [Research Report]. ANSES. https://www.anses.fr/fr/system/files/NUT2014SA0234Ra.pdf

Barret, D., Blundo-Canto, G., Dabat, M.-H., Devaux-Spatarakis, A., Faure, G., Hainzelin, E., Mathé, S., Temple, L., Toillier, A., Triomphe ,B., & Vall, E. (illus.) (2018). ImpresS ex post. Methodological guide to ex post impact evaluation of agricultural research in developing countries. *CIRAD*. https://doi.org/10.19182/agritrop/00006

Caillavet, F., Darmon, N., Dubois, C., Gomy, C., Kabeche, D., Paturel, D., & Perignon, M. (2021). Vers une sécurité alimentaire durable : Enjeux, initiatives et principes directeurs [Research Report]. Terra Nova. https://hal.inrae.fr/hal-03466621

Chiaverina, P., Raynaud, E., Fillâtre, M., Nicklaus, S., & Bellassen, V., (2022). The drivers of the nutritional quality and carbon footprint of school menus in the Paris area. *Journal of Agricultural & Food Industrial Organization*. https://doi.org/10.1515/jafio-2021-0051

CNA. (2017). *Les enjeux de la restauration collective en milieu scolaire*. Conseil National de l'Alimentation.

Comoretto, G., Lhuissier, A., & Maurice, A. (Eds.). (2020). *Quand les cantines se mettent à table… Commensalité et identité sociale*. Quae.

Douthwaite, B., Alvarez, S., Cook, S. E., Davies, R., George, P., Howell, J., … Rubiano Mejía, J. E. (2007). Participatory impact pathways analysis: a practical application of program theory in research-for-development. *Canadian Journal of Program Evaluation*. https://cgspace.cgiar.org/handle/10568/43925

FAO. (2017). Nutrition-sensitive agriculture and food systems in practice. Options for interventions. FAO. http://www.fao.org/3/i7848en/I7848EN.pdf

GEM-RCN. (2007). Recommandation relative à la nutrition du 4 mai 2007. Groupe d'Etude des Mearchés de Restauration Collective et de Nutrition (GEMRCN). Observatoire économique de l'achat public.

GEM-RCN. (2011). Recommandation nutrition Groupe d'Etude des Marchés de Restauration Collective et de Nutrition (GEM-RCN) (completed and updated on 10 October 2011). Obeservatoire économique de l'achat public. https://www.economie.gouv.fr/files/files/directions_services/daj/marches_publics/oeap/gem/ARCHIVE-nutrition/nutrition.pdf?v=1553682981

GEM-RCN. (2015). Recommandation Nutrition. Groupe d'Etude des Marchés de Restauration Collective et de Nutrition (GEM-RCN). Version 2.0, July 2015. Observatoire économique de l'achat public. https://www.economie.gouv.fr/files/directions_services/daj/marches_publics/oeap/gem/nutrition/nutrition.pdf

Guillot, L., & Blatrix, C. (2021). Alimentation, État et territoires. Diffusion et reconnaissance des Projets Alimentaires Territoriaux en France (2014–2021). *Géographie, économie, société*, *23*(4), 437–459.

Lamine, C., Garçon, L., & Brunori, G. (2019). Territorial agrifood systems: A Franco-Italian contribution to the debates over alternative food networks in rural areas. *Journal of Rural Studies*, *68*, 159–170. https://doi.org/10.1016/j.jrurstud.2018.11.007

Lepiller, O., & Valette, E. (2021). Urban food innovations. Scaling and social inclusion issues [Policy Brief]. *So what?*, *14*, 1–4. https://www.chaireunesco-adm.com/14-Urban-food-innovations-scaling-and-social-inclusion-issues

Poinsot, R. (2021). Place de l'offre végétarienne en restauration scolaire pour concilier nutrition et environnement : Le cas français [PhD thesis, Université de Montpellier]. http://www.theses.fr/2021MONTG040

République Française. (2011a). Décret n°2011-1227 du 30 septembre 2011 relatif à la qualité nutritionnelle des repas servis dans le cadre de la restauration scolaire. https://www.legifrance.gouv.fr/jorf/id/JORFTEXT000024614716?r=JWhFQNLUWa

République Française. (2011b). Arrêté du 30 septembre 2011 relatif à la qualité nutritionnelle des repas servis dans le cadre de la restauration scolaire. https://www.legifrance.gouv.fr/jorf/id/JORFTEXT000024614763?r=IZnvkGtjJY

République Française. (2018). LOI n° 2018-938 du 30 octobre 2018 pour l'équilibre des relations commerciales dans le secteur agricole et alimentaire et une alimentation saine, durable et accessible à tous. https://www.legifrance.gouv.fr/jorf/id/JORFTEXT000037547946?r=RhKFAwh9JM

Roudelle, O. (2019). Les impacts d'un projet de restauration scolaire « durable ». Master thesis, Université Toulouse Jean Jaurès, 274 p.

Sanz Sanz, E., Cardona, A., & Napoléone, C. (2022). Motivations of public officials as drivers of transition to sustainable school food provisioning: Insights from Avignon, France. *Journal of Agricultural and Environmental Ethics*, *35*(2), 6. https://doi.org/10.1007/s10806-022-09880-9

Walker, T., Maredia, M., Kelley, T., La Rovere, R., Templeton, D., Thiele, G., & Douthwaite, B. (2008). Strategic guidance for ex post impact assessment of agricultural research. Report prepared for the Standing Panel on Impact Assessment, CGIAR Science Council. Science Council Secretariat.

WFP. (2020). *State of School Feeding Worldwide 2020*. World Food Programme.

6 The potential of Short Food Supply Chains for sustainable urban agri-food systems

The UFIL of Milano Ristorazione

Giulia Bartezzaghi and Federico Caniato

6.1 Introduction

Short Food Supply Chains (SFSCs) are seen as possible sustainable alternatives to long globalized food supply chains. Different SFSC models in the literature are built on the multidimensional concept of *proximity*, which refers not only to *geographical closeness* but also to the relationship between supply chain actors (*relational proximity*) and the degree of information sharing upstream and downstream (*information proximity*). The three dimensions of proximity can produce different sustainability impacts.

This chapter investigates the innovation of introducing SFSC products in the school canteen meals served by Milano Ristorazione (MiRi) in Milan, based on the Urbal framework and the concept of SFSC. We explore this innovation by drawing on interviews with MiRi representatives as well as the results of a participatory workshop with 20 stakeholders. To corroborate our findings, we analyse the MiRi's meal delivery service from production centres to school canteens. We conclude that the geographical proximity of MiRi's food suppliers and kitchen centres to school canteens is not sufficient to guarantee the sustainability of locally sourced products and short-distance logistics systems, but that new forms of vertical cooperation and information sharing constitute key levers for sustainability. Finally, the Urban Food Innovation Lab (UFIL) provides learnings for practitioners and policymakers, towards a new participatory approach for the development of procurement tenders focused on sustainability.

6.2 Short Food Supply Chains and sustainable development: Insights from the literature

Consumers are increasingly asking for high quality standards, product variety, and food safety guarantees, along with information on the origin of products and the sustainability of the whole value chain (Jarzębowski et al., 2020). However, agri-food supply chains operating on the global market must contend with growing distances upstream and downstream of the value chain,

DOI: 10.4324/9781003285441-6

particularly involving long geographical distances and multiple intermediaries, which present challenges for supply chain control and affect consumer trust. SFSCs have emerged as possible sustainable alternatives to global food supply chains. SFSCs are characterized by short geographical distances (Engelseth, 2016), fewer intermediaries, a stronger relationship between producers and consumers (Todorovic et al., 2018), and information closeness (Renting et al., 2003; Caniato et al., 2012). *Geographical proximity* "expresses the kilometric distance that separates two units (e.g. individual organizations or towns) in geographical space" (Torre & Rallet, 2005, p. 4). *Relational proximity* is defined in terms of the number of intermediaries along the chain (Bos & Owen, 2016; Malak-Rawlikowska et al., 2019) and the type of contractual agreements in place between supply chain actors (Edelmann et al., 2019). *Information proximity* is measured according to the type of information shared along the chain (such as product origin, product quality, sustainability practices, and protocols observed), the accessibility of the information, and the level of visibility over products, practices, and processes along the value chain (Garcia-Torres et al., 2019).

Sustainability has come to be closely associated with SFSCs, as has been highlighted by EU Regulation 1305/2013, which defines these supply chains as a production model that generates economic, social, and environmental benefits. Even though SFSCs are considered as alternatives to global and unsustainable food chains, there is often a lack of evidence regarding the actual sustainability of these "shorter" food supply chains.

SFSCs' contribution to the sustainability of food systems should not be taken as a given. The different levers of proximity can reinforce or cancel each other out, generating multiple and interdependent economic, social, and environmental impacts that can also offset one another. For example, SFSCs are often associated with environmentally sustainable practices, as small-scale farming is considered to use less energy than large-scale, industrial agriculture (Woodhouse, 2010). Moreover, the shorter travelling distances can facilitate the prevention of food waste (Jarzębowski et al., 2020). On the other hand, SFSC producers might face economic barriers in accessing the market which, among other things, can stem from a weak organization and limited infrastructure, two key factors affecting competitiveness (Yacamán Ochoa et al., 2019).

Another example is that SFSCs help connect urban and rural areas, enhancing rural development and the revitalization of local communities (Jarzębowski et al., 2020). However, proximity does not automatically imply positive effects on working conditions.

Furthermore, the concept of sustainability is associated with the notion of resilience, defined by Rice and Caniato (2003) as "the organisation's ability to react to an unexpected disruption". Resilience can be considered as a short-term enabler to achieve long-term sustainability (McDaniels et al., 2008): in many cases, resilience and sustainability are affected by the same management practices (Macfadyen et al., 2015). In the context of agri-food supply chains, resilience relates to the ability to maintain the "function" of the system

(Tendall et al., 2015), that is, to guarantee the availability, stability, and accessibility of food over time (FAO & UNICEF, 2020).

The concept of resilience is currently gaining momentum, following the disruptive effects of the COVID-19 pandemic that posed serious threats to the continuity of the agri-food supply chain, as it did in other industries (Cullen, 2020). However, there is no clear consensus on the most relevant factors for achieving resilience in agri-food supply chains (Stone & Rahimifard, 2018). According to Stone and Rahimifard (2018), the qualities central to agri-food supply chains' resilience are collaboration, flexibility, agility, visibility, adaptability, and redundancy and each organization can determine which dimensions of resilience to leverage in a given context, building different resilience strategies. In this regard, SFSCs can play a crucial role in the resilience and sustainability of the agri-food supply chain, by leveraging *geographic*, *relational* and/or *information proximity*.

6.3 The Milano Ristorazione UFIL: Introducing products from Short Food Supply Chains in school canteens in Milan

Given the rapidly evolving regulatory environment and the continuous changes in food consumption habits, the development agendas of cities around the world have started to prioritize reducing the distances between producers and final consumers by creating linkages between urban, peri-urban, and rural areas, as well as promoting more sustainable diets, starting in school canteens.

In 2014, the Milan Municipality established a Food Policy Office in charge of developing a comprehensive food policy strategy for the city of Milan, based on a Memorandum of Understanding signed with the philanthropic organization Fondazione Cariplo. The Milan Food Policy was developed around five priorities:

1) ensuring the supply of healthy food and sufficient drinking water as primary nourishment for everyone
2) fostering the sustainability of the urban food system in Milan, by enabling the conditions necessary for the management of a sustainable food system and promoting the local production and consumption of fresh and seasonal quality food
3) understanding food, by increasing consumer awareness surrounding healthy, safe, culturally appropriate, and sustainable food
4) fighting waste
5) supporting and promoting scientific agri-food research

Since 2015, the Milan Food Policy Office has promoted the development of an international pact on Urban Food Policies—the Milan Urban Food Policy Pact (MUFPP), now signed by more than 210 cities worldwide—with a view to disseminating best practices for urban food policies and activating joint actions towards more sustainable food systems. Moreover, in 2018 the Milan

Municipality joined the "100 Resilient Cities" programme pioneered by The Rockfeller Foundation, which supports cities around the world to integrate resilience measures into their urban development strategies, so as to be able to prevent and face existing and emerging environmental, social and economic urban shocks and stresses (for instance, relating to poverty, unequal access to public services, flooding, air pollution, and climate change). Like the other cities involved in the programme, in 2017 Milan appointed a Chief Resilience Officer in charge of leading the city's resilience efforts, coordinating actions with the other Milan Municipality departments.

Within this framework, MiRi operates as a large public company owned by the Milan Municipality that manages catering for a wide network of public schools and prepares meals for nursing homes, the elderly at home, disability centres, immigration centres, and affiliated private schools in Milan. Its priority mission is to offer children safe, healthy, and nutritious food at school, along with educational activities on adequate nutrition and sustainable consumption. MiRi provides an average 85,000 meals per day, prepared in 26 kitchen centres and distributed to a network of 437 school canteens. It employs 815 people directly (in its kitchens, its offices, etc.), and another 2,900 indirectly (distributing food in the schools, providing cleaning services, etc.) (Milano Ristorazione, 2021). It offers more than 8,500 differentiated ethnic and religious menus (e.g., vegetarian, vegan, pork-free, etc.) and over 2,100 health-specific diets to cater to the multiple cultural practices and specific nutritional diets of its consumers (e.g., for diabetes, celiac, or other allergies).

Over the last few years, MiRi has actively promoted several activities and innovative projects to enhance the sustainability of the whole food chain of the school canteens, from product procurement and logistics to waste management and food education for children and parents. For instance, MiRi has replaced plastic tableware with a biodegradable and compostable alternative, has facilitated the procurement of local and organic products in its public tenders, and has introduced Fair Trade products. This commitment to sustainability is driven by the food policy strategy adopted by the Milan Municipality and is supported by the MiRi senior management's strong commitment to sustainability as well as the obligation to align with current regulations governing public administration at city, national, and European levels, which set strict mandatory requirements regarding food safety, green procurement, and carbon emissions reduction. MiRi's public procurement policy and meal distribution system for school canteens can strongly impact the sustainability of the local urban food system, mainly by regulating the procurement and logistics processes involving suppliers through long-term contracts and tenders. In addition to this, MiRi tenders often define best practices that are then adopted by other Italian municipalities. Furthermore, MiRi's catering service and sustainability awareness initiatives reach a vast population of schoolchildren and their families in Milan.

In line with its strategic food policy goals, the Milan Municipality has invested in defining and implementing a Rural Development Plan aimed at reconnecting the city of Milan with the metropolitan productive agricultural areas, thus facilitating access to sustainably produced food through public tenders.

As part of this, in 2016 the Milan Municipality launched a 12-month pilot initiative in collaboration with the Milan Agricultural District (DAM) and MiRi to establish new arrangements between public administrations and local agricultural enterprises for the development of experimental procedures. Thanks to this institutional innovation, MiRi was able to secure a whole year's supply of rice from the DAM agricultural enterprises (180 tons/year, for a value of €300,000/year), thus introducing this locally sourced product in school canteen menus. Building on the results of this experiment, over the last few years MiRi has been working to scale out the strategy adopted with rice to other 19 food supply chains—including fresh pasta, potatoes, zucchini, lentils, and chickpeas—extending the network of suppliers and partner stakeholders as part of the "Matera Alimenta Urbes" project. This has involved several joint actions on the local territory, including the redevelopment of agricultural land, the modernization of agricultural infrastructure and machinery, the creation of an urban food market with "zero-kilometre" products, and an intense education and communication campaign targeting the school community and civil society.

Given this overall context, the innovation of interest here is the introduction of SFSC products in the menus of the school canteens served by MiRi in Milan. According to the definition of "Short Food Supply Chains" found in the literature, distances between rural and urban areas, as well as distances between producers (agricultural enterprises) and consumers (schoolchildren), can be reduced by mobilizing different proximity levers such as: 1) the sourcing of food that is produced locally, in other words food that is close to the points of consumption (i.e., geographic proximity); 2) the disintermediation of the value chain through new organizational/cooperation frameworks, such as the contractual agreements between MiRi and DAM agricultural companies (i.e., relational proximity); and 3) the sharing of information on products' origin and the associated supply chains, and the development of educational campaigns targeting the school system, institutions, and supply chain actors (i.e., information proximity).

There is however still not a widely shared definition of "local products" within regulation on public procurement. As a result, the boundaries of geographical proximity cannot be clearly identified. The "zero-kilometre" concept is commonly associated with food that is produced within 70 kilometres of the point of consumption, but the definition of "local production" could be extended to cover the whole Milan metropolitan area or the Lombardy Region. Moreover, shortening the supply chain might require some effort from different stakeholders and generate a range of sustainability impacts. Locally produced or zero-kilometre products are not necessarily sustainable; their sustainability depends for instance on how they are produced, transported, and distributed. According to the Urbal framework, sustainability has multiple dimensions, pertaining to the environment, food safety, food security, the economy, society and culture, and governance. The interdependencies between the three pillars of proximity in the context of SFSCs may therefore vary, affecting these supply chains' sustainability performance and the different dimensions of sustainability.

6.4 The Urbal approach and the methodology

The UFIL of MiRi proceeded according to the Urbal approach described in Chapter 1 of this book, considering the key characteristics of the innovator (MiRi) and the local innovation ecosystem. This UFIL focuses on the innovative process of introducing SFSC products in the Milan school canteens served by MiRi by leveraging public procurement tenders.

The research group of the School of Management of Politecnico di Milano (PoliMi) acted as a facilitator for the UFIL, supporting MiRi staff in analysing the scope of the innovation, understanding the innovation context, identifying and involving key stakeholders and establishing the theoretical framework for the adoption of the new SFSC practice. Multiple sources of data were used for the analysis, following the methodological steps of the Urbal framework.

First, MiRi's internal documents were analysed to understand its organizational structure and school canteen network. Moreover, two semi-structured interviews and two meetings with MiRi representatives (the President, the Director of Quality and Food Security, the Director of Operations, and the Director of Procurement and Contracts) were conducted in order to grasp MiRi's procurement strategy and the logistics system underpinning the preparation of meals and their distribution to school canteens.

Second, additional material available online, including reports and policy briefs published on the website of the Food Policy Office of the Milan Municipality, was reviewed in order to enrich the data on the urban context of innovation and to identify relevant stakeholders in MiRi's network.

Moreover, a participatory workshop focused on the MiRi UFIL was organized on 29 January 2020 at PoliMi to identify relevant sustainability dimensions for the innovator and the stakeholders of the UFIL and build the innovation impact pathway map following a participatory approach. Prior to the workshop, a list of three relevant activities connected to the innovation was established by the facilitator together with MiRi so as to focus the map and guide interaction between the stakeholders.

The workshop lasted three hours. It consisted of a preliminary introduction to MiRi's context, the proposed innovation and the Urbal approach, followed by an interactive and participatory session to discuss the key features of the innovation and its implications for sustainability. The workshop was attended by 20 stakeholders relevant to the UFIL: the president of MiRi, a few professors and researchers from PoliMi who took on the role of experts, facilitators, and rapporteurs, an external scientific expert, one representative of the Food Policy Office of the Milan Municipality, a few current partners and suppliers of MiRi, and other food supply chain actors operating in production, processing, retail, and food service, as well as packaging and technology providers. During the interactive session, the innovation of introducing SFSC products in MiRi school canteens was analysed according to the Urbal innovation impact pathway map framework. A new version of the innovation impact pathway map was drawn by the PoliMi research group after the workshop, integrating and detailing the input gathered during the participatory session. The final version of the innovation impact pathway map is shown and discussed in Section 6.5.2. Lastly, the Urbal framework was applied to investigate the sustainability impacts of the innovation and identify key barriers to and drivers of its implementation.

6.5 Analysis of the results of the MiRi UFIL

Building on the preliminary analysis of MiRi's organization and the urban context of the innovation, the UFIL followed a step-by-step approach. First, it identified the key stakeholders involved in the network and their role in the innovation process to produce the network map (Figure 6.1).

Second, it identified the sustainability dimensions addressed by the UFIL (Figure 6.2). Third, it defined the key activities introduced by the innovation as well as the associated changes and impacts surrounding the sustainability dimensions to build the innovation impact pathway map (Figure 6.3). Lastly, it

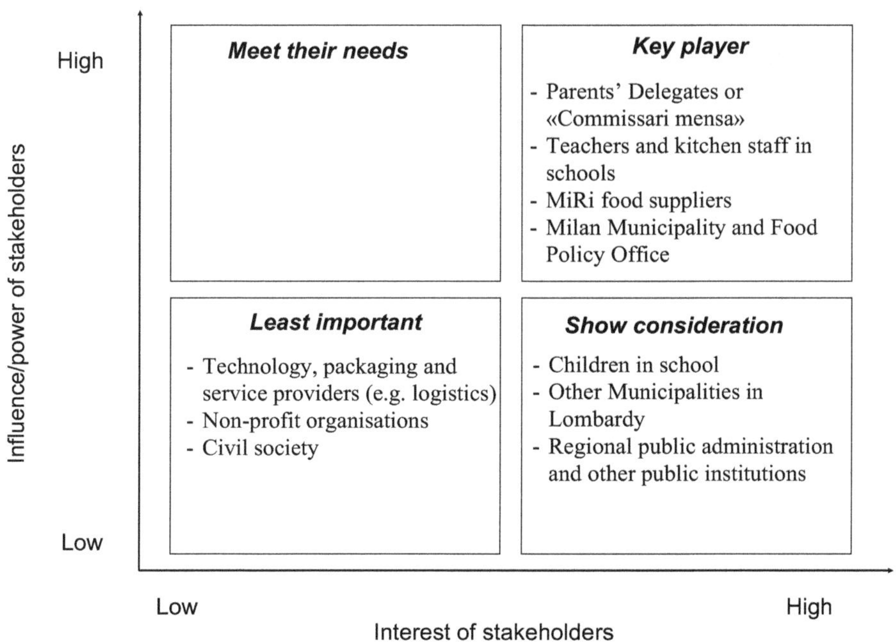

Figure 6.1 Network map.

Authors' own representation based on Reed et al. (2009).

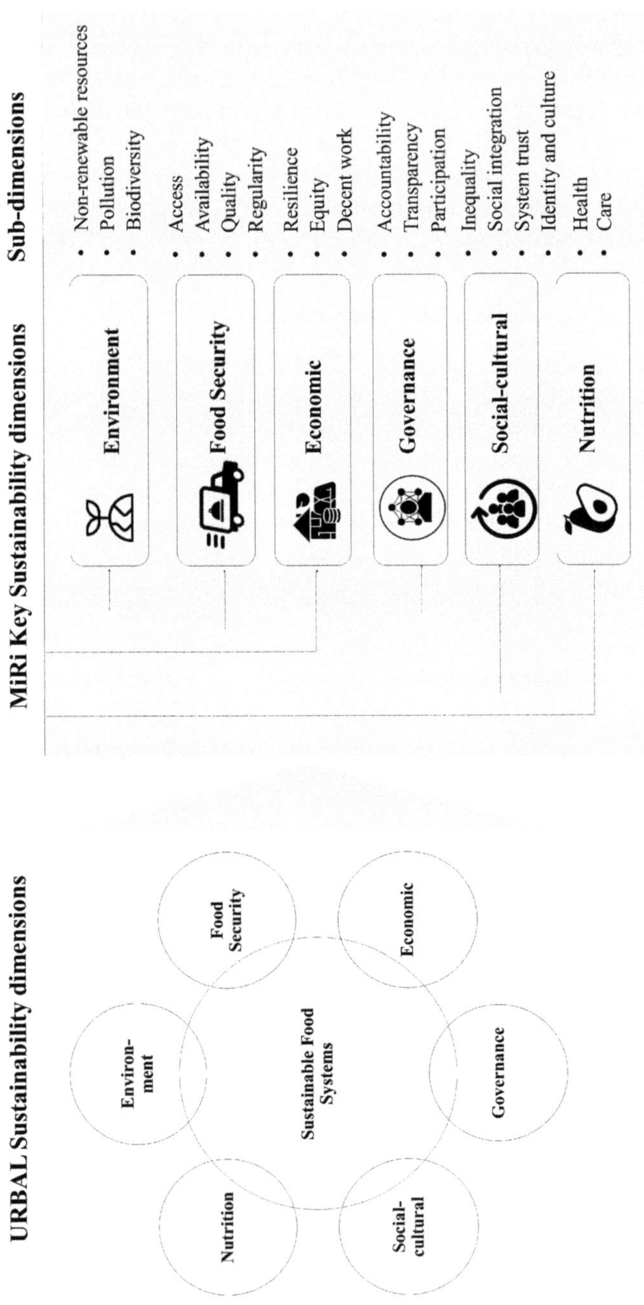

Figure 6.2 Sustainability dimensions.

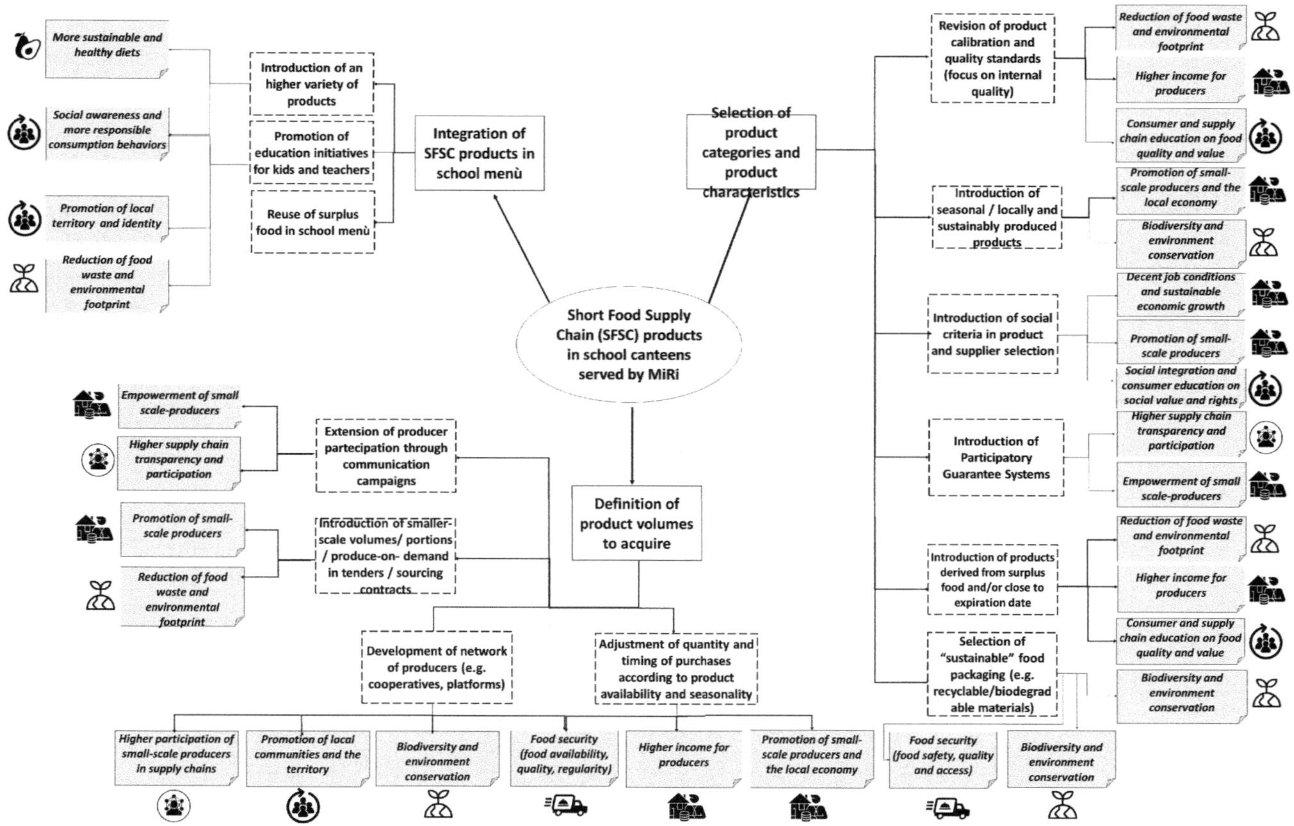

Figure 6.3 Innovation impact pathway map.

identified and discussed drivers of and barriers to the adoption of the innovation, following a multi-stakeholder and supply chain-oriented approach and drawing a comparison with a similar practice, the logistics service delivering meals from MiRi kitchen centres to school canteens.

The results of this step-by-step analysis are discussed within the theoretical framework of SFSCs and presented in the following paragraphs of this chapter.

6.5.1 The stakeholder analysis and the network map

The innovation under study involves different stakeholders who can provide valuable information and insights on the innovation context and/or create a conducive environment for the innovation to be deployed through policy, programmes, and tools. These stakeholders have varying levels of interest in the innovation and capacity to influence it.

The core network of stakeholders includes MiRi's own staff, schoolchildren, parent delegates (so called "Commissari Mensa") acting as consumer representatives, teachers, the kitchen staff in schools, the Milan Municipality administration and the Food Policy Office, and food product suppliers. Other key stakeholders within the urban food system may take part in or influence the innovation, including other public or private collective catering companies, distributors, technology, packaging, and secondary service providers (e.g., logistics providers, consulting firms, and communication agencies), research centres and educational institutions, non-profit organizations, and civil society as a whole.

Based on the information collected through the semi-structured interviews and meetings with MiRi representatives, coupled with the analysis of data gathered from secondary sources, we were able to categorize the stakeholders of MiRi's network involved in the UFIL according to their level of interest in the innovation (high/low) and their power/influence over the innovation process (high/low). According to Reed et al. (2009), "key players" are those who have both a high interest in and strong influence on the innovation. These actors should therefore be managed closely, engaged with and consulted regularly, and possibly involved in the decision-making process (Figure 6.1). Schoolchildren's parents have a strong interest in accessing high-quality and sustainable meals for their children and can influence MiRi's decision-making process through the parent representatives or Commissari Mensa. MiRi food suppliers, the Milan Municipality and Food Policy Office, and teachers and school kitchen staff can each in their own way play a pivotal role in enabling the development of SFSCs, with the final goal of providing more sustainable food to schoolchildren and families in Milan. Other stakeholders may also be highly interested in the innovation, starting with the schoolchildren but also including other municipalities in Lombardy and other levels of governance. These stakeholders, however, have a low level of influence on the specific innovation. Finally, packaging and logistics providers, third-sector organizations and civil society have a low level of interest in and little influence on the innovation.

6.5.2 The sustainability dimensions and the innovation impact pathway map

Given the diverse range of stakeholders involved and the complexity of the innovation ecosystem, several sustainability dimensions may be impacted by the innovation under study.

Figure 6.2 shows the key sustainability dimensions and sub-dimensions defined within the Urbal approach that were identified as relevant for the UFIL: the environmental, food security, nutritional, economic, governance, and social-cultural dimensions of sustainability. The impacts are explained in the description of the innovation impact pathway map, discussed in the following paragraph.

The map depicted in Figure 6.3 is built from the data collected during the workshop and shows the *activities* associated with the new supply chain practice (first level—rectangular boxes in the central part of the map), the *changes* arising from these activities (second level—rectangular boxes with dotted borders, directly connected to the *activities*), and the related *impacts* on the sustainability dimensions (third level—grey rectangular boxes with the lower right corner folded over, directly linked to the *changes* shown in the second level). Each activity and the associated changes can be analysed drawing on the multidimensional definition of SFSCs and can have a potential impact on the different sustainability dimensions identified as relevant, codified in the map using the same icons associated with the sustainability dimensions in Figure 6.2 (see the Note that follows Figure 6.3).

Three key activities related to the procurement of SFSC products for school canteens were chosen prior to the workshop and validated based on the data collected during the participatory session:

1) the selection of product categories and product characteristics
2) the definition of product purchasing volumes
3) the integration of SFSC products in school canteen menus

These activities and the changes they bring about can each be linked to one of the three pillars of proximity (geographical, relational, and information proximity) that allow for reducing distances along the supply chain.

With regard to *the selection of product categories and characteristics*, the main changes arising from the activity are:

1) the revision of calibration and quality standards for the products purchased in order to also include products that do not match traditional commercial standards surrounding size and aesthetic quality
2) the selection of seasonal produce and locally sourced ingredients which are produced following environmentally sound practices
3) the introduction of product and supplier selection criteria pertaining to social dimensions, such as improved labour conditions for producers, support for the employment of vulnerable people in production and distribution activities, and the promotion of small-scale producers and rural territories

4) the selection of products from surplus food sources and/or products nearing their expiry date
5) the introduction of Participatory Guarantee Systems, considered as alternative product certification schemes, which involve the direct participation of producers and consumers in the definition of product specificities as well as the development and implementation of certification procedures. In other words, these are locally oriented product quality protection systems, whereby producers are certified with the active participation of stakeholders and on the basis of trust and reciprocal control, interdependence, and knowledge sharing along the food supply chain
6) the selection of food packaging solutions that ensure food quality and safety while also protecting the environment through the use of recyclable materials

The introduction of new criteria for supplier selection that favour locally produced, seasonal, and sustainably produced ingredients implies geographical closeness between production and consumption, as well as new types of vertical agreements reinforcing relational proximity upstream. Moreover, the sharing and certification of information along the value chain through new participatory guarantees systems contribute to reducing distances upstream and downstream (information proximity).

These changes lead to several impacts on the different dimensions of sustainability:

1) promoting small-scale producers and the local economy
2) reducing the amounts of surplus food and food waste at production sites
3) guaranteeing safe and decent working conditions for producers and fostering sustainable economic growth
4) minimizing the supply chain's environmental footprint to protect biodiversity and reduce carbon emissions
5) increasing consumers' and supply chain actors' awareness surrounding food quality and the value derived from food products' origin and the activities of their upstream supply chain
6) promoting a more transparent and participatory supply chain

In this respect, new regulations and increased transparency in the certification and verification of information regarding products and processes (relational proximity)—also enabled by digital technology—can be *drivers* of sustainability impacts. On the other hand, the limited perception of the added value of products from SFSCs, the lack of incentives for the various stakeholders, and the lack of a collaborative approach among supply chain actors can be *barriers* (and can affect both relational and information proximity).

Regarding *the definition of product purchasing volumes*, the main changes arising from the activity consist of:

1) the revision of purchase quantities and delivery times according to product availability and seasonality

2) the development of networks of local producers, such as aggregation platforms and cooperatives
3) the revision of the volumes specified in procurement tenders and sourcing contracts to favour smaller-scale production and production on demand
4) the expansion of the supplier base by increasing tenders' visibility and accessibility through ad hoc communication campaigns

The revision of the product volume and delivery time criteria in procurement tenders and sourcing contracts to favour small-scale suppliers, along with the development of new forms of producer aggregation, contribute to strengthening the relational proximity of supply chain actors. Greater information sharing on public tenders to broaden the supplier base provides a way to foster information proximity.

The expected sustainability impacts are:

1) the inclusion of a greater number of suppliers with more diverse profiles, and the economic survival of small-scale suppliers
2) the promotion of local products and the local territory
3) guaranteed availability and regularity of the product supply and food quality
4) greater transparency and participation along the supply chain

We identified different drivers and barriers surrounding these impacts. Increased attention paid by consumers to local and sustainable products and the inclusion of small-scale producers can be a *driver* of impact and foster information proximity by enabling consumers to access relevant information on the product and its upstream supply chain. Conversely, the need to supply significant volumes of products to ensure food availability and the regularity of the food service, along with the inclusion of pre-defined size and quality standards within public tenders, constitutes *barriers*. The latter pertain to the selection criteria and the types of vertical agreements reached with suppliers, and therefore to the relational dimension of proximity.

With regard to the third activity selected, namely *the introduction of products from SFSCs in school canteen menus*, the main changes arising from the activity are:

1) the introduction of new products to allow for a more varied diet, which can in turn improve consumption habits
2) the promotion of educational activities and awareness initiatives for children and teachers, focused on sustainable and healthy diets (including "short supply chain" products)
3) the repurposing of edible and safe surplus food in school meals

These activities may mobilize all three dimensions of proximity. The introduction of sustainably produced ingredients implies geographical closeness as well as new contractual agreements and relational dynamics with suppliers.

Education campaigns targeting schoolchildren and teachers help to reduce distances downstream by sharing valuable information and raising awareness.

These changes lead to the following sustainability impacts:

1) social consciousness and awareness, contributing to lasting changes in consumer habits
2) the promotion of healthier diets for children
3) the promotion of the local economy and local identity
4) reduced food waste and a smaller environmental footprint

In this respect, proper and tailored communication along with education initiatives for consumers can be a *driver* of impact, which increases information proximity. On the other hand, cultural resistance to change in habits can constitute a *barrier* (again linked to information access and sharing).

6.6 Discussion of the results

The UFIL revealed that suppliers' geographical proximity to consumers is not the only lever available to reduce distance along the value chain: all three dimensions of proximity can be mobilized. The geographical dimension should be integrated through new forms of producer aggregation and supply chain cooperation schemes (relational proximity) and by promoting information sharing and transparency along the supply chain, from producers to consumers (information proximity). The impacts that can be generated are multiple and interconnected. Different enablers and barriers may arise, mostly associated with social awareness, the regulatory environment, supply chain relationships, and consumption habits.

In order to corroborate these results, we here also analyse the logistics service for meal deliveries from MiRi's kitchen centres to the school canteens, following the Urbal approach and based on the SFSC concept. This activity was selected as a benchmark for two reasons. First, as with product procurement, the logistics service contract is granted by MiRi to third-party logistics service providers through a public tender process. Second, in line with its sustainability commitments, MiRi recently started to focus on improving its logistics service and network, making it more sustainable and resilient to urban shocks by innovating with the mandatory and incentive criteria included in the tender.

The network of stakeholders involved in this logistics service includes MiRi's own staff, schoolchildren and their families, teachers, the school kitchen staff, the Milan Municipality administration, logistics service providers and experts, and technology providers (of vehicles and measurement/monitoring tools).

Based on a preliminary analysis of the context as well as interviews with MiRi representatives and relevant stakeholders, including logistics providers and an external expert, the research team found that innovations around the logistics tender process can have an effect on several of the sustainability dimensions and sub-dimensions identified in the Urbal framework:

- ***Environment: non-renewable sources and pollution*.** The logistics tender can integrate carbon emission reduction criteria and reconsider the means of transportation used in favour of more sustainable solutions (e.g., methane-CNG, hybrid CNG-diesel, electric vehicles), and MiRi's transportation plan can be reviewed.
- ***Food security: availability and regularity*.** The logistics tender should introduce requirements to ensure a continuous and regular meal distribution service to all school canteens in the network on a daily basis. One key strategic lever is the duration of contracts.
- ***Economy: resilience and decent employment*.** Resilience is here understood as logistics providers' ability to promptly respond to unexpected events, such as road congestion due to a car accident or difficult mobility following flooding or snowfall, to guarantee the regular delivery of meals to schools. In this regard, in addition to back-up vehicles in the fleet for emergencies, an incentive criterion could be added to the tender to encourage the introduction of an operative unit for the coordination and management of unexpected events and emergencies.

From an economic perspective, it is important to consider the trade-off between the desire to invest in more environmentally sustainable logistics services and infrastructure, on the one hand, and the need for an economically efficient logistics system with rigid budget constraints on the other.

Moreover, truck drivers must be guaranteed fair working conditions. This could be addressed in the contracts with logistics providers, taking into account different aspects of social sustainability such as appropriate remuneration, training programmes on proper posture when driving and handling goods, forms of integrative insurance, etc.

- ***Governance: transparency and accountability*.** The logistics tender could introduce measurement and monitoring systems to ensure the transparency and traceability of the logistics service and track energy consumption and carbon emissions.
- ***Social-cultural: inequality*.** The logistics tender could include measures to promote diversity and reduce inequality in the work environment.

The analysis of the possible sustainability criteria to be included in the logistics tender reveals that the kitchen centres' geographical proximity to the point of consumption (school canteens) is not sufficient to ensure the sustainability of the logistics service and that other variables should be taken into account at the same time. For example, the reduced geographical distance involved in the meal delivery from MiRi kitchen centres to school canteens says little about the type of labour contracts adopted by the logistics providers or the amount of carbon emissions generated by the vehicles used for the logistics service. The nature and extent of the organizational arrangements between MiRi and the logistics suppliers, and between the latter and their employees, as well as the availability, accessibility, and visibility of information along the value chain up to the final consumers, can play a crucial role in reducing distances and making the logistics chain more sustainable and resilient.

6.7 Conclusions

The UFIL of MiRi proves that the geographic closeness of producers (both MiRi's food suppliers and the kitchen centres) with the point of consumption (school canteens) does not automatically ensure the sustainability of locally sourced products and short-distance logistic systems. The adoption of other sustainability-oriented criteria relating to the selection of products and suppliers (e.g., favouring the supply of seasonal and fresh products, the repurposing of safe and edible surplus food that does not meet commercial standards, fair working conditions, and social integration), as the well as new forms of cooperation between supply chain actors, are key to shifting towards more responsible production and consumption patterns. Moreover, a proper communication and education strategy is needed to foster transparency in the supply chain, increase awareness, and change consumption habits. Thus, relational and information proximity can support geographical proximity to achieve a more sustainable food system.

The sustainability impacts generated by these changes are multiple and intertwined: above all, they involve support to small producers and local production economies, the preservation of cultural and food heritage, the reduction of food waste, the protection of biodiversity in natural ecosystems, and the fostering of innovative participatory production models. New certification schemes and information systems can be a driver of impact, while regulatory and administrative deficiencies, a lack of incentives for stakeholders, limited awareness of the supply chain, strict commercial standards on product quality, and cultural resistance can be barriers to the innovation process.

In conclusion, the UFIL of MiRi contributes to the scientific debate on SFSCs and their potential for building more sustainable and inclusive food systems on an urban level. It provides interesting findings for food supply chain actors looking to build a SFSC and local policymakers wishing to incentivize SFSC schemes, by shedding light on the dimensions and levers of *proximity* involved and providing insights to support the development of a new participatory model for food procurement tenders and contracts with a focus on sustainability.

References

Bos, E., & Owen, L. (2016). Virtual reconnection: The online spaces of alternative food networks in England. *Journal of Rural Studies*, *45*, 1–14.

Caniato, F. F. A., Luzzini, D. G., Crippa, L., & Golini, R. (2012). Short Supply Chain Configurations in the Italian Food Industry. In Esposito, E., & Passaro, R. (Eds.) *Purchasing & supply management in a changing world* (pp. 1–14). Edizioni Scientifiche Italiane.

Cullen, M. T. (2020). *COVID-19 and the risk to food supply chains: How to respond.* FAO: Rome, Italy.

Edelmann, H., Quiñones-Ruiz, X. F., & Penker, M. (2019). Analytic framework to determine proximity in relationship coffee models. *Sociologia ruralis*, *60*(2), 458–481.

Engelseth, P. (2016). Developing exchange in short local foods supply chains. *International Journal on Food System Dynamics*, *7*(3), 229–242.

FAO, & UNICEF (2020). WFP W. Food Security and Nutrition in the World. *IEEE Journal of Selected Topics in Applied Earth Observations and Remote Sensing*, *320*.

Garcia-Torres, S., Albareda, L., Rey-Garcia, M., & Seuring, S. (2019). Traceability for sustainability–literature review and conceptual framework. *Supply Chain Management: An International Journal*, *24*(2), 85–106. https://doi.org/10.1108/SCM-04-2018-0152

Jarzębowski, S., Bourlakis, M., & Bezat-Jarzębowska, A. (2020). Short food supply chains (SFSC) as local and sustainable systems. *Sustainability*, *12*(11), 4715.

Macfadyen, S., Tylianakis, J. M., Letourneau, D. K., Benton, T. G., Tittonell, P., Perring, M. P., … Smith, H. G. (2015). The role of food retailers in improving resilience in global food supply. *Global Food Security*, *7*, 1–8.

Malak-Rawlikowska, A., Majewski, E., Wąs, A., Borgen, S. O., Csillag, P., Donati, M., … Wavresky, P. (2019). Measuring the economic, environmental, and social sustainability of short food supply chains. *Sustainability*, *11*(15), 4004.

McDaniels, T., Chang, S., Cole, D., Mikawoz, J., & Longstaff, H. (2008). Fostering resilience to extreme events within infrastructure systems: Characterizing decision contexts for mitigation and adaptation. *Global Environmental Change*, *18*(2), 310–318.

Milano Ristorazione (2021). https://www.milanoristorazione.it/

Reed, M. S., Graves, A., Dandy, N., Posthumus, H., Hubacek, K., Morris, J., … Stringer, L. C. (2009). Who's in and why? A typology of stakeholder analysis methods for natural resource management. *Journal of Environmental Management*, *90*(5), 1933–1949.

Renting, H., Marsden, T. K., & Banks, J. (2003). Understanding alternative food networks: Exploring the role of short food supply chains in rural development. *Environment and Planning A*, *35*(3), 393–411.

Rice, J. B., & Caniato, F. (2003). Building a secure and resilient supply network. *Supply Chain Management Review*, *7*(5), 22–30.

Stone, J., & Rahimifard, S. (2018). Resilience in agri-food supply chains: A critical analysis of the literature and synthesis of a novel framework. *Supply Chain Management: An International Journal*, *23*(3), 207–238. https://doi.org/10.1108/SCM-06-2017-0201

Tendall, D. M., Joerin, J., Kopainsky, B., Edwards, P., Shreck, A., Le, Q. B., … Six, J. (2015). Food system resilience: Defining the concept. *Global Food Security*, *6*, 17–23.

Todorovic, V., Maslaric, M., Bojic, S., Jokic, M., Mircetic, D., & Nikolicic, S. (2018). Solutions for more sustainable distribution in the short food supply chains. *Sustainability*, *10*(10), 3481.

Torre, A., & Rallet, A. (2005). Proximity and localization. *Regional Studies*, *39*(1), 47–59.

Woodhouse, P. (2010). Beyond industrial agriculture? Some questions about farm size, productivity and sustainability. *Journal of Agrarian Change*, *10*(3), 437–453.

Yacamán Ochoa, C., Matarán, A., Mata Olmo, R., López, J. M., & Fuentes-Guerra, R. (2019). The potential role of short food supply chains in strengthening periurban agriculture in Spain: The cases of Madrid and Barcelona. *Sustainability*, *11*(7), 2080.

7 Studying the impact of e-commerce on the sustainability of food systems in Vietnam

Michaël Bruckert, Olivier Lepiller, Denis Sautier, Nguyen Thi Tan Loc and Nguyen Thi Sau

7.1 Introduction

Food systems in Vietnam are rapidly transforming, in a context of urbanization, economic growth, and trade liberalization. More specifically, with rising mistrust regarding food safety (Wertheim-Heck et al., 2015), the demand for quality food products is growing. Numerous cases of bacterial and chemical contamination and intoxication are reported yearly, along with instances of high use of chemical inputs and a growing number of food safety violations (Hernandez & Lundy, 2020). Scandals surrounding the misuse of fertilizers, pesticides, and food additives often make headlines in local newspapers and spread anxiousness among consumers (Figuié et al., 2019). Additionally, intensive and unsustainable agricultural practices have been blamed since the early 2000s for polluting and degrading agricultural soils, thereby affecting biodiversity, air quality, and water quality (DiGregorio et al., 2003).

Sustainable food systems as an alternative production and consumption approach have not yet gained prominence in the public debate about food in Vietnam (de Koning et al., 2015). To address consumer concerns and health problems, the public authorities have strived to modernize the food sector. They set up a National Food Control System, with the adoption of the Vietnam Food Safety Law in 2010 and the introduction of voluntary private food safety standards (Pham & Dinh, 2020). Meanwhile, consumers have adopted different practices and strategies for buying and handling food in order to navigate the uncertainties around food safety (Wertheim-Heck et al., 2014). A recent study has shown that most Hanoi citizens look for safer food products and demand better food transparency and traceability (Ferrand et al., 2018). Yet many farmers following safety standards face difficulties in finding outlets where their products can be identified as safe and sold at premium prices. Moreover, the proliferation of food safety labels and the reported lack of control by public authorities or third parties have generated a general mistrust among consumers.

Against this backdrop, many actors see e-commerce as an opportunity to connect consumers and producers for the trade of quality food products. The municipality of Hanoi recently launched a public platform to market certified

DOI: 10.4324/9781003285441-7

low-chemical-input food products in the city, while many urban and peri-urban consumers use social media to buy food products online. The online purchase of food products is a recent practice that has so far received little in-depth attention from scholars. Most publications on the subject focus on consumer perceptions and behaviours (Morganosky & Cude, 2000; Quevedo-Silva et al., 2016; Zhao et al., 2017) or implications for management (Murphy, 2002). However, some scholars working on agrifood systems have started to examine the opportunities and limits of leveraging e-commerce platforms, social media, and other digital technologies as instruments to improve the sustainability of food supply networks. Some researchers have assessed the ability of online food retailing to improve economic efficiency by increasing the convenience of order and delivery processes (Wang & Coe, 2021), lowering prices, and diversifying the range of goods on offer (Belton-Chevallier et al., 2014). Others have investigated the potential of e-commerce to facilitate market access for smallholders (Zeng et al., 2017), reconnect food producers and consumers in Alternative Food Networks (Bos & Owen, 2016; Holloway, 2002; Ilbery & Maye, 2006; Renting et al., 2003; Stephens & Barbier, 2021), convey information about the quality of food products (Martindale, 2020), facilitate trust-building mechanisms (Fritz, 2007), or democratize the governance of food systems (Chiffoleau et al., 2018). The impact of e-commerce on the sustainability of food systems has not yet been studied comprehensively in Vietnam. Several articles have highlighted the importance of convenience in the decision to buy online (see for instance Kim Dang et al., 2018; Pham et al., 2018). Studying food shopping practices in Hanoi, Wertheim and Spaargaren observe "a trend of buying online from farmers without direct personal contact" (2016, p. 664) but do not provide a detailed analysis of the drivers and consequences of this new practice.

To bridge this gap, the Urbal research team in Hanoi used the Urbal methodology—which involves conducting interviews and carrying out workshops and innovation mapping with stakeholders—to help characterize and assess the impact of e-commerce innovation on food system sustainability in the region. The Urbal project approaches sustainability as a multi-dimensional concept with environmental, social and cultural, economic, health and nutrition, and governance dimensions (see Chapter 1 of this book). Using the Urbal method, we aimed to answer the following questions: Can e-commerce encourage the sale of quality food products? To what extent can it contribute to the sustainability of urban food systems? And how should market relationships be organized and regulated in order to achieve such goals? The Hanoi team focused on the online sale of "quality food" and studied two different types of e-commerce channels:

1) an informal and horizontal channel: the use of social media (such as Facebook or the more local application Zalo) to buy and sell food products
2) an institutional channel: a municipality-driven platform called Cho Nha Minh, intended for the sale of certified products

In the first section of this chapter, we introduce the e-commerce context in Vietnam and the two innovations we investigated following the Urbal approach. In the second section, we present the results of the discussions on the potential impacts that these innovations may have on different dimensions of sustainability. In the last section, we discuss these results and point out the limits of the Urbal process and the adaptations required in the local context.

7.2 Presentation of the two cases and the use of the Urbal approach

7.2.1 Urban food systems in Hanoi and the development of e-commerce

The urbanization rate in Vietnam has been increasing by nearly 1% yearly, from 30% in 2010 to 37% in 2020 (O'Neill, 2022). In Hanoi, the capital city (with an urban population of 3.6 million), drastic changes have affected food sourcing and consumption practices. Most of the food consumed in Hanoi was long sourced from the fertile urban hinterland. Since the early 1990s, demographic growth, urban sprawl, competition over land use, trade liberalization, private sector investment, and public policies for retail modernization have resulted in longer food supply chains, growing volumes of imports, the development of food processing industries, and greater economic concentration in the food sector (Raneri et al., 2019). New urban ways of life and higher revenues have fostered a nutrition transition, with diets shifting towards more fish, meat, dairy products, fruit, fats, and processed products while consumers are increasingly demanding higher-quality products (Harris et al., 2020). Recent years have been characterized by the development of supermarket chains and convenience stores, which sell processed food but sometimes also fresh products (vegetables, fruit, and livestock products) certified as "safe" by State agencies. However, there is resistance to food system modernization in the "traditional" food sector, which is characterized by informal wet and open markets. As of 2018, between 85% and 90% of fresh farm products were still sold in wet markets and open markets and by street vendors (Loc & Moustier, 2016; The University of Adelaide, 2018).

At the same time, online sales are booming across all industries. The general e-commerce sector has been expanding rapidly in Vietnam, reaching a value of USD 9.5 billion in 2019, representing 5% of the total retail market (Thanh, 2020). The physical distancing policies imposed by local authorities in 2020 to combat the COVID-19 pandemic reportedly boosted this growth. By 2018, 98% of people using the Internet had made purchases online (Saigoneer, 2018). Revenue from online "B2C" (business-to-consumer) sales in Vietnam ranked sixth worldwide (Deloitte, 2019). In 2019, the main actors on the market were Shopee.vn, VinID.net (the e-commerce site of VinGroup), Sendo.vn, Lazada.vn, Tiki.vn, and Lotte.vn. Among other products, food products are often sold online, and following the restrictions introduced during the COVID-19 pandemic, farmers turned to e-commerce platforms to sell their produce (VNS, 2021). While very few fresh food products are found on the aforementioned

B2C online platforms, "C2C" (consumer-to-consumer) e-commerce for food products is becoming increasingly popular in Vietnam. A survey carried out in 2016 showed that in Hanoi and Ho Chi Minh City, 47% of people buy products on social media (VietnamNet, 2017). In Vietnam, an estimated 43.5 million people use Facebook on a regular basis (Degenhard, 2023). The most popular application for online sales is Zalo, an instant messaging and calling application that can be used both on smartphones and on computers.

7.2.2 The methodology used to apply the Urbal approach

The two case studies were explored separately. For the first case study, in 2019 the research team carried out semi-directed interviews with 13 buyers and 6 sellers operating on social media. A participatory workshop was organized in December 2019 to discuss potential impact pathways of these activities, bringing together 24 stakeholders (vegetable, fruit, and meat sellers, fish and honey sellers, researchers, journalists, and governmental officials). The discussions focused on three main sets of activities, identified as important through interviews and a review of the literature, and on these activities' experienced or possible effects:

1) market transactions (online orders, online payments, delivery)
2) trust building and information sharing (sharing opinions, evaluations and comments, posting information and interacting with customers, managing reputation and loyalty)
3) connecting producers and consumers (identifying sellers of specific products, reaching out to consumers)

A second workshop was held in November 2020 to discuss the results. Ten participants attended, including producers, intermediaries, consumers, and public authorities, some of whom had already attended the first workshop. Additional interviews were carried out in early 2021 with 8 buyers and 7 sellers to further explore the question of trust in the context of online retail. In total, individual interviews were carried out with 21 buyers and 13 sellers. Among these 13 sellers, five were professional operators with three who ran brick-and-mortar food shops and two who ran agricultural cooperatives. The others engaged in online retail as a complementary activity.

The second case study, focused on the Cho Nha Minh (CNM) platform, was carried out *in itinere*, over the course of the project's design phase, pilot phase, and initial implementation phase. In 2019 and 2020 the research team conducted three semi-directive interviews with the municipal authorities (the Department of Agriculture and Rural Development (DARD) and the Hanoi Certification Centre), one with the Hanoi Women's Development Support Centre (an organization partnered with the project), and eight with companies and agricultural cooperatives identified by DARD as supplying products on the platform. It also carried out observations and informal interviews at an "offline" physical CNM stall temporarily set up in Hanoi. The team maintained informal relations with DARD in order to follow up on the implementation of CNM. It also collected and translated documents (particularly the rules and regulations of the CNM platform) and newspaper articles about CNM, and ran a participatory workshop in December 2020 with 18 participants, including producer groups' representatives, food retailers, consumers, the head of the Hanoi Certification Centre, the country's representative at the FAO, and researchers specialized in technologies for agriculture, environmental studies, and agricultural economics. The discussions were structured around two main themes and associated activities:

1) setting up a public platform for market transactions (creating a website for online transactions, opening a shop, providing public governance)
2) enrolling participants (attracting new clients and registering local suppliers who comply with the platform's standards)

A workshop was held in September 2021 with 21 participants to discuss the results of the first workshop.

Unfortunately, the research activities were impacted by the COVID-19 pandemic and the subsequent sanitary measures taken by the government. Face-to-face interviews and physical workshops were not possible during most of 2020. The implementation and grand opening of the CNM platform have also been postponed many times due to public health restrictions.

7.2.3 Case study 1: The use of social media to buy and sell quality food products

The first case study of the Urbal project in Hanoi focused on the use of social media for the sale and purchase of quality food products (see Figure 7.1). This practice can be described as a "social innovation", a term which Marques et al. (2018) use to refer to the "activities which aim to change in a significant manner the way that certain goods or services are produced and delivered" (p. 502). When using social media, users mobilize an external and pre-existing technological innovation—the applications and the supporting technological devices—to develop new ways of interacting and trading goods. In this innovation, no group of innovators reflexively coordinates in order to contribute to specific pre-determined goals. The innovation relies on the new economic relations established by isolated actors, rather than on the technical device that supports these relations. It arises from decentralized and polycentric practices that ultimately build up networks of users in a rhizomatic way.

The sellers (producers and intermediaries) and buyers using social media whom we interviewed claimed that they were engaging in a "new practice", but did not consider themselves as innovators. Moreover, concerns relating to sustainability, as defined by the Urbal project, were rarely central to their selling or buying practices. The main driver for using these applications was

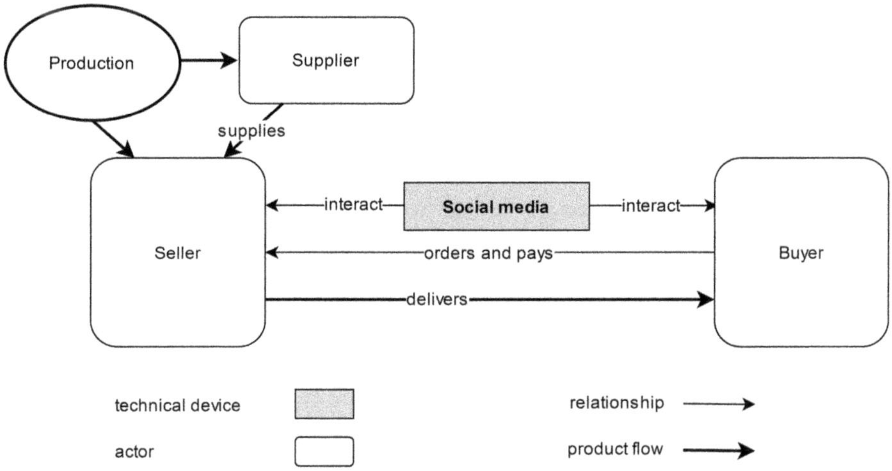

Figure 7.1 Network map of the actors and actions involved in the use of social media to buy and sell quality food products (Case Study 1).

unanimously the convenience of the economic relationship they enabled. Nevertheless, many fresh food products sold online meet different sustainability criteria, such as food safety, organic or "clean" production, palatability (good taste), and connection with origin or cultural identity. The research team focused its attention on the use of social media to trade these types of quality food products. Sellers and buyers usually connect through relatively "weak" linkages, be they physical or digital. However, this is not to say that coordination is absent. As we explain below, communication among buyers is key to creating trust; likewise, sellers sometimes share information about their practices and often use a common Facebook group to sell their products, providing a space for discussion and exchange.

7.2.4 *Case study 2: A municipality-driven e-commerce platform (Cho Nha Minh)*

The second case study relates to the online public-private platform CNM. According to the Hanoi People's Committee (PC) and the Department of Agriculture and Rural Development (DARD), urban consumers have difficulties identifying and sourcing safe food products on the market (interview with DARD, 2019). With e-commerce rapidly developing in Hanoi, they felt that an online platform could be an appropriate tool to connect producers of safe food and urban consumers. In 2018, the public authorities approved the decision to launch the Cho Nha Minh ("our own market") programme, which consisted of creating a transaction centre for producers and intermediaries who abide by food safety standards. Cho Nha Minh (CNM) was initially intended as an online platform managed by the municipal authorities, to be complemented with physical stalls offering the same range of products and promoting the online platform. Public management is seen as necessary to reassure consumers. The authorities argue that buyers trust the products certified and controlled by public authorities more than the ones sold on private platforms which "don't have any public accountability" (interview with DARD representative conducted in 2019). The digital platform was designed in 2018, with a pilot version launched in 2019. It was supervised by the Hanoi Agricultural Products Quality and Certification Centre (hereafter Hanoi Certification Centre), a department of DARD (see Figure 7.2).

In this case study, the innovation is centralized, planned and programmatic, with specific strategies and goals identified by the innovator. However, the innovation was taking its very first steps when the Urbal team started studying it. Moreover, the municipal authorities were initially not fully convinced of the added value of the proposed participatory mapping, as we explain in the last section of this chapter.

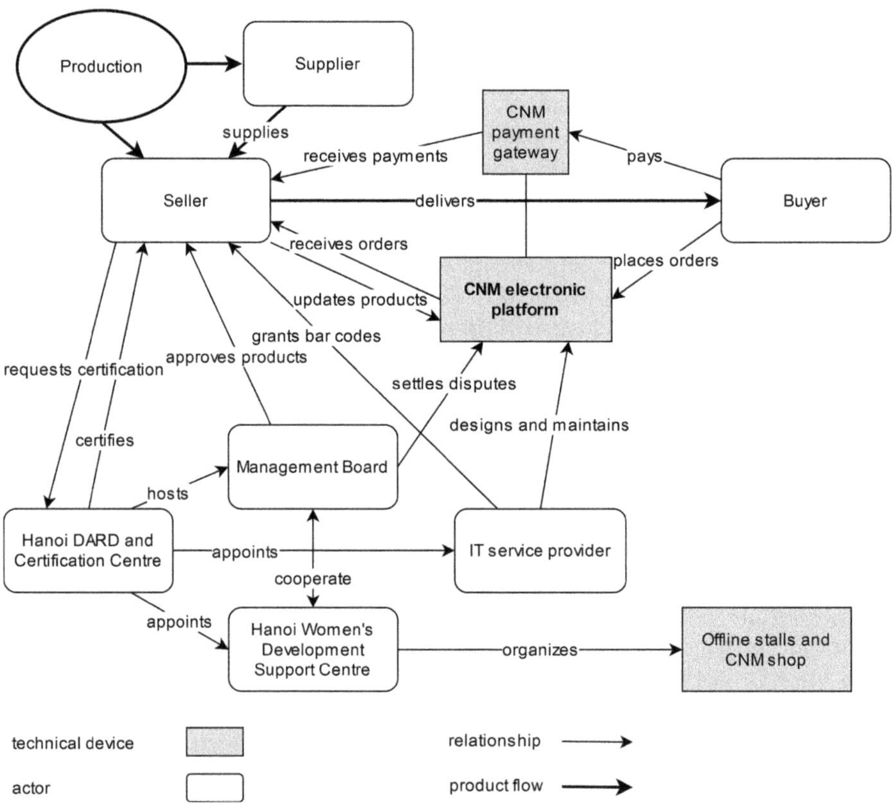

Figure 7.2 Network map of the key actors and actions involved in the municipality-driven platform CNM (Case Study 2).

7.3 Results: Food e-commerce innovations may foster efficiency but raise concerns regarding trust

7.3.1 Defining and characterizing the activities

7.3.1.1 Use of social media

As the team studied the use of social media to purchase food, it found that most of the time, consumers use digital applications and websites to buy fresh food (fruit, vegetables, meat, fish, etc.) or minimally processed food products (cakes, spices, etc.) of presumably higher quality. In this social media context, most of the online sellers are intermediaries, and not primary producers. Sellers tend to point to producers' lack of time and ability to market their production themselves. Usually, sellers publish a post on their Facebook page once they have acquired products, or when they are selling specific foodstuffs. Many sellers post pictures of the products, add at least basic information about them, and specify the price, the minimum order quantity, etc. Buyers can send the seller a private message, reply with a comment, or call or send them a message on Zalo or Messenger to order, specifying the quantity needed. The seller then confirms the order and direct contact is established by phone or via mobile applications to specify the delivery conditions. Facebook and Zalo are the two main channels used. When there is a personal connection between sellers and buyers, payment is made upon delivery. Otherwise, some sellers ask for advance payment, while others get paid through bank transfer. Delivery can be carried out by the seller or by a dedicated delivery service company.

When selecting the participants to invite to the workshop, the team sought to include sellers spanning a diverse range of scales of activity and products sold, and buyers with varied profiles in terms of gender, age, and education. Most of the buyers interviewed had only started using online apps to source food one to three years ago, while the intermediaries had been in the digital business for up to five years. Most of the producers interviewed had just started selling online. Despite our desire to avoid a gender bias, the majority of the online food buyers interviewed were women, as food shopping is still a gendered activity in Vietnam (Kim Dang et al., 2018). Most of them were in their thirties or forties, either married or not, with or without children, and had a professional activity, a decent salary, and a university education. Many had started buying online when they were university students. Some recalled starting this practice unexpectedly as they browsed Facebook, while others were influenced by friends or relatives.

Despite the considerable cost of entry, a growing number of producers, mainly agricultural cooperatives, now sell online in Vietnam. The sellers interviewed fell within two categories: professional organizations, such as agricultural cooperatives and food retailers looking to diversify their retail channels, and non-professional actors acting as intermediaries and selling online as a secondary activity to bring in additional revenue. Most of these non-professional sellers already had direct contact with producers before they started practising e-commerce. Some of them, presently living in Hanoi, came from rural or coastal provinces where their parents or other relatives could buy directly from farmers or fishermen and ship the fresh products to Hanoi. Other sellers had professional experience in the field of rural extension services and agricultural economy. The team met staff members from provincial Departments of Agriculture and Rural Development who sold food online, benefiting from their contacts in production areas upstream and from their colleagues' interest in fresh and quality food downstream. The same was true for many of the agricultural economics lecturers at the VNUA (Vietnam National University of Agriculture) in Hanoi. Interestingly, some "local e-marketplaces" have emerged in these institutions: many staff working in these agricultural research and extension institutions buy online from their colleagues, who source directly from producers with whom they work. These e-marketplaces usually take the form of Facebook groups where sellers post their offer and buyers place their order. In this case, the innovation is a (loosely) coordinated process aiming to achieve certain predetermined goals.

7.3.1.2 The municipality-driven platform "Cho Nha Minh"

Literally, *cho nha minh* means "our own market", an inclusive term that DARD chose to boost buyers' and sellers' sense of responsibility and participation. CNM is supposed to target all kinds of consumers, from lower-middle-class to upper-class backgrounds, and to cater primarily to Hanoi consumers. If successful, it is expected to later be scaled out at the national level. On the supply side, CNM is designed to be centred primarily on producers and retailers from the Hanoi municipality and nearby provinces delivering fresh produce (vegetables, fruit, meat, fish, and seafood). It may also include producers further afield that supply regional specialty products (rice, noodles, tea, oil, fish sauce, spices, honey, etc.). As of December 2020, about 140 suppliers, most of them producers, had registered with the programme, only 44 of whom had been approved by the authorities.

As per the rules and regulations of CNM, the Hanoi Certification Centre is in charge of managing the programme's activities, namely operating the website, vetting and approving the sellers and buyers and ensuring the effective implementation of the rights and obligations of each party. To sell their products on CNM, suppliers must have or apply for food safety certifications such as VietGAP (agricultural best practices certification), VietGAHP (animal husbandry best practices certification), and organic farming certification, all of which also involve enhanced environmental value, or HACCP (Hazard Analysis Critical Control Point) and ISO 22000. Inspections are carried out by the Hanoi Certification Centre. The sellers are required to label the products sold on CNM with the "CNM" registration logo. An IT service provider contracted to support the platform is responsible for designing and maintaining the website, resolving incidents, implementing privacy policies, and opening online accounts for each member. Sellers must post information about the products for sale and their sales policy (shipping policy, exchange policy, etc.) on the CNM webpage. The products must be approved before being displayed online. Transactions can be carried out through CNM's electronic trading portal. After logging in, buyers add products to their shopping cart and select the appropriate shipping and payment method (payment upon delivery, payment via debit card, payment via bank transfer, etc.). The seller must then process the order. Transactions can also happen outside of the digital platform: buyers can use the website to simply search for information about the products and then place their order directly (for instance by phone or email). CNM does however encourage purchasing and selling through the electronic platform, as products are controlled and certified, and users are supported in case of conflicts and complaints.

In the last months of 2018, the municipality launched "offline" CNM stalls in order to raise awareness about safe food and to promote the online platform, which had not yet been developed at the time. The offline stalls consisted of mobile stalls covered by large umbrellas, set up in locations deemed as "strategic" (in front of malls, in upper-end neighbourhoods, etc.) on Saturdays and Sundays. They sold safe food supplied by aspiring sellers on CNM and shared information about CNM.

The CNM programme was reportedly first delayed due to long administrative procedures. The grand opening has been planned and postponed several times. The programme also encountered several unexpected hurdles. The IT company that had been appointed to develop the digital platform was charged over a massive fraud operation in April 2019 (Ba, 2019). In January 2020, the outbreak of the Covid-19 pandemic further delayed the implementation of the programme, as the authorities suspended the offline stall campaign. Ironically, online sales in Vietnam skyrocketed when physical distancing was enforced in late March 2020. According to the interviews conducted with suppliers, the CNM platform has never been fully operational. For a whole year after its launch, the website constantly had to be taken offline. In Spring 2020, hundreds of products were posted on the platform. Yet due to technical issues, it was impossible to place orders online: buyers had to contact the sellers directly (over the phone, through social media applications, etc.) in order to buy products. Most of the products displayed on the website were out of stock and the related information had not been updated in many months. Furthermore, the suppliers were never able to post information directly on the website: they had to email the information to the Hanoi Certification Centre, which would then post it online. This created additional work for the public authorities.

In mid-July 2020, DARD opened a CNM brick-and-mortar shop in Ha Dong district in collaboration with the Hanoi Women's Development Support Centre, where suppliers registered with the CNM programme can sell their safe food products. Women who are potential buyers or potential suppliers are encouraged to take part in this programme.

7.3.2 *Impacts on sustainability: E-commerce as a convenient way to purchase quality food*

The impacts of these innovations on the various dimensions of sustainability were discussed with their different stakeholders during preliminary individual interviews as well as the participatory workshops.

Few stakeholders involved in the two case studies mentioned a specific dimension of sustainability, let alone sustainability in general, as a factor informing their practices. Regarding the CNM platform more specifically, the municipal authorities' vision is clear: their focus is on food safety and securing trust and profitability in the value chain. While it is not explicitly articulated in these terms, the CNM platform therefore contributes to sustainability in the region by providing consumers with access to safe and trustworthy food sources. For their part, the CNM users (sellers and buyers) see the platform not as an opportunity to contribute to a specific dimension of sustainability but as one of a number of devices to access the market and to connect with one another.

7.3.2.1 *Economic impacts and convenience*

Our research confirms the findings of earlier works on online purchases in Vietnam (Kim Dang et al., 2018; Pham et al., 2018): convenience and saving time were the most frequently mentioned reasons for stakeholders engaging in online retailing and shopping. Buying online was usually depicted as "highly convenient" and many buyers with busy schedules argued that they did not have time to go to the "physical" market every day. Some also considered online buying as a trend of which they wanted to be a part. There is clearly an entertainment aspect to online shopping; some consumers saw this activity as "exciting" and "fun". One consumer depicted the videos posted online as being "like cartoons". Special offers and promotions also seemed to bring interest and excitement to many buyers. The benefits were often presented in economic terms: consumers looked for lower prices, due to the presumably higher and fairer competition online. The buyers also mentioned the diversity of available offerings as an attractive feature of e-commerce, with more possibility to compare products and prices. Some buyers and regulators saw the high degree of competition between actors selling online and the possibility for buyers to ask them questions directly as an incentive for suppliers to deliver better products and services.

As for the sellers (producers and intermediaries), they also considered online trading as an efficient way to access the market. They praised e-commerce for enabling direct communication and facilitating access to buyers who lack the time and ability to come to their shops. They hoped to secure higher revenues through more efficient processes and lower transportation and intermediary costs.

7.3.2.2 *Quality food and health*

At face value, e-commerce fulfils the neoclassical function assigned to markets: maximizing utility and satisfaction for all agents. Yet the main stakeholders often also saw it as a preferred way to sell and buy "quality" products. When asked how they defined "quality products", the consumers usually pointed to "tasty", "safe", and "clean" products or, in other words, products free of harmful residues. For instance, freshness of seafood (fish, squid, shellfish, etc.) was equated with safety. People selling sea fish and seafood on social media usually have direct connections with fishermen: fresh fish is bought straight from the boat and shipped to Hanoi, covered in ice cubes in Styrofoam boxes. When it reaches the consumers, it is usually fresher than the sea fish sold through traditional food supply channels, where fish moves from hand to hand, brought from the Hai Phong or Ha Thinh harbour to local wholesale markets where it is kept and handled in conditions that are perceived as "unsafe" and "unhygienic".

While the online buyers acknowledged that there were other ways to buy safe food products, almost all of them expected products bought online to be safe. In other words, although the quest for food safety was not the primary driver of online purchases, safety was usually integrated in the more general concept of quality. As we shall see later, many of the buyers considered that the direct relationship achieved through online purchases enables trust in food quality. The opportunity to ask questions and to get tailored (and sometimes visual) answers and information also reportedly enhances the quality of the food sold online.

The buyers often used online applications and platforms to access food specialty products that are not easily accessible in physical shops and traditional markets. Products such as wild spices (*mac khen*), regional specialty products (*banh da* from Nghe An), renowned products (eel from Nghe An province, seafood from Phu Quoc and Nan Dinh), and fruit associated with specific production places (Dien pomelo, Vinh orange, etc.) are often bought and sold online. While these products can be associated with a "foodie" culture that reproduces social inequalities through distinction (Johnston & Baumann, 2014), they can also convey a specific attachment to culinary diversity, identity and craftsmanship. As for the food sellers, be they producers or retailers, they saw e-commerce and the direct connection with buyers it implies as a way to emphasize the specific qualities of their food products.

As de Koning et al. (2015) argue, "health in combination with food is the most important reason for people to pursue a sustainable lifestyle" (p. 608) in Vietnam. While the quest for quality can be understood as a utilitarian way to enjoy a product with better organoleptic and biochemical properties and a lower (or no) negative impact on health, this concern incidentally contributes to the development of shorter food supply chains, reducing the number of intermediaries, and better connecting producers and consumers. Sustainability is not an intrinsic quality of these food products and food supply chains, but rather an incidental, fortuitous quality that emerges as a by-product. Nevertheless, it is worth taking into consideration. This therefore raises the question of whether sustainability should always be a deliberate, reflexive driver for change, or whether it could be achieved by other, more individualistic, utilitarian, or instrumental means through specific market arrangements.

7.3.2.3 Environment and local development

Some of the consumers had a more "holistic" conception of what constitutes a "good" food product. A retired schoolteacher mentioned that she ordered organic pork online as she was concerned about the farming practices as well as the animal slaughter conditions. Another buyer expressed an interest in "safe vegetables" from Moc Chau and Dalat (cities in mountainous regions), as she felt that the growing environment was cleaner in those regions and the growers' working conditions were better. With the CNM platform, the production and sale of safe food can be more closely associated with environmentally sound practices. Although DARD did not mention this point when the research team interviewed them, some of the producers did allude to it. Not only do lower levels of fertilizer and pesticide use result in safer food for consumers, but they also reduce soil, water, and air contamination, thereby contributing to a healthier environment for the local residents and preserving biodiversity.

Few consumers or buyers spontaneously pointed to the reduction of road traffic facilitated by a more efficient transportation system and consumers making fewer trips to the markets as a positive impact of online sales. However, when specifically asked about it, many of them agreed that this was a potential positive impact.

As fresh food products (such as vegetables or meat) perish quickly, they can be only delivered within a small radius. Food product e-commerce therefore does not induce a placeless food network, as some have argued. On the contrary, it tends to foster the development of short food supply chains and locally sourced food production. This is especially the case when producers sell online without intermediaries. Moreover, as a researcher invited to one of the workshops suggested, e-commerce can indirectly support agroecological practices: by facilitating access to a wider range of fresh products, it encourages diversity in local production.

If it is able to overcome the technical and administrative difficulties mentioned above, the CNM programme could improve territorial cohesiveness and sustainable regional development. During the platform's first few months in operation, the municipality mainly enrolled producers based in Hanoi or in nearby provinces. By facilitating a direct or close connection with consumers, the platform has the potential to provide easy and direct access to the urban market for many local producers who cannot afford a brick-and-mortar shop in the city. In this innovation, the public authorities are not an intermediary *per se*, but rather provide a sociotechnical arrangement to facilitate market connections. The platform may foster the production of safe food and help retain economic value within the urban periphery. If scaled out, it could potentially bring about a more diversified economy and landscape, a dynamic green belt around the city, a cleaner environment, better profits for producers, and job creation in the agricultural sector.

7.3.2.4 Governance, trust, and accountability

The interactions between consumers and sellers are often depicted as more satisfying online than in physical shops. Many consumers praise these "new variants of 'face-to-face' contact" (Renting et al., 2003, p. 400) through e-commerce. Online trading can virtually cancel out physical distance and foster a "relation of regard" (Sage, 2003) between producers and customers. Online market relationships are sometimes contrasted with the trade relationships at traditional wet markets and supermarkets: with e-commerce, consumers can easily give their feedback (which is not the case at supermarkets), and this feedback is taken into account by sellers (which rarely happens at traditional markets). The governance of the food supply chain can therefore be considered as more participative or "democratic" (although the term was not used by our respondents). E-commerce can potentially reinforce the role of stakeholders at both ends of the food network. Through their direct interactions with producers, consumers play an active role in determining the kinds of products sold and, one can speculate, the ways these foodstuffs are produced. E-commerce, especially when it favours direct relations between producers and buyers, reinforces consumers' control over the food chain. At the same time, it can also facilitate access to the market for producers, who thus regain autonomy over the retailing of their products.

Regarding the CNM programme, some interviewees and workshop participants argued that the public governance of the platform could support the government's role in promoting collective action and ensuring the public good. Additionally, the collaboration initiated by DARD with the Hanoi Women's Development Support Centre and the easy access granted to women-run businesses could promote gender equality and the empowerment of women.

While e-commerce is a preferred channel for the sale and purchase of quality products, one of the main challenges with online shopping is ensuring and enhancing trust in the food system. Fritz (2007) argues that "communication of trust between transaction partners is not sufficiently realized in existing e-commerce offers for food networks" (p. 13). This was confirmed by the interviews and workshops held in both case studies. Most of the buyers and sellers thought that, generally speaking, food sold online was less trustworthy than food sold in physical shops. This lack of trust is linked to two main characteristics of e-commerce. The first material characteristic is the distance in time and space between ordering, shipping, and receiving the goods, which may result in poor appreciation of the products (mismatch between expectations and reality) and a deterioration of quality during delivery. Many buyers considered that the inability to physically check a product (by touching it, smelling it, etc.) before buying it is a major drawback of online sales. The second characteristic is more specific to the Vietnamese context. Many stakeholders argued that, contrary to physical retail, online retail is not controlled by the government and therefore opens up a significant avenue for fraud and the sale of low-quality goods. The ease of entry onto the market that online sales permit could thus reinforce this unfair competition and the risk of fraud.

Buyers do however usually trust their sellers. Paradoxically, whereas the products sold online are generally considered as less trustworthy than products sold at physical markets, the specific sellers selected by each buyer are individually considered as more trustworthy than regular sellers. The consumers interviewed expressed both a general mistrust of online sales and an individual attachment to the online sellers they had chosen, making the establishment of trust a personal matter. This is enabled by different choice, calculation, and valuation strategies. For instance, the online sale of honey, a product that exemplifies the risk of fraud through tampering with sugar, proves that trust levels in e-commerce can be very high.

The CNM programme chose to focus on certification: the standards enforced and the municipal control over them are supposed to prevent exposure to chemical and bacterial contamination. Yet personal relationships appear to be one of the most important trust mechanisms, especially when using social media. What is noteworthy in this case is that trust is not built through the practice of buying online but precedes it. Online sales do not generate trust. On the contrary, trust makes online sales possible. Most buyers have prior direct or indirect relationships with the sellers—they met the sellers at food trade fairs, they visited their physical shops, they maintain family, friendship, or professional ties with them, they were introduced through mutual friends, etc. In wet markets, trust is usually embedded in relations of geographic proximity and temporal constancy: the seller down the street is trusted because he/she belongs to the community or has proven to be reliable over time. Digital retail more or less builds on the same patterns of trust. While the economic transaction takes place in a virtual sphere, the market relationship still depends on proximity, constancy, and embeddedness.

Wertheim-Heck and Spaargaren (2016) argue that in Hanoi "social relationships moved from face-to-face contact to online communities" (p. 662). Yet our research reveals that online communities often extend the time- and spatial scales of a pre-existing face-to-face relationship. Still, online trading does reconfigure this relationship. Since consumers see a benefit in sellers having the opportunity to post information, pictures, or even videos online, online purchasing can thus contribute to reducing the physical and economic distance between producers and consumers and to fostering urban-rural linkages, as has already been highlighted in the literature on alternative food networks (Blay-Palmer et al., 2018). Direct contact between suppliers and buyers, as well as the sharing of information online (pictures, description of farming practices, etc.), could also enhance consumers' knowledge of the food they eat and foster trust in the food system.

The products sold online often differ from products bought through mainstream retail channels. Likewise, the food supply system for e-commerce also differs from physical retail. The online food retail innovations considered in the case studies of interest here contribute to the creation of alternative food systems, both through the types of products sold (high-quality and sustainable food items) and through the networks established (direct relationships grounded in personal trust) (see Watts et al., 2005). Our research confirms that, under certain conditions, the online trading of quality food fosters the "socio-material reconnection processes" (Bos & Owen, 2016, p. 1) that occur in alternative food networks (Ilbery & Maye, 2006; Stephens & Barbier, 2021).

7.3.2.5 Potential negative impacts

Beyond trust not being a given in online food retail, the sellers and buyers involved in the case studies did point out other shortcomings. Some stakeholders argued that online retail introduces a kind of unfair competition for the marginalized traders who do not have the means to access and use digital technology. Moreover, some stakeholders saw the ability to order from home and to receive deliveries as driving an increasingly sedentary lifestyle, potentially harming health. Finally, although no participant mentioned this point, we can also argue that online purchases may have negative environmental outcomes: it may increase road traffic in case of lower pooling of food transport flows and induce more electronic waste and energy consumption associated with the use of electronic devices (Figures 7.3–7.5).

7.4 Discussion: The need to adapt to local contexts and understandings

7.4.1 Barriers and enablers

During the workshops, the participants identified several barriers to e-commerce having a positive impact on the different dimensions of sustainability. Many argued that food—and especially quality food—is not the most convenient product for online trade, as sensory appreciation is often necessary before making a purchase. While social media can "explain the material qualities of food" (Martindale, 2020), they cannot physically convey them. The lack of trust in the products sold online was also unanimously mentioned as an obstacle. This was often associated with the difficulty for public authorities to control online sales, mainly owing to a lack of resources. The CNM platform was conceived as a way to counter this alleged lack of trust in the transactions that take place on social media. However, as mentioned earlier, the difficulties it has encountered highlight the shortage of financial and human resources with which the public authorities must contend. Many stakeholders also considered that smallholders and small suppliers lack the knowledge, time, and financial

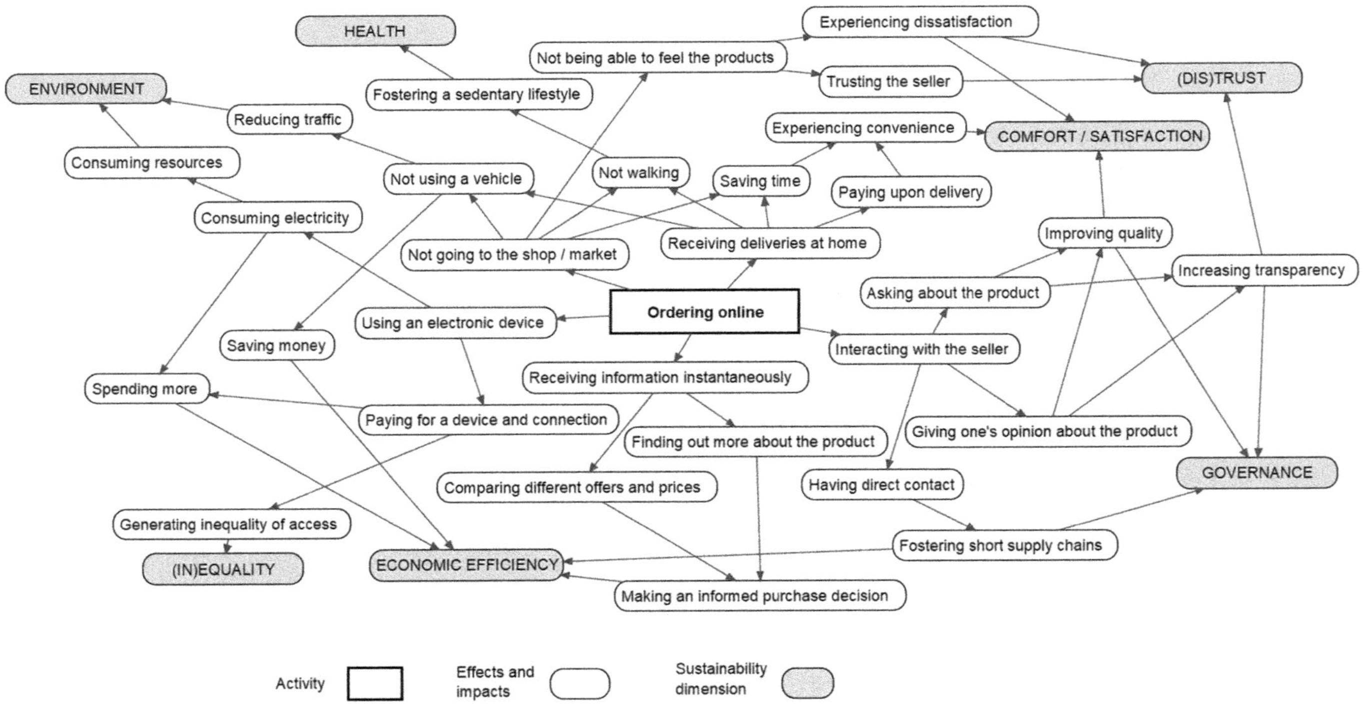

Figure 7.3 Potential positive and negative impacts of ordering on social media (Case Study 1), mapped before the workshop.

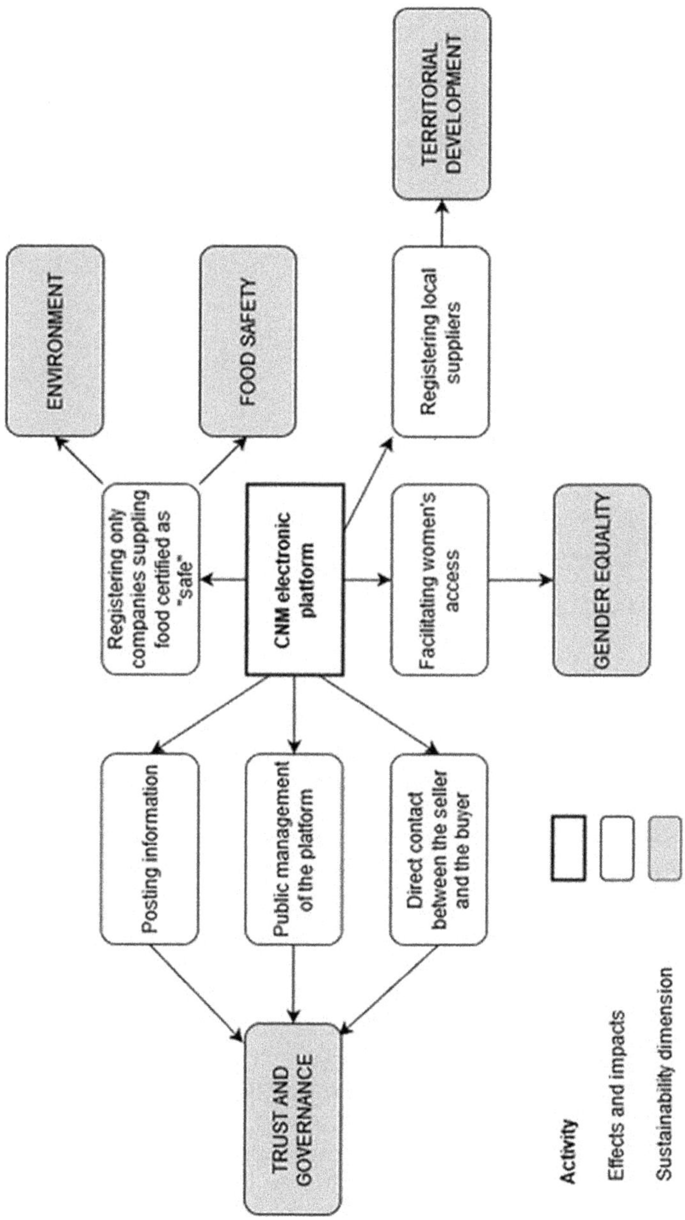

Figure 7.4 Potential positive impacts of the municipality-driven platform (Case Study 2), mapped before the workshop.

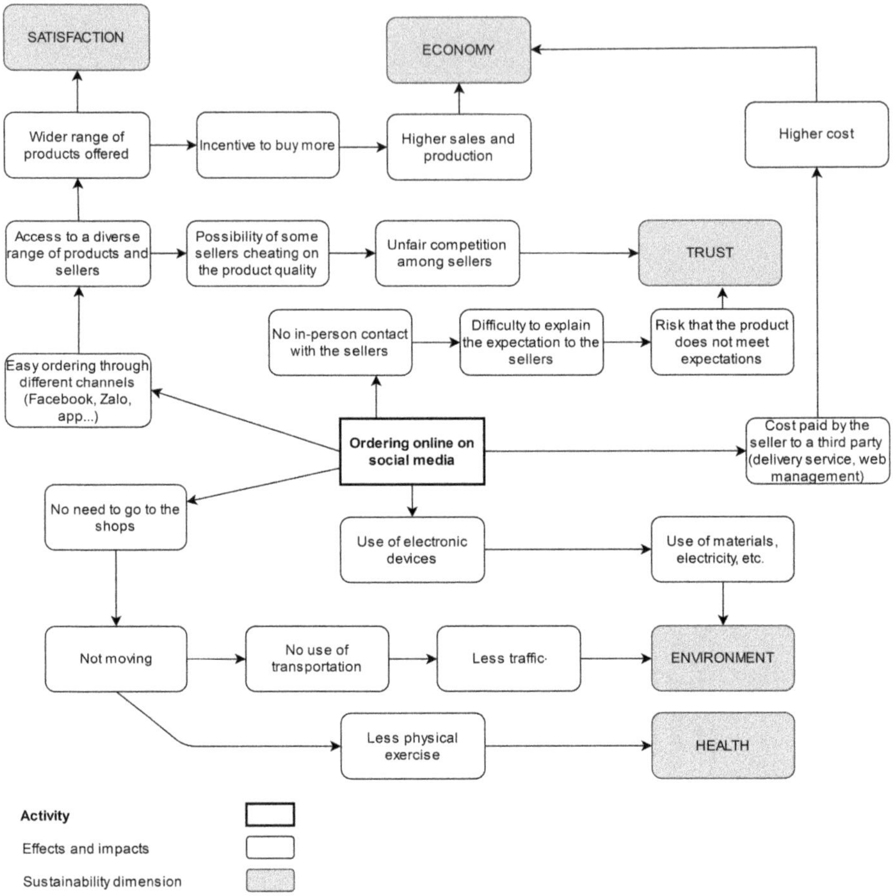

Figure 7.5 Positive and negative impacts of ordering online on social media (Case Study 1), mapped during the participatory workshop.

resources to engage in e-commerce. Many pointed to the digital divide between those who master the technology and those do not or cannot access it.

Some suppliers expressed their dissatisfaction with online trading. They argued that it raises logistical and organizational difficulties, including a reliance on delivery companies to ship small quantities due to the high costs associated with handling deliveries and that updating the information online is time-consuming. They also identified securing buyers' loyalty as a challenge since the vast majority of consumers prefer going to the traditional market. Adapting to buyers' requirements for flexibility in terms of delivery times or payment methods was likewise a big concern.

Accordingly, many stakeholders called for more public interventions not only to introduce control measures or taxes but also to involve the private sector in setting up appropriate technological solutions. Capacity-building programmes were suggested to enable small actors to engage in e-commerce. Many participants also stressed the fact that e-commerce is not a purely virtual relationship—it requires efficient and reliable infrastructure to ensure the proper shipping of the goods ordered.

7.4.2 The question of trust and the participants' instrumental understanding of sustainability

Although the workshops focused on sustainability in general, the research team noticed that there was no shared understanding of sustainability among the participants. The concept was explained at the beginning of the workshops, but the stakeholders did not use it when expressing their views on the innovations discussed. The facilitators had to break down sustainability into its different dimensions (health, social, economic, ecological, etc.) as defined by Urbal, in order to stimulate discussions about non-economic dimensions. Despite regular reminders, environmental and equity issues were rarely addressed, and the stakeholders mainly focused on "instrumental" or economic-driven dimensions such as convenience, customer satisfaction and market opportunities for producers. Interestingly, the concept of "sustainability" itself is hardly translatable into Vietnamese. "Sustainable" is translated as *bền vững*, which denotes something that "lasts a long time", without any ecological connotation *per se*. Most of the participants therefore merely expressed their views on how these innovations could "last a long time". It is clear that the "holistic" and "multi-dimensional nature of the concept of sustainability" (Béné et al., 2019, p. 127) is not taken as a given in non-Western and non-academic contexts. Thus, discussions about the necessary trade-offs between specific dimensions of sustainability did not emerge in an explicit way.

As mentioned above, many stakeholders referred to trust as a major issue for the e-commerce of quality food, either blaming online retail for failing to generate trust or calling for mechanisms to guarantee trust. In the discussions, the participants explored the potential of different activities involved in e-commerce (posting information online, public control over online sales, etc.) to ensure more trust in the quality of the products sold. Through the interviews and the workshops, we identified four main mechanisms to build and sustain trust in online sales:

Institutional trust:

1) **Expertise**: trust is enabled through controls and the granting of certifications, labels and brands by third-party corporations or State bodies.
2) **Reputation**: trust is enabled by the recognition and praise of the seller's features by a larger community.

Interpersonal trust:

3) **Relationship**: trust is ensured by the buyer knowing the seller prior to the market transaction or, in an intermediated and less direct way, by someone whom the buyer trusts expressing their confidence in a seller they know.

4) **Experience**: trust is sustained by the buyer having already bought from the seller and being satisfied with the quality of the products.

In the discussions, trust was seen as both a necessary condition of food systems' sustainability and an outcome of specific market relations. In the tentative Urbal approach, trust was not identified as a specific dimension of sustainable food systems. Yet the literature on alternative food networks often presents trust as a product of local and "embedded" food systems (see for instance Sage, 2003). According to this body of work, the face-to-face relationship between sellers and buyers produces a kind of personal trust that conventional and placeless food systems cannot provide. Based on the Urbal workshop discussions and data collected through the interviews, we argue that trust is not only an outcome of sustainable food systems, but also an enabling condition of sustainability. In so-called "conventional food systems", while trust is not absent, it is of a different kind. Direct information sharing between retailers or producers and consumers in e-commerce may lead to a more satisfactory mechanism for ensuring trust. However, some online market relations mobilize more conventional trust-building mechanisms, such as labels and certifications. Trust is therefore a mechanism, a process that pervades all the different dimensions of sustainable systems. It mediates transactions between producers and consumers and makes these transactions possible, and in return, the trust that sustains the transactions generates positive effects for both the producers and the consumers. Trust needs to be understood as a dynamic system of relations that is constantly reinforced and re-enacted in a cumulative way through satisfactory and meaningful relations.

7.4.3 Difficulties encountered and adaptations to the local context

We identified two types of limits in the implementation of the methodology: "incidental" difficulties and more "structural" difficulties. Incidental difficulties are due to unexpected factors that may arise during the research process. First, the team encountered difficulties in identifying the innovations to study. For one case study, it successively selected and abandoned two different innovations due to difficulties in accessing information and stakeholders, before deciding to focus on the CNM programme. The COVID-19 crisis affected the implementation of the programme and consequently the research process. Finally, convincing the public authorities and geographically distant producers to take part in time-consuming workshops was a challenge and the team had to rely on long-term relationships with those actors to successfully enrol them in the process. As is customary in Vietnam, a small financial compensation was given to the stakeholders for their participation in the workshops.

Structural difficulties relate more to the specific context in which a methodology is implemented. We have already discussed the difficulties encountered in translating the concept of sustainability linguistically and culturally. Likewise, terms such as "impact" and "pathways" had to be adapted and explained.

Moreover, participatory methodologies are not frequently applied in Vietnam, and the power imbalances arising from explicit and/or tacit authority dynamics as well as the strong state-driven context sometimes made it difficult for some stakeholders to express their views freely in public. However, the individual interviews carried out prior to the workshops afforded rich insights from the actors (especially smallholders) with less power and a smaller voice in the systems of innovation studied. During the workshops, the facilitators managed to create space for each participant's voice to be heard. More generally, they were able to strike a balance between a participatory approach attentive to the stakeholders' understandings of the objectives and their knowledge of the innovation on the one hand, and a more directive approach with incentives and reminders to address sustainability at large on the other.

Several elements from the tentative Urbal process were adapted to the local context. Due to time constraints and the above-mentioned difficulties in translating the concepts, the conceptual framework was not presented in depth during the workshops. Instead, the Urbal diagram of sustainability, which depicts the different "dimensions" encompassed within the concept, was used as a medium for discussion. However, this may have promoted a "reductionist" understanding of sustainability. During the workshop discussions, the facilitators had to constantly remind the participants of the focus on sustainability in general as a holistic concept and not just on its instrumental and functional dimensions.

The study of the CNM programme had to adapt to its work-in-progress situation and to the difficulties it had encountered. The first workshop did not directly address impacts and impact pathways, for the programme was still in its initial stages with no tangible and measurable outcomes thus far. As the innovation had met technical and organizational difficulties, the research team prioritized discussions on how to adapt and modify the activities and the structure of the programme in order to make it work better and, if possible, achieve greater impact. Thus, the focus was more on what *had to be* done rather than on what *had been* done.

This strategy also helped involve the public authorities in the process. At first, the municipality was not convinced about the benefits of the participatory approach. Instead, it was expecting the team to provide its expertise, which posed a challenge for the community-driven methodology. After showing the municipal authorities that the goal was not to assess their innovation but to support them in improving it, the team managed to get them on board. The second workshop to discuss the results focused not on CNM as such but on institutional e-commerce platforms more broadly and their capacity to support sustainability in food systems.

7.4.4 *Benefits of the workshops*

Beyond the discussions about the impact pathways arising from the two innovations studied, the workshops were useful in building connections between different stakeholders, allowing them to share their experiences and fostering a sense of community among the different actors. Above all, the participants benefited from the workshops by identifying barriers to and solutions for enhancing the innovations' performance. Although sustainability was not central to the stakeholders' concerns, the workshops were a good opportunity to disseminate a holistic understanding of the concept and to raise awareness about the way in which innovations in urban food systems can potentially result in positive impacts on several interconnected dimensions.

7.5 Conclusion: Strengths and weaknesses of striving for sustainable food systems through digital technology

Digital technology affords a range of new relations between food producers and consumers in the urban space. Vietnamese consumers have increased their online food purchasing as a result of the COVID-19 pandemic. Buying directly through social media apps and digital platforms, as described in this chapter, are examples of such innovations. In Hanoi, consumers using such technologies tend to be young, active, and highly educated women. Sellers are mostly intermediaries, although suburban producers are now also entering the online market. Many operators use these digital technologies to trade quality food products. This reduces the distance between producers and consumers through the sharing of written and visual information and by enabling direct feedback and complaints. Furthermore, e-commerce could promote a territory-based food production system, especially for fresh and perishable products delivered to urban consumers.

The reliability of these new relations is however contingent on a number of conditions being met, such as the service remaining operational, consistently successful deliveries, and governance fostering the participation and coordination of a large number of local producers. Interestingly, the online trading networks that seem to have worked well so far in Hanoi connect sellers and buyers who already knew each other before engaging in a trading relationship. Even though they do not always target specifically sustainable food products, these new marketing channels have the capacity to convey more and better information on food quality attributes as well as production and processing techniques, through direct and personalized communication or the certification of safe products.

References

Ba, D. (2019, July 10). Runaway tech company chief now faces money laundering charges—VnExpress International. https://e.vnexpress.net/news/news/runaway-tech-company-chief-now-faces-money-laundering-charges-3950873.html

Belton-Chevallier, L., Motte-Baumvol, B., Belin-Munier, C., Carrouet, G., Chrétien, J., Dablanc, L., Coninck, F. de, Fortin, F., Jégou, A., Morganti, E., Reinhard, N., & Thévenin, T. (2014). *Les effets de la vente en ligne sur les inégalités territoriales d'accès au commerce. Vers un nivellement des disparités urbain-périurbain?* [Report, Université de Bourgogne; IFSTTAR]. https://hal.archives-ouvertes.fr/hal-01108851

Béné, C., Oosterveer, P., Lamotte, L., Brouwer, I. D., de Haan, S., Prager, S. D., Talsma, E.F., & Khoury, C.K. (2019). When food systems meet sustainability – Current narratives and implications for actions. *World Development*, *113*, 116–130. https://doi.org/10.1016/j.worlddev.2018.08.011

Blay-Palmer, A., Santini, G., Dubbeling, M., Renting, H., Taguchi, M., & Giordano, T. (2018). Validating the city region food system approach: Enacting inclusive, transformational city region food systems. *Sustainability*, *10*(5), 1680. https://doi.org/10.3390/su10051680

Bos, E., & Owen, L. (2016). Virtual reconnection: The online spaces of alternative food networks in England. *Journal of Rural Studies*, *45*, 1–14. https://doi.org/10.1016/j.jrurstud.2016.02.016

Chiffoleau, Y., Bouré, M., & Akermann, G. (2018). Les circuits courts alimentaires à l'heure du numérique: Quels enjeux? Une exploration. *Innovations Agronomiques*, *67*, 37. https://doi.org/10.15454/FDWTG6

De Koning, J. I. J. C., Crul, M. R. M., Wever, R., & Brezet, J. C. (2015). Sustainable consumption in Vietnam: An explorative study among the urban middle class. *International Journal of Consumer Studies*, *39*(6), 608–618. https://doi.org/10.1111/ijcs.12235

Degenhard, J. (2023, March). Vietnam: Facebook users 2018–2027. *Statista*. https://www.statista.com/forecasts/1136459/facebook-users-in-vietnam

Deloitte. (2019). *Retail in Vietnam. Navigating the digital retail landscape*. https://www2.deloitte.com/content/dam/Deloitte/vn/Documents/consumer-business/vn-cb-vietnam-consumer-retail-2019.pdf

DiGregorio, M., Rambo, T., & Yanagisawa, M. (2003). Clean, green, and beautiful: Environment and development under the renovation economy. In V.L. Hy (Ed.), *Postwar Vietnam: Dynamics of a Transforming Society* (pp. 297–323). Rowman & Littlefield.

Ferrand, P., Guillonnet, R., & Vagneron, I. (2018). *Consumer perceptions towards good and safe food in Myanmar and Vietnam*. Conference Greening Agri-food Systems, Ensuring Rural Sustainability and Promoting Healthy Socioeconomic Transformation in Southeast Asia, Chulalongkorn University, Bangkok.

Figuié, M., Moustier, P., Bricas, N., & Nguyen-Thi Tan, L. (2019). Trust and food modernity in Vietnam. In J. Ehlert & N.K. Faltmann (Eds.), *Food anxiety in globalising Vietnam* (pp. 139–166). Palgrave Macmillan. https://doi.org/10.1007/978-981-13-0743-0

Fritz, M. (2007). E-commerce partnering due diligence: A methodology for trust in e-commerce in food networks. *Food Economics – Acta Agriculturae Scandinavica, Section C*, *4*(1), 13–20. https://doi.org/10.1080/16507540701192493

Harris, J., Nguyen, P.H., Tran, L.M., & Huynh, P.N. (2020). Nutrition transition in Vietnam: Changing food supply, food prices, household expenditure, diet and nutrition outcomes. *Food Security*, *12*(5), 1141–1155. https://doi.org/10.1007/s12571-020-01096-x

Hernandez, R., & Lundy, M. (2020). *Vietnamese food systems profile* (p. 22) [Country Brief]. CIAT.

Holloway, L. (2002). Virtual vegetables and adopted sheep: Ethical relation, authenticity and Internet-mediated food production technologies. *Area*, *34*(1), 70–81. https://doi.org/10.1111/1475-4762.00058

Ilbery, B., & Maye, D. (2006). Retailing local food in the Scottish–English borders: A supply chain perspective. *Geoforum*, *37*(3), 352–367. https://doi.org/10.1016/j.geoforum.2005.09.003

Johnston, J., & Baumann, S. (2014). *Foodies: Democracy and distinction in the gourmet foodscape*. Routledge.

Kim Dang, A., Xuan Tran, B., Tat Nguyen, C., Thi Le, H., Thi Do, H., Duc Nguyen, H., Hoang Nguyen, L., Huu Nguyen, T., Thi Mai, H., Dinh Tran, T., Ngo, C., Thi Minh Vu, T., Latkin, C., Zhang, M., & Ho, R. (2018). Consumer preference and attitude regarding online food products in Hanoi, Vietnam. *International Journal of Environmental Research and Public Health*, *15*(5), 981. https://doi.org/10.3390/ijerph15050981

Loc, N.T.T., & Moustier, P. (2016). Toward a restricted tolerance of street vending of food in Hanoi districts: The role of stakeholder dialogue. *World Food Policy*, *2/3*(2/1). https://doi.org/10.18278/wfp.2.2.3.1.5

Marques, P., Morgan, K., & Richardson, R. (2018). Social innovation in question: The theoretical and practical implications of a contested concept. *Environment and Planning C: Politics and Space*, *36*(3), 496–512. https://doi.org/10.1177/2399654417717986

Martindale, L. (2020). 'I will know it when I taste it': Trust, food materialities and social media in Chinese alternative food networks. *Agriculture and Human Values*. https://doi.org/10.1007/s10460-020-10155-0

Morganosky, M. A., & Cude, B. J. (2000). Consumer response to online grocery shopping. *International Journal of Retail & Distribution Management*, *28*(1), 17–26. https://doi.org/10.1108/09590550010306737

Murphy, A. (2002). The emergence of online food retailing: A stakeholder perspective. *Tijdschrift Voor Economische En Sociale Geografie*, *93*(1), 47–61. https://doi.org/10.1111/1467-9663.00182

O'Neill, A. (2022, December). Vietnam—Urbanization 2021. *Statista*. https://www.statista.com/statistics/444882/urbanization-in-vietnam/

Pham, H. V., & Dinh, T. L. (2020). The Vietnam's food control system: Achievements and remaining issues. *Food Control*, *108*, 106862. https://doi.org/10.1016/j.foodcont.2019.106862

Pham, Q., Tran, X., Misra, S., Maskeliūnas, R., & Damaševičius, R. (2018). Relationship between convenience, perceived value, and repurchase intention in online shopping in Vietnam. *Sustainability*, *10*(2), 156. https://doi.org/10.3390/su10010156

Quevedo-Silva, F., Freire, O., Lima-Filho, D. de O., Brandão, M. M., Isabella, G., & Moreira, L. B. (2016). Intentions to purchase food through the internet: Developing and testing a model. *British Food Journal*, *118*(3), 572–587. https://doi.org/10.1108/BFJ-09-2015-0305

Raneri, J. E., Kennedy, G., Nguyen, T., Wertheim-Heck, S., Do, H., & de Haan, S. (2019). *Determining key research areas for healthier diets and sustainable food systems in Viet Nam*. IFPRI Discussion Paper 01872, CGIAR Research Program on Agriculture for Nutrition and Health.

Renting, H., Marsden, T. K., & Banks, J. (2003). Understanding alternative food networks: Exploring the role of short food supply chains in rural development. *Environment and Planning A*, *35*(3), 393–411. https://doi.org/10.1068/a3510

Sage, C. (2003). Social embeddedness and relations of regard: Alternative 'good food' networks in south-west Ireland. *Journal of Rural Studies*, *14*, 47–60.

Saigoneer. (2018, December 21). Nearly every Vietnamese internet user shops online: Report. *Saigoneer*. https://saigoneer.com/vietnam-news/15314-nearly-every-vietnamese-internet-user-shops-online

Stephens, R., & Barbier, M. (2021). Digital fooding, cashless marketplaces and reconnection in intermediated third places: Conceptualizing metropolitan food provision in the age of prosumption. *Journal of Rural Studies*, *82*, 366–379. https://doi.org/10.1016/j.jrurstud.2020.11.009

Thanh, V. (2020, March 11). Vietnam's e-commerce market to exceed $17 billion in 2023. Vietnam Investment Review – VIR. https://vir.com.vn/vietnams-e-commerce-market-to-exceed-17-billion-in-2023-74647.html

The University of Adelaide. (2018). The Vietnam urban food consumption and expenditure study, Factsheet 6. https://www.adelaide.edu.au/global-food/ua/media/101/Urban_Consumer_Survey_Factsheet_06.pdf

VietnamNet. (2017, February). Saigonese, Hanoians prefer buying goods online via Facebook. *Ministry of information and communications of the socialist republic of Vietnam*. https://english.mic.gov.vn/mra/Pages/TinTuc/133733/Saigonese--Hanoians-prefer-buying-goods-online-via-Facebook.html

VNS. (2021, November). Agricultural products go online. *Vietnamnews.Vn*. https://vietnamnews.vn/economy/899756/agricultural-products-go-online.html

Wang, Y., & Coe, N. M. (2021). Platform ecosystems and digital innovation in food retailing: Exploring the rise of Hema in China. *Geoforum*, *126*, 310–321. https://doi.org/10.1016/j.geoforum.2021.08.007

Watts, D., Ilbery, B., & Maye, D. (2005). Making reconnections in agro-food geography: Alternative systems of food provision. *Progress in Human Geography*, *29*(1), 22–40. https://doi.org/10.1191/0309132505ph526oa

Wertheim-Heck, S., & Spaargaren, G. (2016). Shifting configurations of shopping practices and food safety dynamics in Hanoi, Vietnam: A historical analysis. *Agriculture and Human Values*, *33*(3), 655–671. https://doi.org/10.1007/s10460-015-9645-4

Wertheim-Heck, S., Vellema, S., & Spaargaren, G. (2015). Food safety and urban food markets in Vietnam: The need for flexible and customized retail modernization policies. *Food Policy*, *54*, 95–106. https://doi.org/10.1016/j.foodpol.2015.05.002

Wertheim-Heck, S. C. O., Spaargaren, G., & Vellema, S. (2014). Food safety in everyday life: Shopping for vegetables in a rural city in Vietnam. *Journal of Rural Studies*, *35*, 37–48. https://doi.org/10.1016/j.jrurstud.2014.04.002

Zeng, Y., Jia, F., Wan, L., & Guo, H. (2017). E-commerce in agri-food sector: A systematic literature review. *International Food and Agribusiness Management Review*, *20*(4), 439–460. https://doi.org/10.22434/IFAMR2016.0156

Zhao, X., Deng, S., & Zhou, Y. (2017). The impact of reference effects on online purchase intention of agricultural products: The moderating role of consumers' food safety consciousness. *Internet Research*, *27*(2), 233–255. https://doi.org/10.1108/IntR-03-2016-0082

8 Ecofriendly farmsystems

Testing the Urbal approach in Berlin

Lucas Hövelmann and Undine Giseke

8.1 Introduction

As an Urban Food Innovation Lab (UFIL) of the Urbal project, Ecofriendly Farmsystems (ECF) in Berlin provides an example of an alternative food chain operation impacting different dimensions of sustainability. This aquaponic urban farm breeds perch and grows basil in an increasingly closed-loop production system at the Berlin city centre. This food is largely distributed within Berlin through a national grocery retail chain and can also be purchased locally at the farm. Since its inception, ECF has consulted on the installation and construction of two turnkey projects outside of Germany—one in Brussels and the other in Switzerland.

This chapter investigates how technical innovation in urban food systems can be broadened to address social dimensions of sustainability in addition to environmental and economic considerations as part of a more holistic approach to sustainability. Since the Urbal approach was designed to enable stakeholders to consider multiple dimensions of sustainability concurrently, the case of ECF helps to test and develop a more comprehensive sustainability assessment framework for urban food system innovations.

Furthermore, we explore how interactions within and through spaces—what we call "inside–outside" dynamics"—lead to unique sustainability configurations in the places where they are located, and we consider whether a connection to the regional scale can be established, focusing especially on the relationships between different spaces of the same food system inside and outside cities.

The ECF Farm project provides an example of how urban agriculture is linked to its urban context and the surrounding region, and how the turnkey operations it installs in other cities are connected to these cities' communities and regions, as well as other places. We also shed light on how the project integrates socio-cultural dimensions by investigating the motivations and efforts of the ECF Farm and evaluating additional steps that could enable these efforts to be further developed as part of private sustainability initiatives.

DOI: 10.4324/9781003285441-8

As an Urbal UFIL focused on private enterprise, supply chains, and sustainability, the case of ECF also provides an opportunity to consider avenues for further developing theories surrounding the environmental and technical context of sustainability, such as the theory of socio-technical transitions and the circular economy approach, to include the social and health dimensions of sustainability.

The application of the Urbal framework during an innovation workshop (see Section 8.4) at the ECF Farm facilities provide insight on a range of environmental and socio-economic considerations surrounding scalability as well as obstacles encountered during the development phase of the venture, specifically for businesses working in the field of food production in urban areas. The participants, key findings from the discussion, and tailored process diagrams focusing on past and future innovations are presented in Section 8.5, followed by a description of how the method was adapted to the specific case of the ECF Farm.

8.2 Context

8.2.1 Literature review: Multi-level perspectives and trans-scale considerations regarding regional food and distribution networks

Faced with pressing global challenges—climate change, biodiversity loss, pandemics, rising food insecurity, and diet-related disease—there are ongoing discussions on how sustainable transitions can take place and be fostered. The socio-technical transitions literature offers a point of entry into this discussion. Within this literature, the multi-level perspective (MLP) analyses the factors that enable or hinder sustainability. According to this theory, radical, transformative innovation can move from being a niche innovation to becoming part of the socio-technical system where, if a window of opportunity exists, it can overcome existing lock-ins. These lock-ins are the result of market conditions, policy, science, and existing technology. If it is successful at the system level, this radical innovation then has the potential to influence the larger socio-technical landscape. Innovation can thus be scaled out (Westley et al., 2011). In the context of MLP analysis, social dimensions are limited to the norms, cultural expectations, and discourses connected to socio-technical innovation (Geels, 2019).

While the MLP approach is useful to better understand environmental and economic dimensions of sustainability transitions, it lacks a robust social justice component.

In parallel, the threefold focus on economic, social, and environmental sustainability advocated by the Sustainable Development Goals (SDGs), for example, has gained traction on the global stage (United Nations, 2021, p. 3). While such frameworks cover all the key dimensions of sustainability, articulating the three pillars together can be a challenge in both practice and theory.

Food offers a concrete and relatable theme for understanding and acting on sustainability. As a fundamental human right, a cultural touchstone, a key economic factor, and a major contributor to environmental degradation, food constitutes a crossroad between these three important facets of sustainability. Food is a unifying starting point that helps us to consider how the SDGs can be achieved, simultaneously improving food security (Goal 2), providing decent work and economic growth (Goal 8), boosting industry, innovation, and infrastructure (Goal 9), building sustainable cities and communities (Goal 11), and increasing responsible consumption and production (Goal 12). However, the SDGs need to be enacted across multiple scales at the same time, at global, sub-national, and local level. This involves constantly shifting power and scales:

> [S]ocio-spatial processes change the importance and role of certain geographical scales, re-assert the importance of others, and on occasion create entirely new scales. These scale redefinitions in turn alter geometry of social power by strengthening the power and control of some while disempowering other. … Scale also emerges as the site where co-operation and competition find a (fragile) standoff.
>
> (Swyngedouw, 2002, p. 8)

This shifting from one scale to another is consistent with socio-technical regime theory as innovations move from being niche to impacting the socio-technical system and ultimately, if they are impactful enough, to transitioning their landscape and associated exogenous conditions to a new scale. Expanding beyond MLP theory, Swyngedouw (2002) points to the changing nature of power and control across different geographies and locations, providing a more detailed basis for the analysis of the ECF Farm's innovation. Furthermore, we take into account the connecting role of distribution, which involves more than the mere "process of transport of raw and processed food products and organic waste between the places of food production, processing, sale, consumption, disposal and reuse respectively" (Kasper et al., 2015, p. 47). Distribution ensures "the connection between industry, farmers and consumers on household level and commercial consumption in restaurants or canteens" making it a connecting infrastructure between a city and its region (Kasper et al., 2015, p. 47).

In this chapter, we investigate the spatial correlation between locations of production, logistics, and distribution, based on economic, ecological, and social factors. We particularly explore how the shifts from the local to the regional scale through food production and consumption impact businesses' ability to focus on ecological and social justice considerations inside Berlin, and how these shifts offer the potential to engage with the city's outer region, Brandenburg, as well as other parts of the European Union. We perform this "inside–outside" analysis based on the case study of an emerging food technology as defined by the Urbal framework, a new approach that maps innovation to better understand how change is enabled or challenged.

8.2.2 The ECF Farm in the context of the Urbal approach

Urbal, as described in the introductory chapter of this book, is an evolving approach designed to help innovators, policymakers, and financial backers understand how urban innovation takes place in sustainable food systems. It is participatory, bringing together practitioners, the public, and scientists. Mapping the pathways of the different dimensions of sustainability helps to shed light on the enablers of and barriers to sustainable innovation pathways of change and impact. The ECF Farm in Berlin is a model that uses high-tech management tools and the concept of circular economy, focusing on the economic, food security, nutrition, and environmental dimensions of sustainability.

8.3 Understanding the innovation pathway: The ECF urban food innovation lab

One of the key challenges for minimizing food imports and shortening the associated long food chains is creating highly productive spaces within cities through food system innovations (Nicholls et al., 2020, p. 1592). The ECF Farm is an example of a socio-technical innovation originating from the private sector that offers a new way to produce protein in an urban setting. Perch and basil are farmed together in an aquaponic system to create a circular flow of water and nutrients. Diverse distribution and marketing strategies provide connections to the regional food system. As this innovation is furthermore intended to provide a social benefit through public tours as well as its contribution to food security and nutrition in cities, we explore the ways in which this example helps broaden the literature on socio-technical innovation to include social considerations.

In the subsequent sections, we describe ECF and its innovations to assess how four dimensions of urban food system sustainability, namely the economic, food security, nutrition, and environmental dimensions, are addressed by the project. Definitions of food security typically include food quality, quantity, safety, and cultural acceptability (Leroy et al., 2015). In the Berlin UFIL, food quality is the main point of focus regarding food security: a key goal is to provide more locally produced, high-quality protein through aquaponics. We show how ECF's local production and shorter supply chains impact the food system and how the economic dimension of the chain is structured (for more information about short food supply chains, see Chapter 6, this book). We also explore the question of whether high-tech efficiency is congruent with social inclusiveness. Finally, we consider which sustainability goals are reached and where development potential exists. With this outline in mind, we first turn our attention to the history of ECF (Figure 8.1).

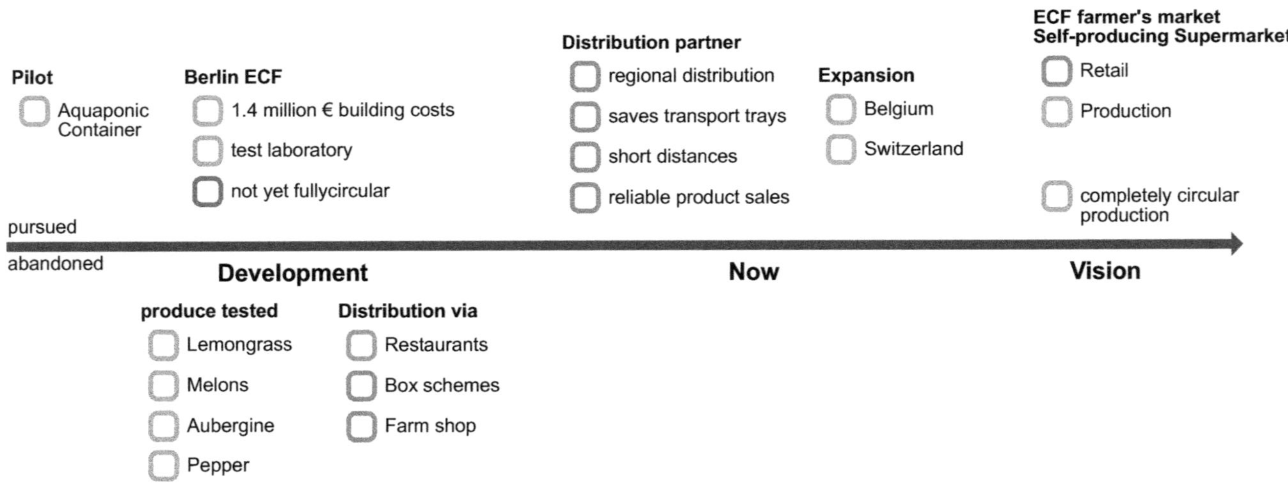

Figure 8.1 Timeline of the innovations pursued and abandoned during the development phase of the farm, and future innovations envisaged.

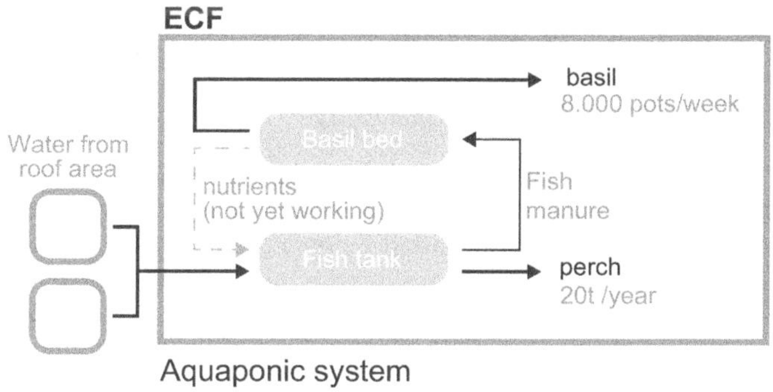

Figure 8.2 Integrated aquaponic and hydroponic systems at the ECF Farm in Berlin.

8.3.1 ECF's background, history, and actors: Inside–outside Berlin

The ECF Farm was founded by Nicolas Leschke and Christian Echternacht in 2012. Leschke studied International Management at the European Business School in London and is a self-taught agriculturalist. He is the CEO of "IGG Malzfabrik MBH", which manages the factory building where ECF first started and where other small businesses are located, and is also the CEO of ECF. Echternacht is an Internet entrepreneur with a background in software development. While the project attracted significant public interest, there were technological challenges and expertise in the field was lacking. For example, plants require more nutrients than fish and the pH levels needed to be calibrated through an innovative two-cycle system (see Section 8.5 and Figure 8.2).

ECF has since relocated within the site and occupies a 1,800 m^2 surface. This includes both the farm itself and office facilities, where turnkey farms are designed for other developers. As of 2018, the ECF farm employed seven farmworkers and five aquaponic system planning experts, along with several interns (Terpitz, 2017; ECF Workshop, 2019). Through its distribution partner, a large German supermarket chain, ECF markets its products, "Capital City Perch" and "Capital City Basil", in local branches in and around Berlin. For commercial reasons, further information on market arrangements like capacity, prices, and general agreements are not publicly accessible and must remain vague. The fish is also occasionally sold through other supermarket brands and to local restaurants that pick up the produce from the farm. Earlier attempts at direct retail to consumers or box schemes were abandoned, due to limited demand (ECF Tour, 2018). The farm connects with the community by providing public educational guided tours as well as classes and tours for students at the ECF facilities, during which the technical aspects of the aquaponic systems are explained and the products are presented (ECF Tour, 2018).

8.3.2 Sustainability innovations and shifting scales: From inside to outside Berlin

8.3.2.1 Food chain innovation and sustainability

The main innovation of the project relates to production and distribution. Based on circular economy principles, it addresses the environmental dimension of sustainability goals (as detailed below). Some aspects of the nutrition and food security dimensions of sustainability are also addressed. As stated by the initiators, the main innovation principles are as follows: local production and the establishment of local employment; the closed-loop production of nutrients through the aquaponic system; pesticide- and antibiotic-free farming; alternatives to overfishing the oceans; and contributing to healthy nutrition by providing a supply of omega 3.

8.3.2.1.1 PRODUCTION

The term "aquaponic" stems from a combination of "*aqua*culture", the farming of fish and other marine animals in large basins on land, and "hydro*ponic*", which refers to a cultivation method whereby plants are grown not in soil but in an inorganic substrate in greenhouses and fed an aqueous solution. An aquaponic system is considered highly resource-efficient, as the nutrient-rich excrement of the fish can be processed and used for the production of vegetables and herbs (Baganz et al., 2021, p. 253). With agriculture and processing accounting for 70% of the freshwater used by humans, aquaponics provides an appealing alternative. With the aquaponic system used by the ECF Farm, food production requires up to 90% less water consumption than in conventional agriculture. The high water efficiency is further enhanced by the use of circulatory systems for the fish and vegetable production (ECF, 2018). Some fish varieties are among the most sustainable sources of animal protein and can be bred in comparatively resource-minimal conditions. Only 1.2–1.4 kilogrammes of feed, which is imported from Denmark, is required for 1 kilogramme of fish farmed at the ECF Farm (ECF, 2019). By comparison, beef production requires about 11 kilogrammes of feed for 1 kilogramme of meat. Given the high resource consumption and carbon emissions associated with animal feed production, this new production structure can afford significant environmental benefits. For example, the CO_2 generated by the fish farm is captured and channelled to the greenhouse. CO_2 would normally have to be purchased in bottles, but in this case it can be easily sourced from the fish farming activity. In addition to the fish feed, the fish larvae needed for breeding must also be imported from other EU countries. Unfortunately, the nutrient-rich fish excrement cannot be repurposed at the ECF Farm facilities: as the fish are not native, this would violate national regulations. At present, this residual matter is discharged into the Berlin sewer system and only the nutrient-rich water is used for fertilization (ECF, 2018; ECF, 2019).

The aquaponic system consists of two interconnected circular flows. This technique enables the urban farmers to monitor them separately and to apply an individual pH value to each one, optimized for either fish or plants. Moreover, each circuit can be shut down independently of the other for cleaning and maintenance, thereby minimizing production risk (Figure 8.3). The aquaculture circuit uses advanced filtration systems, oxygen reactors and 20 fish tanks of various sizes, partly filled with rainwater collected from the farm's roof area. Optimal water temperatures and feed quantities calculated by the control technology increase animal welfare, strengthening the immune system of the fish and reducing mortality. This allows for continuous harvesting while maintaining consistent calibration and quality. In order to meet the demand for perch, every month a batch of fry is introduced and farmed for eight months, producing approximately 30 tons per year (ECF, 2018).

The hydroponic circuit in the laboratory uses a cultivation method that is optimized for the different plant species grown: ebb-tide systems for herbs and drip irrigation for experiments with tomatoes. These systems are supplemented with the use of assimilation lighting in the growing room, which uses LED lighting with specific wavelengths that stimulate the plants' photoreceptors and extends the hours of sunshine. Water quantities, nutrient compositions, and irrigation rhythms are continuously monitored and controlled by the central control technology. Due to the high and continuous demand from the farm's distribution partner, the main system is optimized for the production of basil and produces approximately 7,000 to 8,000 pots per week. The farm's current mode of production uses organic soil for the cultivation of basil, and is therefore not classified as conventional hydroponics (ECF Tour, 2018).

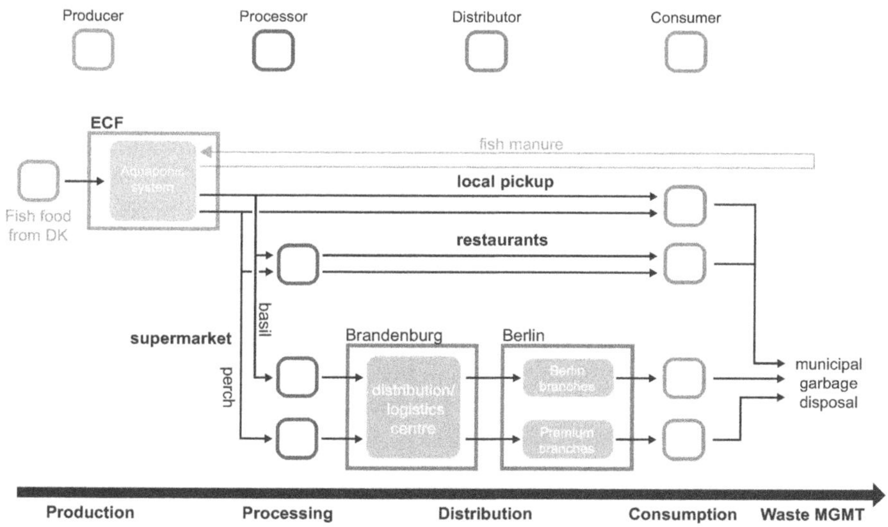

Figure 8.3 Network map showing the five stages of food production and the different distribution methods of the ECF Farm Berlin.

Central to the quality of the products is the complex specialized control technology that analyses and efficiently controls all the aquaculture and hydroponic processes, as well as their supply facilities. In ECF's aquaculture cycle, innovative filter units measure the systems and oxygenation levels to ensure steady water quality, healthy fish growth and optimal output. Since the farm is a largely closed system and external threats such as harmful plant parasites and diseases can be kept out, the cultivation of GMOs and the use of antibiotics and pesticides can be avoided (ECF, 2018).

At the time of the interviews in 2018, ECF was working to upgrade the aquaponic system to strengthen the connection between the aquaculture and hydroponic systems. Due to the different plant species grown, the hydroponic system requires specific pH values and nutrients which currently cannot be recycled back into the fishponds (ECF Tour, 2018).

8.3.2.1.2 DISTRIBUTION

Owing to the business partnership with the ECF's distribution partner, both the "Capital City Perch" and the "Capital City Basil" are available in selected retail outlets in Berlin and nearby Brandenburg and Mecklenburg-Vorpommern. The aquaponic farming method makes it possible to grow numerous plant varieties flexibly for the local market, applying variety-specific cultivation methods (ECF Tour, 2018). The ECF Farm argues that it offers "upscale and authentic food that preserves the environment through high standards of environmental protection, resource efficiency and transparency" and by eliminating additives (ECF Tour, 2018).

Local cultivation reduces transport distances and cold chains for a more sustainable and fresher offer, which is a decisive advantage, especially in an urban environment with many customers. Furthermore, thanks to the shorter transport times, the plants do not require additional irrigation during transport. This reduces not only resource consumption but also the use of transport trays, which are made of plastic. The fish and the basil have somewhat different supply chains. The fish is processed and prepared at the ECF Farm facilities, and then sold in regional grocery chains as a fresh or frozen product and to local restaurants as fresh produce. The basil replaces basil sourced from the global food network, especially from the Netherlands, thus substantially reducing food miles (Terpitz, 2017). The products of the ECF Farm are positioned in the higher-priced market segment due to its cost-intensive production methods, higher wages, and comparably small production quantities. Furthermore, due to current federal regulations, the product cannot yet receive and be marketed with an organic label (ECF, 2019).

8.3.2.2 Economic structure and marketing strategies

The "IBB Beteiligungsgesellschaft Berlin und Brandenburg", a joint venture by the development bank of the State of Berlin and a private investor, has provided financial support to the enterprise since 2014 (Boldt, 2018). During its development phase, which started with a concept for aquaponic systems in shipping containers (Boldt, 2018), the UFIL initially tested different types of produce (Figure 8.4). In 2014, it was able to build the ECF Farm Berlin as a test laboratory and reference site for future deployment (Terpitz, 2017).

While it has been dependent on investors for its initial development phase and the construction of the ECF facility, the UFIL is striving for economic stability in the future. The main revenue streams come from its farmed produce sold locally and its global offering of planning services, know-how, and turnkey factory construction (see Figure 8.5). A successful collaboration agreement with a large supermarket chain gives ECF access to the chain's franchisees throughout Germany, while a collection of selected local retail options as well as ECF's branding and marketing strategy have opened up the Berlin market. Although the "Capital City Basil" is available in nearly every branch of the supermarket in Berlin, the "Capital City Perch" is marketed in premium branches only (ECF Tour, 2018). Being part of a large retail network however also means having to submit to the rules of logistics. A large proportion of the produce sold to the supermarket chain is collected from the farm by truck, redistributed via the logistics centres outside of Berlin, and delivered to the individual stores (ECF, 2019), thus substantially increasing the delivery distances.

ECF is using the knowledge about cultivation methods, control technology and control systems is has gained at its production facility in Berlin to improve the marketing and functionality of the turnkey factories it offers. Sales, including planning, project study, construction management, support at the start of production and after-sales service, is another pillar of the UFIL's activity (ECF, 2017).

Recent activities include the spread of the aquaponic system to independent sites in Switzerland and Belgium, where the company has built one of the largest aquaponic facilities in Europe. The Swiss site was installed for an existing fruit and vegetable wholesaler, ecco-jägger. The rooftop garden and aquaponic farm began production in 2014 as part of a renovation. The rooftop installation captures waste heat from the ground-level cold-store operation. The greens, herbs and trout farmed on the roof complement the existing line of 2,500 fresh, processed, and frozen fruits and vegetables delivered to approximately 1,600 customers in food retail, direct customers, and restaurants (ecco-jägger, 2021). At the time of construction, the cost of the renovation was forecast to be recovered within three years.

The second turnkey project, with the Belgian firm BIGH, combines the aquaponics and greens operation with growing vegetables outdoors on a rooftop in the city centre, located on a historic abattoir site. Founder Steven Becker is a cradle-to-cradle architect who has led international architectural projects and circular economy projects in the real estate sector since 2011. Other BIGH team members include aquaponics, operations, and horticulture managers along with supporting technicians, as well as marketing, communications, and

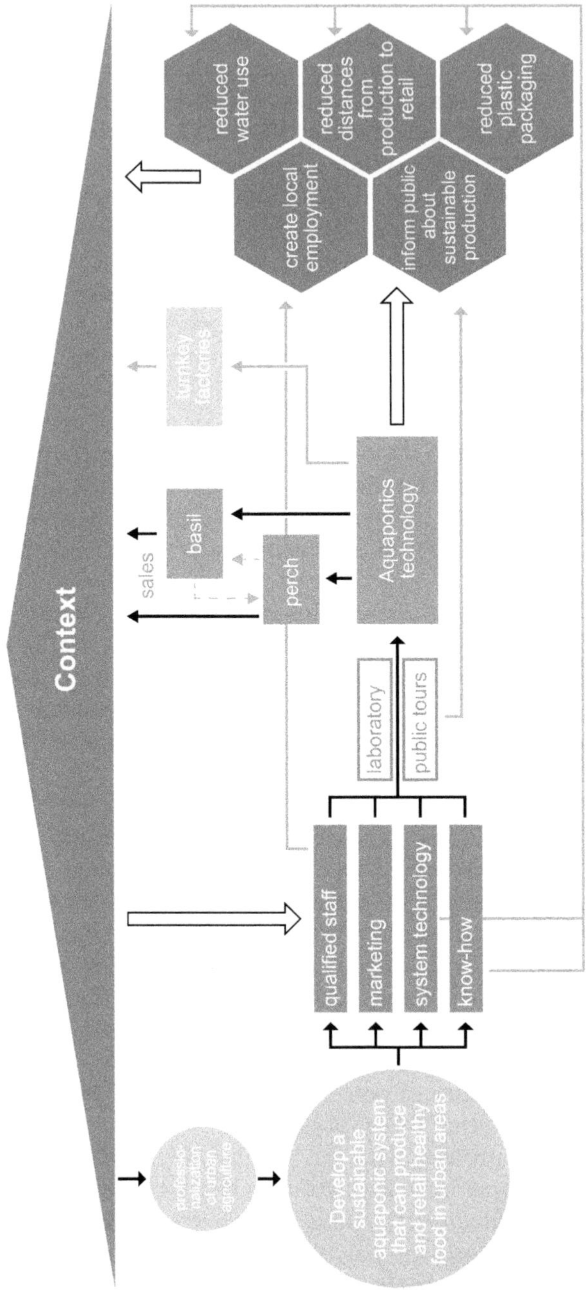

Figure 8.4 Innovation process, consequences, and interactions of the aquaponic food production and technology development of the ECF Farm.

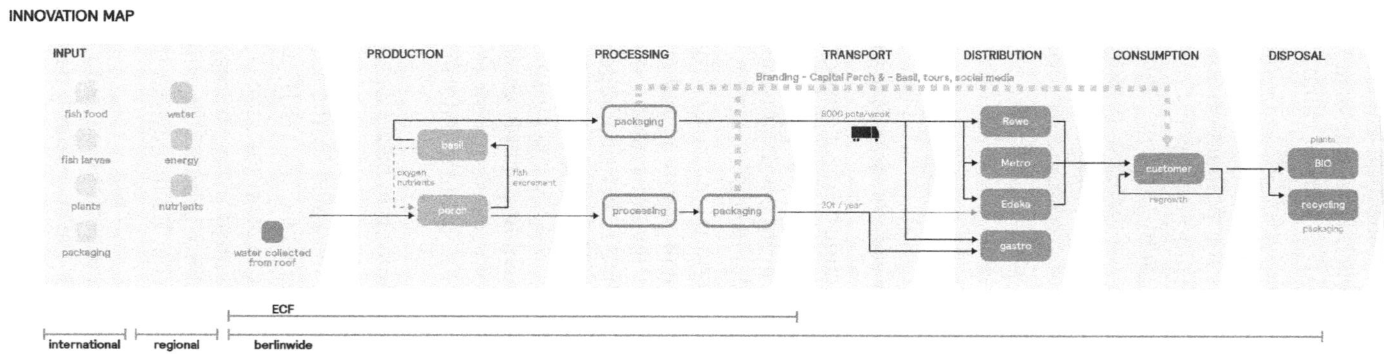

Figure 8.5 Innovation map showing the processes, inside–outside dynamics, technical features, and geographical scales of ECF's food system.

events managers. BIGH also captures waste heat and supplements its energy needs with solar panels. The organization captures rainwater to minimize water demand. The greenhouse/fish farm was completed in 2018. The aquaponic operation can produce up to 23 tons of rainbow trout annually. The fish are fed plant and animal-based, non-GMO certified organic pellets. In the 2,000-m^2 greenhouse, herbs and greens are grown chemical- and pesticide-free, relying instead on bumble bees for pollination and biological controls for pests. The aquaponic and greenhouse operations are complemented by outdoor rooftop gardens to expand the fruit and vegetable offerings. The greenhouse employs physically challenged persons, providing them with employment and skill development opportunities. The enterprise places a premium on public education about sustainable food systems. BIGH hopes this model will be taken up elsewhere and provides its expertise to others through public education campaigns and more targeted tours for professionals (BIGH, 2021).

8.3.3 Dimensions of sustainability and cross-scale innovation transfer

With its innovative and production-ready aquaponic technology, the ECF Farm addresses various subcategories of the dimensions of sustainability of food systems, including the environmental, nutrition, and economic dimensions. The ECF Farm reports a significant impact on the environment, through the reduction of production emissions compared with conventional agriculture by capturing CO2 emissions from fish farming and repurposing them in hydroponics. The use of rainwater for the aquaculture operation, the space-saving build, and the possibility of adding to existing buildings, make for an efficient use of valuable open space in highly compact urban areas. Furthermore, the shorter distance to supermarkets and the end customer, as well as the replacement of longer, more energy-demanding supply chains, have a potentially positive effect on the products' ecological footprint (ECF, 2018), although the farm itself was unable to provide detailed information or precise data on this topic.

The ECF Farm's product selection is based on the production conditions required, especially for perch, and on the marketing strategy of the farm and its distribution partner. It is not informed by the scarcity of or need for these specific types of products. Nonetheless, the UFIL and its turnkey operations produce nutritious, pesticide-free protein that can contribute to a healthy diet (ECF Tour, 2018). Largely decoupled from external influences, the farm can yield a safe harvest and high-quality produce throughout the year. The products' distribution in supermarkets in Berlin ensures their availability to a wider group of consumers.

Owing to its high-tech production technique and its unique position in the urban context of Berlin, the ECF Farm creates a particular set of specific new job opportunities at the crossroads between tech and agriculture, located not in rural but in urban areas. The farm's two-pronged, diversified market approach, running its own fish and basil operation as well as marketing and selling turn-key operations, gives it more financial stability for the future.

8.4 Applying the Urbal methodology—the ECF Farm workshop

In September 2019, the Berlin UFIL workshop was held at the premises of the ECF Farm. Along with scientists from various disciplines and an expert in innovation management, the founder of the farm, Christian Echternacht, was present to discuss the development of past and future innovation in urban aquaponic production. The workshop was split into three thematic sessions: 1) the preparation of the participants; 2) the analysis; and 3) the discussion of the innovations implemented to date and of possible future innovations. Each thematic session was supported with pre-prepared process diagrams showing the detailed production cycle of the farm, the inside–outside dynamic and, for the discussion of past and future innovation, a marker indicating where in the process the innovation might take place and a short description (see Figures 8.6 and 8.7).

8.4.1 Selection of the participants

Discussing past and future innovations with different actors, experts, and researchers brings broader yet more specialized opinions and suggestions to the table and enables small businesses focusing on their expertise to further develop their place and connections within the food system. The participating experts were chosen for their backgrounds in and knowledge of aquaponic systems, logistics and markets, innovation management, spatial design and city development, urban gardening initiatives, and urban rural food systems.

8.4.2 Structure of the workshop

8.4.2.1 Preparation of the participants

Information material was sent out prior to the workshop to inform the various participants about the ECF's history and production methods, the hurdles it faced in the development phase, and the farm's production processes. In addition to this, the workshop started with a tour of the fish and basil production facilities. A blank innovation map showing the production cycle (see Figure 8.6) was prepared and handed to the participants, as a basis for the discussion that would follow.

8.4.2.2 Analysis and discussion of the innovations to date

Following the introduction and a presentation of the Urbal process, Dr. Susanne Schön briefly described the defining characteristics of innovations in general and how these could provide a framework for discussing the ECF

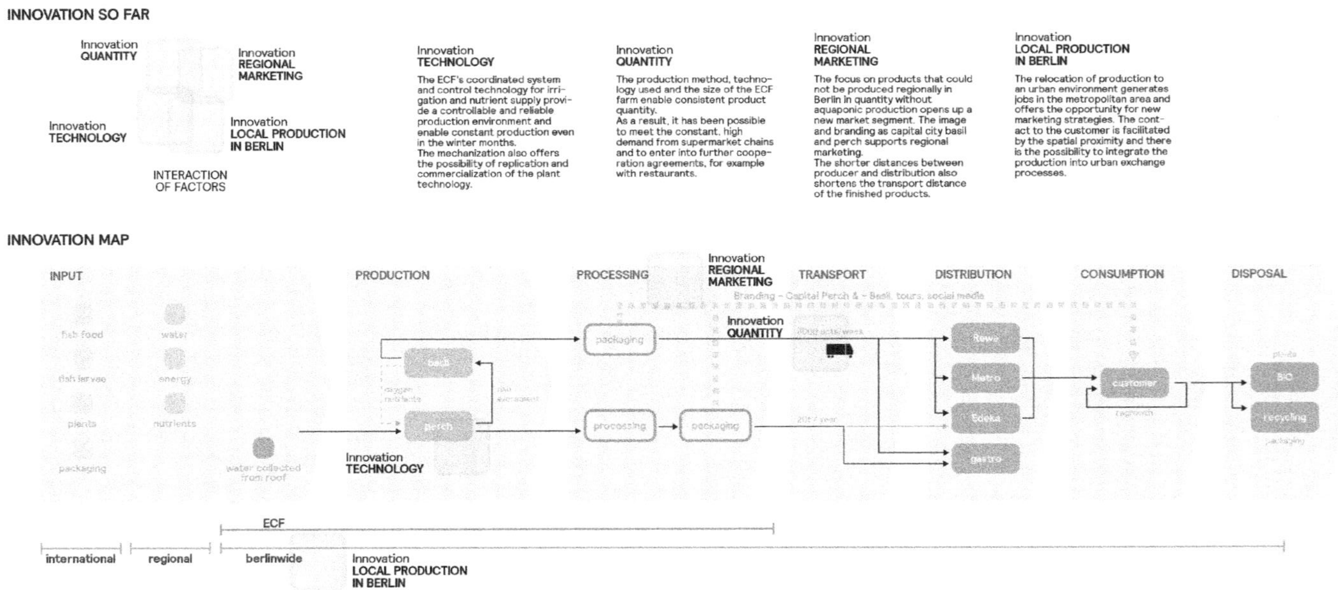

Figure 8.6 Innovation map describing and representing the past innovations and their location within the production cycle.

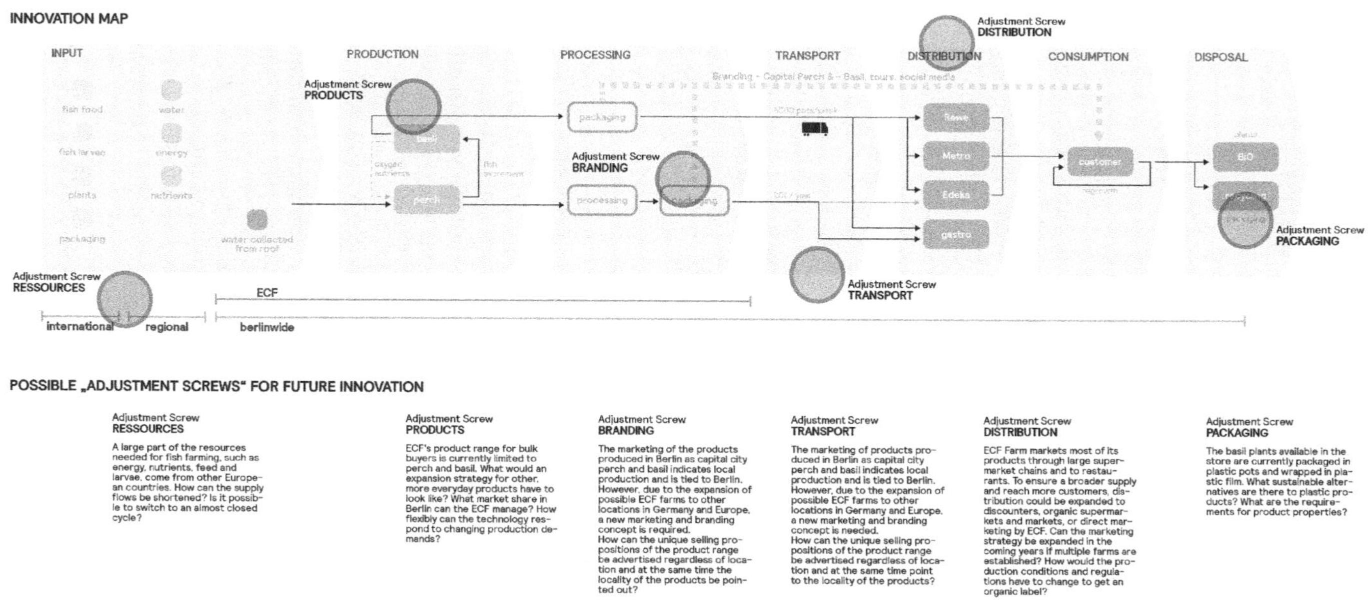

Figure 8.7 Innovation map describing and representing "adjustments" that could lead to possible future innovations, and their location within the production cycle.

innovations presented. The participants were enabled to draw comparisons and the innovation was made more accessible by defining the innovation and its potential according to the following four questions:

1) What is new?
2) What is perceived as being better?
3) Is it accepted (i.e. in the market environment)?
4) What role does sustainability play?

Different past innovations were then discussed, categorized, and situated on the pre-prepared innovation diagram. However, the different cases had multiple development stages and often proceeded by trial and error, making it harder to define the innovation pathway. The participants' diverse range of expertise helped to engage with the different dimensions of sustainability.

8.4.2.3 Discussion of possible future innovations

The third session of the workshop focused on future innovation, introducing a third iteration of the diagram displaying possible "adjustments" that could lead to future innovation. The suggestions presented were drawn from the discussion and debated among the participants, also concentrating on the circumstances needed to enable development and the sustainability dimensions that could possibly be affected.

8.4.3 Adaptation of the methodology – capabilities, challenges, and limits of the workshop

As the workshop took place at the production site, and due to the unique case of the ECF Farm—a producing, commercial company with strong business ties to larger supply chains—only experts and researchers were invited to participate in the workshop. Including private citizens in the discussion, to represent the public interest, could yield different arguments and perspectives. However, although ECF engages with the public by offering tours, the farm does not yet have a steady connection to a public community invested in its production method or in the location of the production facility. This limits the possibilities of public engagement with private citizens invested enough without being in the employment of ECF. The company's request not to invite direct competitors to take part in the workshop so that it could speak more freely about internal processes and its economic connections was complied with.

The creative process of identifying future innovations was highly focused and, given the participants' backgrounds in food systems, logistics, and design, the barriers to grasping the topics at hand were limited. Focusing on predefined innovations helped to steer the discussion towards delving deeper into certain topics rather than remaining broad, and to stay within the time limit of the workshop. Nevertheless, the participants did not follow the Suggestion to focus on the innovation pathways and to represent them in the diagrams, as the requirements and factors that led to the innovations were not linear and had a wide range of ramifications and were therefore not easy enough to represent within the limited timeframe of the workshop. The participants addressed the dimensions of sustainability in relation to each part of the innovation.

Having a shared understanding of what innovation means afforded clearer discussions on the possibilities and outcomes of potential interventions on the processes and system of production. The fact that ECF's economic success so far has been dependent on its connection to large supermarket brands and their conditions of supply and logistics is one of the reasons that makes the farm an interesting UFIL. However, in the workshop, there was limited room for internal discussions and for these to inform different perspectives on future and past innovation, due to ECF's request for confidentiality.

8.5 Discussion: practical insights to improve sustainable food system innovation theory

In addition to economic independence, ECF is also striving to achieve other sustainability goals, including reducing its environmental footprint, reducing water and chemical use, educating the public, and addressing nutrition security. The two turnkey projects demonstrate the range of dimensions of sustainability that can be addressed by an aquaponic business. On one end of the spectrum, ecco-jägger sells 2,500 different products, has minimal enviro-sustainability goals, and does not seem to emphasize social justice considerations. BIGH, which sits more towards the middle of the spectrum, is focused on minimizing its environmental impact through waste heat capture, solar panels, and reduced water use, and on enhancing its social impact by hiring and training workforce with disabilities as well as engaging in public education actions and spreading its model beyond Brussels. The ECF Farm itself offers public guided tours as well as tours for school groups and students at its facilities, in which it explains the technical aspects of aquaponic systems and presents the products.

8.5.1 Place-based urban agriculture: The local scale

The site of the ECF Farm Berlin has various specificities that cannot be directly replicated in other regions, cities, or spaces, and thus reflects the particular spatial context of its urban area. The Berlin-based ECF plant does not include in-house large-scale distribution, it is limited to produce pick-ups by a very small number of private customers, and although the farm produces for direct retail on the local market, parts of the site are still reserved for research and testing of the technology. Its use as a laboratory also allows ECF to market its turnkey installations (ECF, 2018). Unlike the locations in Switzerland and Belgium, the company's headquarters and the production facilities in Berlin are on a former industrial site that offers limited access to the public, other than for the guided tours and when the farm is rented out as an events space (ECF Tour, 2018).

As it develops, ECF must also contend with place-specific challenges. ECF's focus on profit and economic feasibility as well as the marketing of the technology to investors in other locations achieves economic sustainability, but this is reflected in the pricing. ECF's products rely on high-tech farming methods and are positioned in the higher-priced segment of the market, and hence not widely affordable for disadvantaged customers (ECF Tour, 2019). It could however be argued that an increase in the number of production facilities in urban areas might reduce retail prices, thus making the products accessible to a broader audience, which could be seen to contribute to food security in urban areas. German law presents a further constraint. According to current interpretation, products from aquaponic cultivation are not yet classifiable as organic products, as there are no standards for classification. Moreover, the focus on production costs means the innovators must rely on a narrow range of foods, making perch and basil the best option (ECF Workshop, 2019). From a non-human perspective, the project has received some criticism concerning the conditions of animal keeping. The German branch of People for the Ethical Treatment of Animals (PETA) has argued that perch are regarded as a highly intelligent species, and that the breeding cycle and living conditions do not comply with animal welfare, and might thus be deemed to violate the Animal Welfare Act (Stich, 2018).

8.5.2 Scalability: ECF's inside–outside dynamic as a socio-technical innovation

From containers and roof top gardens to the 2,400-square-metre aquaponic farm in Brussels, ECF's facilities cover a wide range of layouts and production capacities (ECF Tour, 2018). The Urbal assessment of the company's network, timelines, and impact pathway mappings shed light on key enablers of and barriers to this innovation, both within Berlin and beyond with its turnkey sites. This range of projects carried out, as well as the possibility of adding to existing structures such as supermarkets and industrial buildings, make the farms easy to implement and adaptable to different urban spaces. The vision of ECF, to establish a farm in every major city in Germany and to create farms worldwide, speaks to their possibilities in terms of transferability and scalability. ECF offers an example of a socio-technical niche innovation that has found a small window of opportunity. Whether this results in landscape change through significant scaling out remains to be seen.

Returning to Swyngedouw (2002), cited at the beginning of the chapter, "[s]cale also emerges as the site where co-operation and competition find a (fragile) standoff" (p. 8). The ECF case study helps us to understand how urban

Table 8.1 List of participants in the UFIL workshop at the ECF Farm in September 2019

Name	*Firm*	*Expertise*
External participants		
Prof. Katrin Bohn	Senior lecturer at the University of Brighton, co-founder of Bohn and Viljoen Architects	food systems, productive cities, architecture, design for circular cities and regions
Toni Karge	Scientific employee at the Senate of Berlin, Department for the Environment, Transport and Climate Protection, Department of Open Space Planning and Urban Greening	urban gardening initiatives
Dr. Susanne Schön	inter_3 - Institute for Resource Management	resource and innovation management
Angelica Coll	Technical University Berlin (TUB), Department of Logistics	food logistics, supply chain management
Dr. Thomas Nehls	TUB, Department of Ecohydrology & Landscape Assessment	Chair of Ecohydrology
Christoph Kasper	TUB, Department of Landscape Architecture and Open Space Planning	urban and rural food systems, urban planning
Peter Werner	Student at TUB	metabolic design, urban planning
ECF Farm		
Christian Echternacht	ECF	founder of ECF, production manager
Urbal researchers		
Prof. Undine Giseke	TUB, Head of the Department of Landscape Architecture and Open Space Planning	
Lucas Hövelmann	TUB, Department of Landscape Architecture and Open Space Planning	
Team		
Magdalena Grienig	TUB, Department of Landscape Architecture and Open Space Planning	documentation, protocol

food system innovations remain within the city or cross over to other scales. ECF provides a concrete example of an ostensible food system innovation inside a city and shows how this innovation fits within innovations outside the city (Table 8.1). For this UFIL, the urban site allows the company to have a production system that is transparent to the public. It also enables the collaborating supermarket chain to brand the fish and basil as "Capital City" products, thereby developing a niche it can sell into and sustaining the products' market viability. However, the supermarkets' rigid supply chain require the fish and basil to be delivered to their central warehouses outside of Berlin. Given the market power of the retailer, the need for financial stability and the lack of other market outlets, ECF must comply with these delivery demands. In this sense, the retailer can dictate its terms to ECF, such that its vision of an urban farm is threatened. While future innovations could include regional marketing in other cities (ECF Workshop, 2019), this dilemma demonstrates the negotiations necessarily at play within food systems and the power dynamics between different actors. The case of the ECF Farm shows how the conventional food networks and large-scale logistics systems of supermarket chains work around the world and how small-scale interventions like urban food production for a bigger market can be subsumed by these networks. To counter theses dynamics, Ana Moragues-Faus et al. (2020) call "for a more fluid, place-based and interactive conceptualization of food infrastructures as bridging material and socio-political devices that allow reconfiguring foodscapes into more diverse and distributive economies", showing "the potential of developing more resilient infrastructures co-constituted by multiple stakeholders, sectors and scales" (p. 35) (Table 8.2).

In the case of the ECF Farm, following this approach could help strengthen diverse local partnerships for distribution, a distributed network of small-scale food production facilities and farms or other aquaponic-related practices throughout Berlin, and could lead to the establishment of a public food community and an alternative food network.

Furthermore, waste management regulations mean that the fish manure cannot be captured and repurposed but must instead be discharged into the local sewage. These lock-ins impede the innovation's success and challenge its capacity to break through (Geels, 2019). Yet this innovation could enable a reversal of the dominant food system's dynamic, whereby food comes from outside and is brought into cities through distribution centres. With urban production, the logic of large-scale food networks is turned on its head, as the flow of products shifts from originating outside the urban centre to arising directly inside this centre, shortening the links between production and consumption. As the turnkey operations have demonstrated, with the emergence of more alternatives over time, farms can be added to existing buildings, integrated into existing supply chains (as was the case in Switzerland), or dedicated exclusively to the city (as in Brussels). This in turn raises questions about the size of greenhouse operations within cities, given the competition for land. The urban identity of urban food production sites as educational showrooms is important to both ECF and BIGH. In this sense, consumers provide a tipping point that justifies urban production. As part of the social sustainability missions central to the identities of ECF and BIGH, productive urban sites can provide clear answers to consumers' questions about where their food comes from. Providing skilled work and training within urban settings is another identifying economic and social contribution of the innovation.

Table 8.2 Examples of how the inside–outside dynamic operates within the ECF UFIL

	Inside	*Outside (turnkey operations)*		
	ECF Berlin	*Brandenburg and proximate regions*	*BIGH Brussels*	*eco-jägger Switzerland*
Environment	1. - Reduced water use • Imported basil is replaced with “Capital Basil” • Reduced food miles with locally sourced protein		• Reduced food miles with locally sourced protein	• Reduced food miles with locally sourced protein
Economy	• Increased employment • Development of technical skills	• Logistic centres and distribution back to Berlin • Contribution to the regional natural fish supply		• Supply of 2,500 products throughout Switzerland
Society	• Locally available (upscale) protein, improved nutrition security • Public education regarding sustainability		• **Public education regarding sustainability**	

Source: (BIGH, 2021; ecco-jägger, 2021; ECF, 2018; Terpitz, 2017)

8.6 Conclusion

In the context of food production, scale-appropriate sustainable food system innovations that work in urban contexts challenge traditional notions of food coming from rural areas outside of cities to where the demand is located. With populations becoming increasingly removed from their food and nature in general, moving closer to the source of their food can help sensitize people to pressing environmental issues linked to food production, such as climate change. The ECF Farm's innovative production technology, site selection, and distribution method make it a unique actor in the Berlin food system. Through its focus on a specific upmarket selection of produce that is usually imported, the UFIL's impact can be considered as a viable substitute for food imports, thus having a recognizable impact on food's carbon footprint and on food security. However, the reduction of transportation distances through local production does not apply to the larvae and fish food, which are still being imported. Furthermore, the objective of the ECF Farm's aquaponic system is not to replace traditional native produce grown regionally.

With regard to ECF's capacity to develop and implement more sustainable and resource-efficient systems that take into account the diverse range of stakeholders in the food system—particularly small food businesses and disadvantaged consumers—the greater expenses associated with high-tech production must be taken into consideration, along with the development and research involved. Due to its need for economic profitability, its pace of growth, and its bold vision, ECF requires a stable distribution partner with consistent demand, something which small businesses cannot necessarily reliably provide. As an Urban Food Innovation Lab, ECF helps us to understand the potential for urban food innovations to support sustainable transitions. It also provides insight on how to better integrate social considerations into urban food sustainability frameworks.

The workshop and its results have shown where the importance of the ECF Farm as an urban food producer lies, and revealed both avenues for innovation development already pursued and others that could be explored in the future. In order to further advance our understanding of urban food system innovation and the associated changes and impacts, we here draw on the workshop's results to reflect on possible questions for future research. On the production side, it is worth considering the offering of other products, such as microgreens or tomatoes. Is there a way to make the products more affordable or accessible? Does local gastronomy offer an entry point? At present, there are still only a few buyers who pick up fish directly at the farm. The high price point makes the product too expensive for standard catering. COVID-19 has added another pressure on the gastronomy front, as restaurants have closed. A way forward could be to form partnerships with like-minded enterprises such as sustainable public canteens, for example Kantine Zukunft in the Berlin region, and to leverage the density and innovativeness of Germany's largest city. There is considerable spatial potential for food production in urban areas, still largely untapped. The ECF UFIL shows that its urban location is not the only decisive factor: integration in the distribution network also plays a crucial role. In what capacity can these innovative, so far small-scale urban farms be articulated with distribution spaces? Do they have the potential to change the way we deliver and distribute produce in cities or even to establish alternative distribution methods in dense urban areas?

Future research could also explore questions surrounding sectoral thinking, legal regulations, marketing, and organic labelling: the ECF Farm is aiming to further connect the two production systems and to minimize the use of plastic packaging; however, due to the company's unique production process, neither basil nor perch are entitled to organic labelling or government subsidies. Adapting legal regulations and introducing prototypes in the urban food system could lead to further innovation by showing the system's weak points, bottlenecks and potential for larger-scale improvements, while also opening up the market to more innovative food start-ups.

The sectoral thinking applied to the regulation of individual themes like wastewater, feed water, rainwater, energy, and food production, including the aforementioned regulations, makes for a system that hinders cross-sectoral innovation and leaves little room for variation.

Finally, on the social justice side, while the upscale market is currently served through retail and restaurants, making this product more affordable could open access to a broader share of the market and enable more equitable distribution within society. Envisaging different distribution strategies, including different supply chain markets, along with suggestions for preparation, could make the fish more accessible.

Using the Urbal approach to understand more about the ECF Farm as a sustainable urban food system innovation reveals existing and potential impacts on sustainability dimensions. It also contributes to the theory of socio-technical innovations by adding somewhat more explicit consideration for social aspects. Furthermore, the process allows us to approach scale and power relations as more deliberate reflections on how food innovations operate across space, both inside and outside urban centres. However, each UFIL, project, or case has a different set of circumstances, other prerequisites, and unique conditions that must lead to adaptation. Being a young enterprise, the ECF Farms' settings place it at the crossroads between start-up culture, an ideological drive to change the way cities produce food in the future, and the need to build a self-sustaining company that can compete in the marketplace. The openness of the methodology and ability to adapt to the distinctive profile of the ECF Farm as a UFIL was imperative to producing the findings presented in this chapter.

References

Baganz, G.F.M., Junge, R., Portella, M.C., Goddess, S., Keesmann, K.J., Baganz, D., Staaks, G., Shaw, C., Lohrberg, F., & Kloas, W. (2021). The aquaponic principle—It is all about coupling. *Reviews In Aquaculture*, *14*, 252–264. https://doi.org/10.1111/raq.12596

BIGH. (2021). *Brussels Aquaponic Farm*. https://bigh.farm/farm/

Boldt, B. (2018). Schweizer Geld für Berliner Aquaponik-Farm. https://biooekonomie.de/nachrichten/schweizergeld-fuer-berliner-aquaponik-farm

ecco-jägger. (2021). http://www.ecco-jaeger.ch/

ECF. (2017). *ECF baut die nächste urbane Aquaponik-Farm, jetzt im Herzen Europas*. http://www.ecf-farmsystems.com/ecf-baut-die-naechste-urbane-aquaponik-farm-jetzt-im-herzen-europas/

ECF. (2018). *Planning, Construction & Operations*. http://www.ecf-farmsystems.com/

Geels, F. (2019). Socio-technical transitions to sustainability: A review of criticisms and elaborations of the multi-level perspective. *Current Opinion in Environmental Sustainability*, *39*, 187–201. https://doi.org/10.1016/j.cosust.2019.06.009

Kasper, C., Brandt, J., Lindschulte, K., & Giseke, U. (2015). Food as an infrastructure in urbanizing regions. In G. Cinà & E. Dansero (Eds.), *Localizing urban food strategies. Farming cities and performing rurality*. (pp. 42–56). Politecnico di Torino.

Leroy, J.L., Ruel, M., Frongillo, E.A., Harris, J., & Ballard, T.J. (2015). Measuring the food access dimension of food security: A critical review and mapping of indicators. *Food and Nutrition Bulletin*, *36*(2), 167–195.

Moragues-Faus, A., Marsden, T., Adlerová, B., & Hausmanová, T. (2020). Building diverse, distributive, and territorialized agrifood economies to deliver sustainability and food security. *Economic Geography*, *96*(3), 219–243. https://doi.org/10.1080/00130095.2020.1749047

Nicholls, E., Ely, A., Birkin, L., Parthiba, B., & Goulson, D. (2020). The contribution of small-scale food production in urban areas to the sustainable development goals: A review and case study. *Sustainability Science*, *15*, 1585–1599. https://doi.org/10.1007/s11625-020-00792-z

Stich, J. (2018). *Fische sind kein Gemüse*. https://www.focus.de/regional/berlin/tierschutz-in-berlin-barschzucht-unter-widrigen-bedingungen-fische-sind-kein-gemuese_id_8441791.html

Swyngedouw, E. (2002). Scaled geographies: Nature, place, and the politics of scale. In E. Sheppard & R.B. McMaster (Eds.), *Scale and geographic inquiry* (p. 8). https://doi.org/10.1002/9780470999141.ch7

Terpitz, K. (2017). Auf den Barsch gekommen - Berliner Fischzucht-Start-up ECF. *Handelsblatt*. https://www.handelsblatt.com/technik/energie-umwelt/circular-economy/berliner-fischzucht-start-upecf-auf-den-barsch-gekommen/20374012.html?ticket=ST-965267-Vcxm5qhhzxilnZJ1nKme-ap4

United Nations department for economic and social affairs. (2021). *The Sustainable Development Goals Report 2021*. United Nations. https://unstats.un.org/sdgs/report/2021/The-Sustainable-Development-Goals-Report-2021.pdf

Westley, F., Olsson, P., Folks, C., Homer-Dixon, T. Vredenburg, H., Loorbach, D., Thompson, J., Nilsson, M., Lambin, E., Sendzimir, J., Banerjee, B., Galaz, V., & van der Leeuw, S. (2011). Tipping toward sustainability: Emerging pathways of transformation. *AMBIO*, *40*, 762–780. https://doi.org/10.1007/s13280-011-0186-9

9 Agricultural districts as tools for sustainable urban food systems

The case of Milan

Valerio Bini and Giacomo Zanolin

9.1 Introduction

The chapter explores how "agricultural districts",[1] an Italian institution that federates farmers to promote local development, has influenced the urban food system of the city of Milan. The districts take part in a form of multi-level governance (Gemmiti & Conti Puorger, 2008) that produces significant political, economic, and socio-cultural effects. The authors used the Urbal process to assess the impact of this innovation in the governance of the urban food system, by establishing a participatory Impact Pathway Map (see Chapter 1).

On a theoretical level, the topic of agricultural districts fits within a more general branch of research on local development, which stresses the strategic role of local networks and resources in promoting development processes (Becattini, 1987; Dematteis & Governa, 2005; Porter, 1990). More specifically, in the agri-food sector, several researchers have highlighted the need for food "relocalisation" around Alternative Food Networks (Watts et al., 2005), theorizing the development of localized agri-food systems (Muchnik et al., 2008). With regard to cities in particular, Morgan (2015) has shown how agri-food networks are underpinned by socio-spatial patterns that integrate both rural and urban areas.

The geographical context of this research is the area of the Metropolitan City of Milan (MCM), a region of about 1,500 km^2 with over three million inhabitants, which can be roughly split into three main sectors: the city of Milan itself; the northern part of the region, mostly urban and with an economy mainly built around industry; and the southern part, which is more sparsely populated and has a predominantly agricultural landscape.

The MCM region is characterized by large, protected areas surrounding the city: the South Milan Agricultural Park (SMAP), the Ticino Valley Regional Park to the west; and the two Adda Parks (Adda North and Adda South) to the east. The presence of these protected areas—especially the first two—has supported the development of the districts by limiting urban sprawl, the main challenge for agricultural activities in the region.

Five rural districts operate in the MCM area: the Milan Agricultural District (DAM), the Adda Martesana District (DAMA), the Olona Valley District

DOI: 10.4324/9781003285441-9

(DAVO), the Neo-rural District of the Three Waters of Milan (Dinamo), and the Rice and Frogs District.

This chapter is organized into six sections. Following the introduction, we present the research methodology in Section 9.2 and the institutional framework underpinning the rural districts of the MCM in Section 9.3. In Section 9.4, we outline the basic characteristics of the five districts. In the fifth section, we discuss the results of the research, showing the impact of the districts on four major areas of analysis identified through the elaboration of the Impact Pathway Map. Finally, in the conclusion, we share some remarks about the potential and challenges of the agricultural districts within the Milan urban food system.

9.2 The Urbal approach: Building an impact pathway map for agricultural districts

Since the main objective of this research was to assess the impact of agricultural districts on the governance of the urban food system, we used the Urbal approach to produce a participatory Impact Pathway Map of this innovation. The map was initially intended to be the result of several focus groups with the key players in the sector, but the constraints surrounding the COVID-19 pandemic partially hindered the organization of public meetings. Consequently, the authors decided to adopt a mixed strategy.

First, drawing on the results of two meetings[2] and on a first round of in-depth interviews, we produced a draft Impact Pathway Map. Then, this draft map was discussed in a second round of semi-structured interviews with eight relevant actors from the rural district system.

The first focus group meeting aimed to identify the opportunities available to the rural districts to develop a short supply chain within the mass retail system, a crucial part of the strategy adopted by the districts (see Sections 4.1 and 4.2). The meeting involved three representatives of mass retailers (LIDL, Carrefour, Coop) and a number of researchers active in this field of study.[3]

The second meeting focused on the commercial network of the rural districts. Representatives of all five districts were present and provided basic information about the structural characteristics of each district, their strategies, and their commercial ties. The interviews were conducted in two stages. The first stage focused on understanding the context and identifying the issues most relevant to the development of the districts. The first interview was with the Lombardy Region official in charge of the rural districts system (September 2019), who outlined the institutional framework and the recent change in the legislation (D.g.r. 31 July 2019 - n. XI/2040). The other interviews in this first stage were with leading figures of the rural districts (January–March 2020), and were geared towards understanding the characteristics and strategies of the districts. Specific questions were asked to shed light on three dimensions of the potential benefits of rural districts for the farmers: 1) the empowerment of farmers in their relationship with institutions; 2) the support in accessing public funds; and 3) the enhancement of commercial networks.

Following this first round of interviews, a draft Impact Pathway Map was produced. This map was presented to the leaders of all the districts and discussed in a second round of semi-structured interviews (December 2020–January 2021). Lastly, we established the final map, the features of which are presented in Section 9.5 of this paper.

9.3 Institutional framework

According to Italian legislation, agricultural districts are groups of farmers that come together to secure better economic outcomes (e.g., economies of scale, public fundraising), enhance their communication (e.g., visibility), and achieve greater political influence (e.g., advocacy for policies supporting the farmers). The Italian government started developing the "district strategy" about 30 years ago, first in the industrial sector with the 317/91 law "Interventions for innovation and small enterprise development", and later in agriculture, with the 228/01 legislative decree "Orientation and modernization of the agricultural sector". Further legislative acts (289/02; 80/05) created specific forms of public support for agricultural districts, and the European Commission ultimately endorsed this form of aid in 2008 (C 2008 7843). The Regional Council of Lombardy developed the district strategy with a specific law in January 2007 and regulated the issue with the deliberation 8/10085 (August 2009), creating three categories of agricultural districts: rural districts, high-quality agri-food districts, and supply-chain districts.[4]

In 2017, the Italian government modified the 228/01 decree (205/17 law), creating the "food district" category and expanding the range of typologies to include rural districts, agri-food quality districts, organic districts, and five types of local production districts. Following the 205/17 law, in July 2019, the regional government reclassified the agricultural districts into six new categories: rural, peri-urban productive system, high-quality agri-food, productive system with a high concentration of SMEs, organic productive system, and supply-chain districts. This recent reclassification did not result in any significant changes in operating procedures. However, it is worth noting that among the five districts involved in this research, four have remained "rural districts" while one has been re-labelled as a "peri-urban productive system" district (the DAM).[5] Compared to the other categories, "rural districts" and "peri-urban productive system districts" are less focused on a specific product (unlike supply-chain districts, for example) or a specific production quality standard (e.g., high-quality agri-food districts), and more concerned with the development of a synergistic relationship between the farmers and the local socio-environmental context.

Regarding governance, two legal frameworks need to be highlighted. The first is the Milan Urban Food Policy (MUFP), which aims to systematically address all matters relating to food that usually fall under the jurisdiction of separate administrative bodies. The MUFP guidelines set out five priorities: 1) providing healthy food for everyone; 2) promoting the sustainability of the food system; 3) understanding food; 4) reducing waste; and 5) supporting and promoting scientific research in the agri-food sector. While these priorities are all interconnected, Priority 2 relates closely to the topic discussed here. The guidelines of the MUFP were approved in 2015, the year of the World Expo “Feeding the Planet, Energy for Life”, and later became what is commonly known as the Milan Food Policy. The Food Policy Office, created in 2017, supports the districts by coordinating their political action (see Section 4.1) and assisting them in development projects (see Sections 4.2 and 4.4).

The second legal framework directly relating to the governance of the urban food system is the Framework Agreement for Local Development (Accordo Quadro di Sviluppo Territoriale, AQST), approved in 2014. The agreement brings together the agricultural districts, the municipality of Milan, the Metropolitan City of Milan, and the Lombardy regional government,[6] and provides a channel to coordinate strategies on a wider scale, beyond that of individual districts. The AQST was established to enhance the rural characteristics of Milan’s metropolitan area by promoting sustainable development, integrating local economic activities, and carrying out environmental restoration.

9.4 The districts

The research focuses on the five districts of the MCM (Figure 9.1). Four of these districts were created in 2011–2012, a period that saw profound changes in the municipal agri-food strategies, while the DAMA district is the outcome of a more recent effort by local farmers and institutions.

Formally, the districts are consortium organizations with a light management structure and a low operating budget. Four of the districts were established based on geographical attributes (three are connected to waterways and one to the city of Milan), while one is more defined by its farmers’ produce (Rice and Frogs).

9.4.1 Milan Agricultural District (DAM)

The Milan Agricultural District (DAM), created in 2011, now counts 34 farms spanning around 1,500 hectares of agricultural land, mostly situated within the boundaries of the city. The main activities of the farmers are those typical of the area—rice (10,000 t), maize (5,000 t), and milk production (2,000 t)—although a horticultural operation also started recently. On the whole, these farms’ approach to agriculture is rather conventional: the farmers have adopted integrated farming techniques, but organic farming is essentially absent, with the exception of the horticultural production.

The DAM’s focus is on building a positive relationship between urban and rural areas and integrating agricultural activities in the city. The district’s development plan identifies its primary objective as the protection of the commons, particularly water and soil, along with landscape and peri-urban environmental rehabilitation.

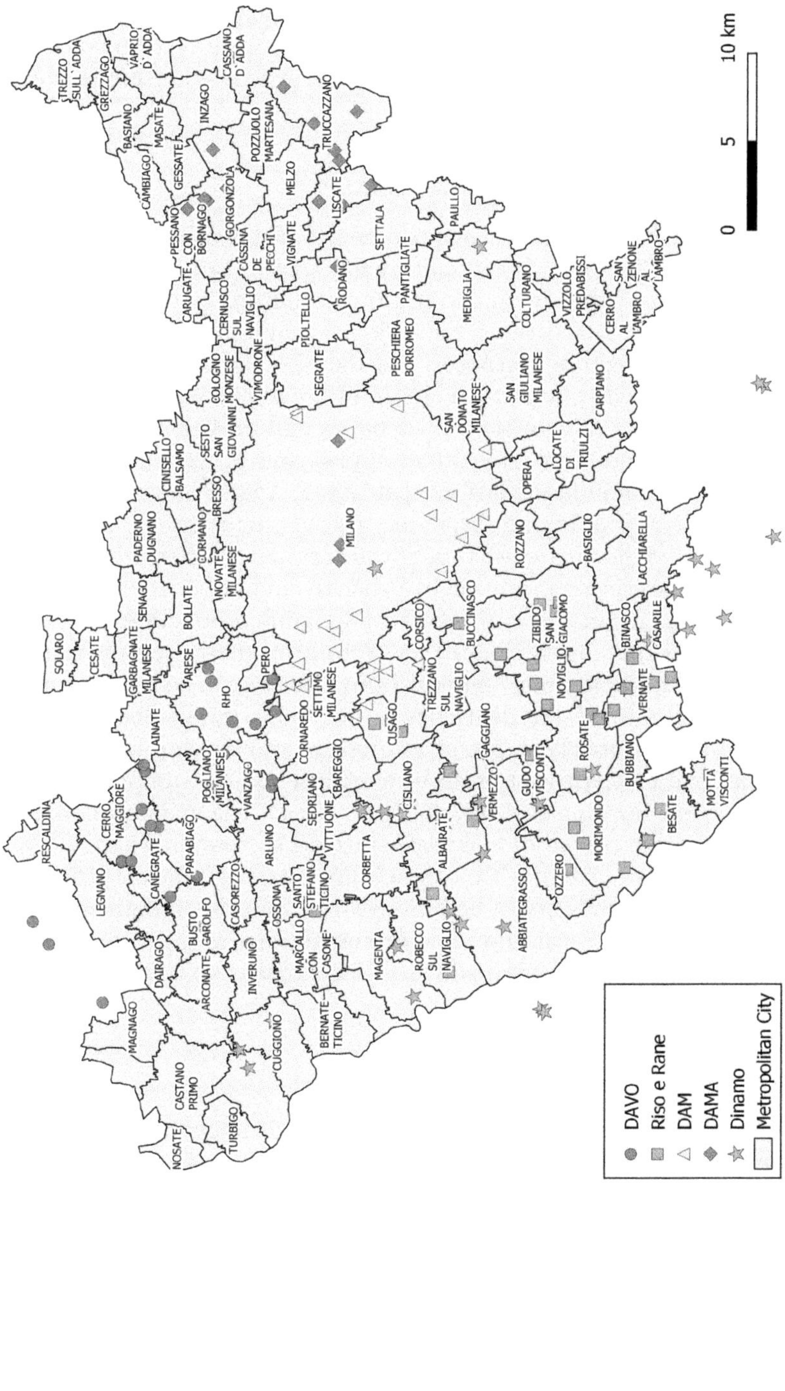

Figure 9.1 Member farms of the agricultural districts of the MCM.

(Map by Valerio Bini based on data collected by Valerio Bini, Giacomo Zanolin, Chiara Pirovano, and Luna Alice Rolle)

The location of the farms is a key feature of the district, in terms of both opportunities and threats. On the one hand, the area is characterized by strong pressure from urban activities—associated with real estate speculation and social and environmental externalities—that have eroded the quantity and quality of agricultural spaces, especially during the period between 1950 and 1990. On the other hand, the city represents an opportunity to enhance the production and distribution of food, in a new synergetic relationship between rural and urban actors.

9.4.2 *Adda Martesana Agricultural District (DAMA)*

The DAMA was established in 2017, and consists of 25 members, mostly based in the eastern part of the MCM. Agriculture has traditionally had an important place in this part of the region and the area is marked by the presence of two crucial hydraulic infrastructures: the Villoresi channel, built at the end of the 19th century for irrigation purposes, and the Naviglio Martesana Canal, built in the 15th century to connect the city of Milan with the Adda river.

Although agricultural activities still cover nearly half of the total area (Istat, 2010), they are now threatened by urban sprawl and infrastructure—most notably two highways built in the last 10 years (A35; A58)—which are further fragmenting the already shrinking rural area. Agriculture is weaker here than in the DAM area, and the district was specifically created to defend these residual spaces against the erosion produced by urban dynamics. Most of the members are farmers engaged in conventional farming (grain production and cattle breeding), but the district also includes a few non-farm enterprises, such as the service company "La Madonnina" and the fair-trade store in Agrate Brianza.

The general objective of the district plan highlights the conflict between agriculture and urban sprawl, as it aims to preserve and develop high-quality farming "as a form of territorial protection against soil consumption" (*Distretto Agricolo Adda Martesana (DAMA)*, 2017, Art.1). The first line of action is focused on increasing cooperation between farmers surrounding agricultural activities (new crops or techniques) and communication (e.g., the creation of a district label). A second category of action is geared towards strengthening the ties between farmers and local and regional institutions. Finally, the district strives to enhance its environmental and historical heritage, in part to promote tourism.

9.4.3 *Olona Valley Agricultural District (DAVO)*

The Olona Valley Agricultural District was created in 2012 by the Olona River Consortium, one of the oldest river management institutions in Italy (founded in 1606). At present, the district counts 39 members from a fairly large area in the north-west part of the MCM and the southern part of the Province of Varese. Due to the natural characteristics of the area, agricultural activities are less prominent in the northern part of the MCM than in the rest of the region, and urbanization is far more extensive.

Like in the first two districts, grain production and cattle breeding are the dominant activities in the area, but a wider range of products are made in this district than in the DAM and the DAMA. The first strategic pillar of the district plan focuses on territorial regeneration through projects that encourage people to visit and use the area. The second strategic pillar aims to develop services for citizens, companies, and users. Finally, the district strives to improve farm performance through collective and coordinated actions.

Given its specific nature, this district prioritizes environmental actions, especially relating to water issues, and it is involved in important territorial management projects (see Section 4.1). At the same time, like all the other districts, the DAVO has developed more typical activities such as the promotion of local products in local markets and through mass retailers.

9.4.4 Rice and frogs

The "Riso e Rane" (Rice and Frogs) district was founded in 2011 in the south-western part of the MCM. The 23 municipalities involved cover an area of 30,513 hectares (19.37% of the Metropolitan City of Milan) and specialize in intensive rice cultivation: productive agricultural soil accounts for 80% of the area, and 60% of the land used for rice-growing in the metropolitan area of Milan is located in the municipalities within this district.

The Rice and Frogs district was created in order to build a network of local farmers, to distinguish their presence on the market by certifying the high quality of the food they produce. To this end, the district has developed a marketing strategy mainly targeting the MCM urban and peri-urban markets, focused on the high quality of its agricultural products. It has also created a specific label for its rice, which has proven useful for penetrating large markets by using recognizable packaging that enables consumers to choose high-quality food certified by the district.

Moreover, to promote the image of the rice produced in this area, the district has developed actions to ensure the quality of the food and its unique value. As part of this work, in 2016 the district launched an important project called the "DNA-controlled brand". The aim of the project is to certify the quality of the local rice with genetic analysis identifying the specific characteristics of the different varieties grown by the farmers (Carnaroli, Arborio, Volano, Baldo, S. Andrea, and Vialone nano).

Finally, an objective specific to the "Rice and Frogs" approach to federating farmers is to motivate them to cooperate rather than compete. The underlying premise of this objective is that an individual farmer cannot compete on the global rice market on their own. The district exists essentially to generate economic opportunities to foster cooperation between farmers who can grow stronger if they buy and sell as a single economic actor.

9.4.5 Neo-rural district of the three waters of Milan (Dinamo)

Dinamo was founded in 2012 by 42 farmers in an area delimited by three watercourses: the Ticino River, the Villoresi Channel, and the Naviglio Pavese Canal. At present, the district counts 36 farms located in two provinces, Milan and Pavia, across an area that partially overlaps with the Rice and Frogs district. The main crop is rice, but in this case the district's strategy is more geared towards diversifying agricultural activities rather than focusing on a single product.

The main aim of this district is to combine high-quality production with agriculture and environmental restoration. These two dimensions are intertwined in the district's vision. In line with the European Union's Common Agricultural Policy, it considers the environment and the landscape as strategic ecosystem services that can generate added value and make local products more competitive in the global economic system. According to the vision of Neo-rural Group, an organization that includes some of the largest Dinamo farms, biodiversity is the key factor distinguishing high-quality food produced in the MCM from low-quality food that could have been produced anywhere in the world. Biodiversity is thus far more than an ethical goal for the district: it constitutes an economic strategy to try to sell agricultural products at higher prices than those set by national and international markets.

In connection with this, a second aim of the district is to promote local products on a local scale, through marketing and branding strategies focused on generating economic demand for high-quality products grown in a high-quality environment and landscape. It has launched two specific brands to this end: "Riso dell'anno mille" and "Cavaliere d'Italia". These brands, geared towards two different sales channels (large-scale distribution and upscale restaurants respectively), illustrate Dinamo's strategy of generating added value through biodiversity and environmental quality.

A final focus specific to Dinamo's work in the MCM is multifunctionality: Dinamo runs several projects focused on building networks to complement food production with proximity rural tourism, social and educational services, and wellness activities.

9.5 The impact of the agricultural districts on the governance of the urban food system

The institution of the agricultural districts in the metropolitan area of Milan has fostered multi-level governance, empowering local farmers and generating a number of positive impacts on the development of a more sustainable urban food system. In the Impact Pathway Map we drew with the farmers (see Section 9.2) following the Urbal process, we grouped these impacts into four areas of action: 1) territorial planning; 2) economic activities; 3) socio-cultural dynamics; and 4) project design (Figure 9.2).

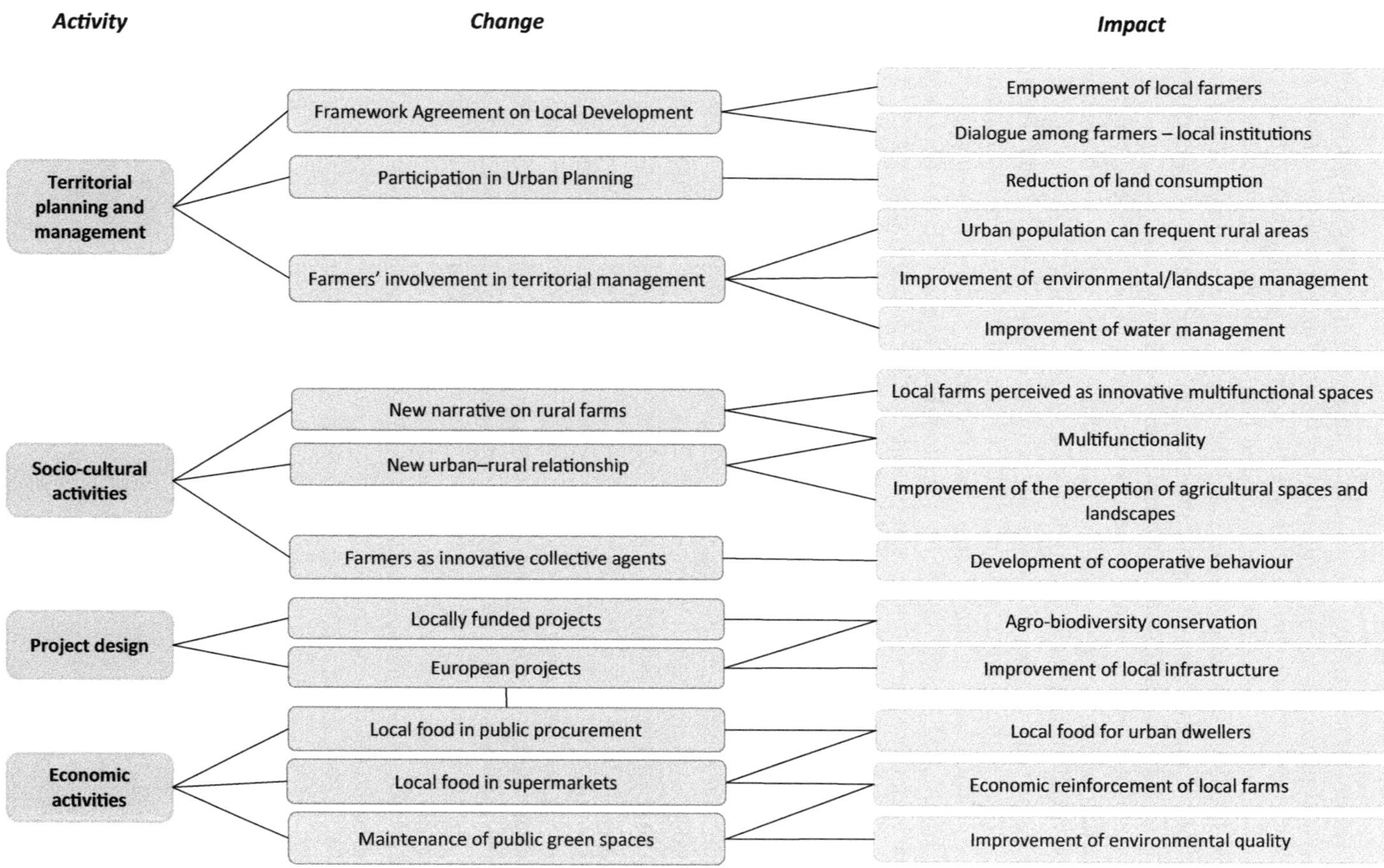

Figure 9.2 Impact pathway map (Bini et al., 2019).

9.5.1 Territorial planning

Agricultural districts provide a useful framework for addressing some of the structural problems facing contemporary agriculture, bringing together farmers who would otherwise have very little agency. For instance, districts have played a role in the negotiations around land-use policies at local level, and some districts, especially Dinamo and the DAM, have emphasized this political dimension, explicitly approaching their role as a force opposing the massive land-use conversion currently witnessed in the region.

Increasing farmers' power in negotiations on land-use policies is an essential precondition for the permanence of agriculture in the region, and consequently for the development of a sustainable urban food system.

The districts' impact on territorial planning can be observed on three different scales: at the municipal level, districts can lobby for sound land-management policies; on a broader scale, districts participate in the management of intercommunal spaces; lastly, on a regional scale, the districts contribute to defining development strategies, especially in the agricultural sector.

On a municipal scale, the negotiations around land use plans highlight the role played by the districts. The MCM is simultaneously an important centre of agricultural production and one of the largest urbanization areas in Europe. The tensions between rural and urban activities are therefore particularly high in this region. This competition has been a source of constant negotiations and conflicts in which, with the exception of occasional initiatives such as the creation of the South Milan Agricultural Park (SMAP) in 1990, urban development has largely prevailed.

As a result of this dynamic, more than 30% of the land in the MCM is covered by artificial surfaces (Ispra, 2020), one of the highest rates in Italy (third, after the neighbouring province of Monza and the metropolitan city of Naples). While this trend has now virtually stabilized (+0.5% artificial surfaces in the last seven years), conflict has been particularly fierce in the past, with documented cases of corruption to influence political actors to convert agricultural land into real estate development areas.

The Milan Agricultural District (DAM) was created in response to one of these scandals: the cheap sale of public farmland to private developers in the 1980s. In 1984, a real estate company bought Cascina Campazzo, a farm owned by the municipality and managed by the first president-to-be of the DAM, as part of a larger operation that was to lead to the construction of a new residential neighbourhood and an urban park. In 2003, after the neighbourhood was built, with the park still in the pipeline, the developer started the process of evicting the farmers from the area. Between 2003 and 2014, pressure from farmers and civil society organizations led the municipality to expropriate the land and the farm from the developer, in order to create an agricultural urban park called Parco Ticinello. This process culminated in the DAM being temporarily entrusted with the management of the 88-ha area. The Ticinello Park Association, that now manages the area, played a crucial role in the institution of the DAM in 2011, and the municipality's radical change of strategy was made possible by the district's lobbying.

On a larger scale, some districts also participate in the land-use planning of environmentally sensitive areas. This is the case of the DAVO, which is part of the working group monitoring the Olona river, an initiative of the regional government that also involves local municipalities (Legnano, Canegrate, San Vittore Olona, Parabiago), the Olona River Consortium, and the Regional Agency for Agricultural and Forestry Services (Ersaf). The area is at the centre of a decade-long controversy relating to the construction of lamination tanks[7] to control the effects of river flooding. In the last few years, the DAVO and Dinamo have been working together to obtain authorizations to manage the landscape of the Olona floodway channel, turning this hydraulic work with a high environmental impact into a tourism trail useful for strengthening spatial cohesion and supporting local farmers' economic development through multifunctionality (e.g., educational farms, restaurants, agritourism).

The last dimension of the districts' participation in territorial planning is their contribution to the Framework Agreement for Local Development (AQST). After an initial period of activity by the districts, which mostly coincided with the World Expo 2015, the framework agreement went through a period of relative stagnation until 2019, when the Milan Food Policy office took charge of the process to revise the agreement, leading to the approval of its updated version in June 2020. The updated AQST action plan is structured in seven macro-actions: 1) the improvement of the irrigation system; 2) landscape rehabilitation; 3) land-management improvement; 4) innovation; 5) multifunctionality; 6) the promotion of rural culture; and 7) the consolidation of development strategy. At present, of the 94 actions envisaged by the framework agreement, 42 are coordinated by a district (12 by the DAVO, 10 by the DAM, seven by Dinamo, seven by Rice and Frogs, five by the DAMA, and one by the five districts collectively). The macro-action in which the districts are most involved is the promotion of "product, process and supply chain innovation" (AQST, 2020, pp. 109–137). The action collectively managed by the five districts is the promotion of supply agreements with mass retailers and public catering, which is particularly relevant to achieving a sustainable urban food system.

9.5.2 Economic activities

Italian legislation considers the districts primarily as instruments to enhance competitiveness by creating economies of scale and network effects. Thus, many farmers in the MCM joined the districts with a view to strengthening their position on the market in a context of global competition.

Most of the farmers involved in the five districts practise rather conventional farming, producing grain (e.g., rice, maize), and dairy. Global competition on the market for these products is particularly strong. This keeps prices low, making agriculture a problematic activity in an area in such high demand for other uses. In many cases, the districts provide innovative answers to address these structural challenges. While the five districts each have quite different situations, the economic dimension is present in all of their strategies.

We can highlight two main pathways through which the districts produce economic benefits for the farmers: 1) strengthening their position on the private-sector market; and 2) activating public-private partnerships with local authorities.

To strengthen the farmers' position on the private-sector market, the districts have produced many initiatives with interesting potential, even if their economic impact is still limited. The easiest way to leverage the districts to enhance the farmers' competitiveness is by creating a district label that distinguishes the products as "local" and/or "high-quality" food. The idea behind this strategy is to make consumers more aware of the quality of the food they eat, based on the premise that a conscious consumer is willing to spend more to buy high-quality food. All the districts have in different ways promoted a label to market part of their products in specific contexts (e.g., farmers' markets, farm shops, conventional stores, large retail stores, etc.) In this way, the districts help by creating a recognizable identity, fostering economies of scale and facilitating the fulfilment of bureaucratic practices.

The Rice and Frogs district has developed the most structured actions in this regard, for instance with the "DNA-controlled brand" project aimed at highlighting the uniqueness of the rice produced within the boundaries of the district. Four districts have chosen to commercialize their products in the large-scale distribution circuit, Rice and Frogs, Dinamo, the DAM, and the DAVO. In these cases, the presence of a district is essential for negotiating with mass retailers and being able to guarantee the quantities required by such distribution channels.

While this strategy has great potential, the total amount of products commercialized through this channel is currently still low. The farmers of Rice and Frogs, which is the strongest district in this respect, produce around 20,000–25,000 tonnes of rice per year, yet only 1% is commercialized through the district to mass retailers. The situation is similar for Dinamo, with approximately 1% of the certified rice produced by its farmers being sold through the high-quality channels ("Riso dell'anno mille" and "Cavaliere d'Italia"). Moreover, competition among the districts for the same markets (particularly rice) weakens their position on these markets. For this reason, the AQST has envisaged the creation of a special brand for the products of the MCM districts, but the negotiations are still underway.

Another strategy pursued by the districts to enhance their position on the private market is the development of autonomous commercial channels, especially through online platforms. This is exemplified by Agricibo, the website developed by the Dinamo district to sell products directly, with a potential economic benefit for both the producer and the consumer. A wide range of products is available on the website and the district delivers the products within a 10 km radius of the logistics centre, a partner farm of the district located in Rosate (MI).

The second pathway developed by the districts to enhance their economic position is the activation of public-private partnerships, either in the food sector or in the environmental services field. In the last few years, many projects have been launched to connect the districts with urban school canteens. In the focus group discussions, the representatives of the districts identified this as the strategy with the highest growth potential for food distribution. The most advanced project is the partnership between the DAM and the food service company "Milano Ristorazione" (see Chapter 6, this volume), which is 99% owned by the municipality of Milan. This project started in 2016, when DAM members were asked to supply rice for the local school canteens (180 tonnes/year for a value of €300,000). The municipality is now extending this model to other products—particularly legumes, vegetables, and cereals—with the double purpose of enhancing the local component of the urban food service system and stimulating a transition in peri-urban agriculture from cereal monoculture to more diverse production (see infra, Section 4.4, the "Mater Alimenta Urbes" project).

As for the public-private partnerships around the environmental services provided by the districts to local municipalities, they cover a wide range of activities, from small interventions in urban green management to more complex partnerships, as in the case of the DAVO district which has been appointed to manage the land expropriated for the construction of the lamination tanks on the Olona River (par. 4.1).

9.5.3 Socio-cultural dynamics

The institution of the five rural districts has also produced a number of socio-cultural impacts, both internally on the farmers' identity, and on the urban perception of rural spaces. Many interviews identified the individualist and competitive attitude among the farmers as a relevant barrier to the development of a truly integrated urban food system. The districts have helped foster the emergence of cooperative behaviour, even if the issue of individualism is still perceived as a constraint for the development of the districts themselves. On a deeper level, some interviewees pointed out that the districts are changing the way in which farmers perceive themselves, from upholding a traditional and rather conservative stance towards more active and innovative interpretations of their role.

The emergence of these cooperative behaviours is linked to the economic benefits afforded by the districts, but also to a shared cultural *milieu* that facilitates social relationships among the farmers. The research area is characterized by a significant cultural heritage, with both architectural assets and a distinctive landscape shaped by centuries of farming, especially in the Southern part of the MCM. All the districts are involved in the preservation and restoration of this heritage: the RDP project "Mater Alimenta Urbes", for instance, has developed a specific focus on this theme, striving to rehabilitate places of significance to the identity of the local community.

The restoration of this cultural heritage should also be read as a way to promote tourism as a part of a broader multifunctionality strategy. Dinamo farmers in particular have leveraged tourism and environmental education as two strategic pillars for the promotion of their projects. Multifunctionality is part of an ongoing socio-cultural shift in urban-rural relationships fuelled by the districts, from competitive "zero-sum" interaction with the city to a win-win dynamic. This approach sees the two spaces as no longer separate or in competition for the same areas, but instead as having the opportunity to develop synergies that can benefit both urban and rural populations.

This cultural shift is still ongoing, but many districts are explicitly pursuing this objective in their plans and actions. Only Rice and Frogs—the "single-product" district—seems to remain focused on a rather conventional cultural framework and less geared towards the kind of radical change described above. This district's strategy is more focused on economic and productive impact, fostering change in consumer attitudes rather than a broad cultural shift.

To promote a new narrative, the districts organize public meetings and participate in scientific conferences focused on urban-rural interaction, such as the "Agriculture, Community and Climate" conference of 20 February 2020 organized by the Dinamo district, involving the South Milan Agricultural Park, the Ticino Park, the University of Milan and the Polytechnic University of Milan. In addition to this conference, we should also mention more practical initiatives such as "Cascine aperte" (Open Farmhouses), an annual event aimed at allowing citizens to get to know the farmhouses in the South Milan Agricultural Park (SMAP). Initiatives like this aim to overturn the traditionally closed-off positioning of the agricultural world and the corresponding indifference of the urban population towards rural life.

9.5.4 Project design

The last type of impact that we wish to highlight pertains to the farmers' ability to access external funding through project design work. The socio-economic environment of the MCM provides many opportunities for this kind of activity, in both the public and the private sector. However, farmers often cannot easily access this funding, due to operational barriers such as a lack of time to work on project design or difficulty expressing their needs and their solutions in the project design language. The districts thus represent powerful tools to aggregate the farmers' needs and to achieve economies of scale, allowing the farmers to benefit from this kind of opportunity, whether to support everyday activities or to develop innovative strategies.

In the private sector, the Cariplo Foundation has played a crucial role. Based in Milan, the Foundation is the philanthropic branch of one of Italy's leading banking groups (Intesa Sanpaolo) and the largest private donor in the area. It typically funds projects based in Lombardy with a specific focus on the MCM, and in the last ten years it has backed at least ten projects that have contributed to the development of the districts and of an urban food system in the MCM.

The institution of the DAM, for instance, is directly linked to the project "For an Agri-Cultural District in Milan", funded by Cariplo Foundation in 2010.

The existence of the districts makes farmers more visible to other actors in the area, thereby facilitating the creation of partnerships with institutions and civil society organizations to initiate projects for developing and protecting the territory. This is the case of the "Olona entra in città" project, developed in cooperation between the municipality of Rho (MI) and the DAVO from 2014 to 2018, or the "Librarsi" project, launched in 2016 by Legambiente, one of the biggest environmental organizations in Italy, in collaboration with Dinamo.

The importance of the districts is even more visible in the case of institutional projects such as those of the EU Rural Development Programme (RDP), which requires applicants to have specific project design and management skills. In this regard, the most interesting case is the project "Mater Alimenta Urbes" (Measure 16 "Cooperation", Action 16.10.02 "Integrated Area Projects"), approved in 2019. This project represents an innovative form of collaboration between local bodies (six municipalities of the MCM are directly involved in the project), farmers (21 farms), and agricultural districts (the DAM and the DAMA). The project aims to strengthen collaboration between farmers and local institutions in the public food service sector, promote landscape restoration activities (hedge and tree-row restoration), and improve slow-mobility infrastructure (signage and cycle lanes).

Neo-rural projects promoted by Dinamo are also closely informed by the EU Rural Development Programme, for example Measure 214 (Agri-environment payments) of RDP 2007–2013 and Priority 4 of RDP 2014–2020 (Restoring, preserving and enhancing ecosystems related to agriculture and forestry). Biodiversity and rice production have been promoted by Dinamo through these instruments (Bogliani & Della Rocca, 2014), deeply transforming the landscape in a large area between MCM and the province of Pavia, and offering a unique example of the potential of agro-ecological ecosystems to produce high-quality food and regenerate the environment (Assandri et al., 2018).

The RDP also funded the institution of the Rice and Frogs District in 2011 and its flagship initiative, the "DNA trademark" rice certification project. This initiative was recognized as best practice by the Lombardy region in the project "Rural-Urban partnerships Motivating Regional Economies" (Rumore), an international initiative co-financed with ERDF funds from the Interreg Europe Programme.

9.6 Conclusion

The five rural districts presented here emerged in the same socio-political context, but evolved in slightly different ways, emphasizing one or another of the dimensions of food system sustainability addressed by the Urbal project (environment, society and culture, economics, health, nutrition, and governance) based on very local characteristics.

The political dimension is evident in the districts that are more exposed to pressure from the urbanization process, such as the DAM, which sits within the boundaries of Milan. On the contrary, the Rice and Frogs District, which is deeply embedded in an agricultural landscape, has focused on the economic aspects of sustainability. The environmental dimension is crucial for a "river-based" district such as the DAVO and for the more innovative, neo-rural Dinamo district, the strategy of which explicitly strives for a new form of agriculture and an integrated relationship between urban and rural spaces (Van der Ploeg, 2018).

The environmental dimension introduces a decisive challenge for the development of a sustainable urban food system. On the one hand, the districts are crucial instrument for protecting agriculture from urban sprawl and developing a locally anchored food system; on the other, many members of the districts still practise rather conventional agriculture with a significant environmental impact. The MCM involves widely diverse configurations, ranging from single-product conventional districts (e.g., Rice and Frogs) to more experimental and agroecology-oriented farmers (e.g., Dinamo). The conflict between local and agroecological agriculture represents a potential fault line within districts in the future. The relative heterogeneity of the districts can be a strength that fosters inclusiveness, but it also has the potential to hinder coordinated action by the districts and limit their action on small-scale projects. In terms of scale, the districts have prioritized local action based on micro-interventions, and the main challenge for the future will be to scale up these initiatives to have a bigger impact on the region's socio-spatial dynamics. In this regard, the RDP project developed by the DAM and the DAMA could provide a template for these actors' development, showing the potential role of the districts in larger projects funded by bigger players, such as the EU.

On the whole, the districts offer an excellent opportunity to innovate with the food production process (Calori & Magarini, 2015), activating Alternative Food Networks (AFNs) (Dansero & Pettenati, 2018) that are capable of reshaping the relationship between the city and the peri-urban countryside (Donadieu, 2013). Districts are bearers of a creative vision with strong innovative potential, underpinned by two fundamental elements: 1) the ability to create and manage multi-level governance tools; and 2) an approach to land-use policies guided by landscape agriculture (Poli, 2013). District farmers recognize the value of the landscape in which their farms are located, which not only plays a role in grounding production activities, but is also a crucial factor of production capable of generating a fundamental surplus value for local food and making it competitive on the global market and attractive to city dwellers, who are becoming increasingly interested in buying good and healthy food.

These are key issues that lead us to reflect on the role of agricultural districts from the point of view of land governance: through the districts, farmers transcend their role as workers of the land and become protagonists of a movement for radical change in land-use policies. The districts work to promote access to the tools and funds of the Common Agricultural Policy, provide technical support for the implementation of projects that have concrete effects on food production and distribution, and contribute to the maintenance and production of the local environment and landscape.

Measured in purely econometric terms, their impact is still very limited. Nevertheless, at present, the agricultural districts can be considered as emerging actors that are playing a crucial role as innovators of metropolitan food systems governance, and forerunners of change in the making.

Notes

1 In Italian legislation, the denomination of "agricultural district" has changed over time and differs according to the scale of analysis (e.g., agricultural districts, rural districts, agri-food districts, food districts, etc.). This chapter will use the term agricultural districts to refer to the general concept and the other terms to identify particular forms of organization defined by specific regulations. For example, the five districts analysed in this chapter have been labelled "rural" by the local legislation (see Section 3).
2 The two focus groups were organized before the COVID-19 outbreak, in collaboration with the Milan Food Policy Office.
3 The meeting was co-organized with the Food Policy Office of the City of Milan, in order to develop one of the strategies identified in the Framework Agreement for Local Development (AQST, see Section 3 and 5.1), namely strengthening the districts' commercial networks.
4 In this case, the first term refers to more general and diverse farm clusters, while the other two denote districts more specifically linked to particular products.
5 The name change reflects only the location of the districts and did not result in changes to the way they operate.
6 In 2016 two more institutions signed the agreement: the East Ticino-Villoresi Consortium and the Olona River consortium.
7 A lamination tank is a temporary rainwater storage tank.

References

Accordo Quadro Sviluppo Territoriale (AQST). (2020). *Piano D'Azione 2020*. Milano Metropoli Rurale. https://www.milanometropolirurale.regione.lombardia.it/

Assandri, G., Bogliani, G., Pedrini, P., & Brambilla, M. (2018). Beautiful agricultural landscapes promote cultural ecosystem services and biodiversity conservation. *Agriculture, Ecosystems & Environment*, *256*, 200–210. https://doi.org/10.1016/j.agee.2018.01.012

Becattini, G. (1987). *Mercato e forze locali: il distretto industriale*. Il Mulino.

Bini, V., Mastropietro, E., Pettenati, G., & Zanolin, G. (2019). Urban food policies and metropolitan spaces: The case of Milan. *Revista Urbano*, *22*(39), 26–41. http://revistas.ubiobio.cl/index.php/RU/article/view/3322

Bogliani, G., & Della Rocca, F. (Eds.). (2014). *Biodiversity and rice production in rice agro-ecosystem_The Action Plan*. International Rice Field Ecological Network. https://doi.org/10.13140/RG.2.1.2524.7205

Calori, A., & Magarini, A. (2015). *Food and the cities. Politiche alimentari per città Sostenibili*. Edizioni Ambiente.

Dansero, E., & Pettenati, G. (2018). Reterritorialization, proximity, and urban food planning: Research perspectives on afns. In A. Corsi, F. Barbera, E. Dansero, & C. Peano (Eds.), *Alternative food networks* (pp. 273–301). Palgrave Macmillan.

Dematteis, G., & Governa, F. (Eds.). (2005). *Territorialità, sviluppo locale, sostenibilità: il modello SLoT*. Franco Angeli.

Distretto Agricolo Adda Martesana (DAMA). (2017). *Piano di distretto*. https://distrettoagricoloaddamartesana.it/wp-content/uploads/2019/07/Piano_distretto_DAMA.pdf

Donadieu, P. (2013). *Campagne urbane. Una nuova proposta di paesaggio della città*. Donzelli.

Gemmiti, R., & Conti Puorger, A. (2008). Governo, governance, sussidiarietà e territorio. In L. Scarpelli (Ed.), *Organizzazione del territorio e governance multilivello* (pp. 13–46). Pàtron.

ISTAT. (2010). *6° Censimento dell'agricoltura*. Istat. https://www.istat.it/it/censimenti-permanenti/censimenti-precedenti/agricoltura/agricoltura-2010

Istituto Superiore per la Protezione e la Ricerca Ambientale (Ispra). (2020). *Consumo di suolo, dinamiche territoriali e servizi ecosistemici*. Ispra. https://www.isprambiente.gov.it/it/archivio/eventi/2020/07/consumo-di-suolo-dinamiche-territoriali-e-servizi-ecosistemici

Morgan, K. (2015). Nourishing the city: The rise of the urban food question in the Global North. *Urban Studies*, *52*(8), 1379–1394. https://doi.org/10.1177/0042098014534902

Muchnik, J., Sanz Cañada, J., & Torres Salcido, G. (2008). Systèmes agroalimentaires localisés: état des recherches et perspectives. *Cahiers Agricultures*, *17*(6), 513–519. https://doi.org/10.1684/agr.2008.0251

Poli, D. (2013). Agricoltura paesaggistica: un arredo fittizio della campagna o un'opportunità di sviluppo per il mondo rurale in evoluzione? In D. Poli (Ed.), *Agricoltura paesaggistica. Visioni, metodi, esperienze* (pp. 1–31). Firenze University Press.

Porter, M.E. (1990). *The competitive advantage of nations*. Free Press.

Van der Ploeg, J.D. (2018). *The new peasantries. Rural development in times of globalization*. Routledge.

Watts, D.C.H., Ilbery, B., & Maye, D. (2005). Making reconnections in agro-food geography: Alternative systems of food provision. *Progress in Human Geography*, *29*(1), 22–40. https://doi.org/10.1191/0309132505ph526oa

10 The Urbal approach and the after-life of a food systems innovation process

The Nourish to Flourish governance process in Cape Town, South Africa

Gareth Haysom and Jane Battersby

10.1 Introduction

The Western Cape Government's draft Household Food and Nutrition Security Strategy (commonly referred to as "Nourish to Flourish"), published in 2016, was developed to address the multiple dimensions of hunger, food insecurity, and malnutrition in the region. As a strategic framework document, Nourish to Flourish aims to improve food system governance by bringing stakeholders in communities together to address interconnected issues relating to food, ensure effective coordination of State and non-State actors, leverage existing programmes to identify ways to capitalize on positive outcomes, and promote greater efficiencies and synergies for stakeholders actively supporting the reduction of food insecurity.

On a policy level, despite claims of integrated policy approaches, the reality is that South African food security governance remains deeply embedded in a production-as-solution approach, which overlooks the fact that South Africa is over 65% urbanized. This rural- and production-oriented approach to food security not only misunderstands the challenge, but it also draws fiscal resources into redundant programmes.

The Household Food and Nutrition Security Strategic Framework was chosen as the Cape Town innovation for the Urbal project as it was considered to represent a dramatic departure from South African food security policy and programming, calling for explicitly transversal governance approaches to address food security through food system interventions. Not only was the approach of the strategic framework novel, but the roadmap for the framework's development also represented a significant innovation. The strategic framework was extensively workshopped within government and beyond. The driver of the innovation, the Western Cape Government, and expressly the Department of the Premier, then sought to develop a sustainable food system implementation strategy through a series of facilitated stakeholder engagements.

DOI: 10.4324/9781003285441-10

During the Urbal innovation assessment review, however, other processes were observed. These specifically involved other localized food systems actions aligning with, supporting, and generally further developing one another, informed largely by the processes that emerged as the Nourish to Flourish process unfolded. These cross-scale and cross-sector actions are also new in the context of South African food systems governance and policy processes. Additionally, the Urbal approach not only helped capture the intricacies of the innovation, it also supported the innovators in unexpected ways. The diverse benefits of the Urbal approach are documented in this chapter.

The chapter begins with an explanation of the context-specific interpretation of what constitutes a sustainable food system. This chapter defines sustainable food systems slightly differently to most other framings, particularly the Triple Bottom Line approach, which situates sustainability at the crossroads of social, ecological and economic imperatives. Given the context of the review, South Africa, a country with significant inequality and where negotiating the trade-offs between the three bottom lines is more challenging, a nuanced approach was adopted. The role of governance in mediating the intersections between the different components of sustainability (social, ecological, economic) further aligned with the specific innovation under review, a specifically governance-related innovation. In what follows, we discuss the Urbal methodology, offering the reader a sense of the innovation review process, who was involved in the consultation processes, and additional engagement activities, including the virtual workshop. The workshop helped to provide feedback to those consulted in this process, but also enabled further inquiry and the refinement of specific actions. As the Cape Town Urban Food Innovation Lab (UFIL) involved a review of a food system governance process, the chapter then provides an overview of conventional policy development processes. Next, we introduce and explain the innovation, the Western Cape Household Food and Nutrition Security Strategy, also providing supporting information on the context of the innovation. This contextualization is twofold. First, we situate the innovation within the landscape of food system challenges encountered in the Western Cape of South Africa. Second, we explain the origins of the innovation and how it evolved, the various consultation processes that took place, and the novel governance approach applied. The chapter then reflects on other aligned and mutually supporting food system innovations that emerged in the region, either as a result of the innovation under review, or owing to the significance of this innovation enabling them to act more boldly. Finally, we examine the utility of the Urbal approach to innovations under review and to other innovations aligned with them. The chapter concludes by reflecting on how the Urbal process of documenting, rather than assessing or judging, was a particularly powerful tool to capture such unique governance processes, which allowed the innovators to showcase their work without the risk of critique and, at the same time, to co-produce an assessment of the innovation.

10.2 On what constitutes a sustainable food system

For the Cape Town UFIL, it was deemed important, prior to the interviews but also throughout the review of the innovation, to articulate how sustainability as a broader concept needed to be framed. Clarifying a sustainability position, in relation to the context as well as the original Urbal framing, helped to situate the study both in context and within the wider framework of the impact assessment of the innovation under review. The Urbal project framing of food system sustainability proved to be particularly weighted and geared towards specific components of sustainability. Given the location of this review, in South Africa, sustainability priorities, or the weighting of the specific dimensions, needed to be clearly articulated and aligned with contextual needs. Additionally, since the innovation under review was a governance process, embedded within government processes, it seemed valuable to align the review with existing policy and governance frameworks.

For this reason, the Cape Town UFIL adopted the South African Sustainable Development Framework (Department of Environmental Affairs and Tourism, 2008) as an overarching conceptual framework for sustainability. Earlier conceptual framings of sustainability, still very much evident in the way sustainability tends to be framed, describe sustainability as a balance between the three key pillars of sustainability, namely society, the environment, and the economy (the proverbial "milking stool"). From this perspective, sustainability can sometimes be viewed as a trade-off between these different dimensions.

For the Cape Town UFIL, sustainability needed to be approached as interconnected and causal. Due to the high levels of inequality in the country, society needed to be central to the concept rather than peripheral, as is often the case in more ecological or economic framings of sustainability. Given the focus on a governance innovation, our framing of sustainability needed to account for how tensions between and across the different dimensions of sustainability were governed. For this reason, the articulation of sustainability provided by the South African Sustainable Development Framework proved useful. This articulation is guided by the premise that the different sustainability dimensions are co-dependant. From this perspective, financial sustainability, when considered broadly in terms of equity and justice rather than just profit, is contingent on societal justice, wellbeing, equity, and cohesion. This in turn is contingent on ecological sustainability, in other words equitable and regenerative resource consumption. Governance is necessary to mediate the competing demands of the different dimensions, for instance to regulate unsustainable use, to ensure greater equity, and to counter existing hegemonic views regarding entitlement. Through legal, policy, and associated intervention processes, governance needs to mediate the tensions that arise in trying to reconcile different priorities associated with the sustainability dimensions. This Embedded Spheres model is depicted in Figure 10.1, countering the more traditional Triple Bottom Line concept.

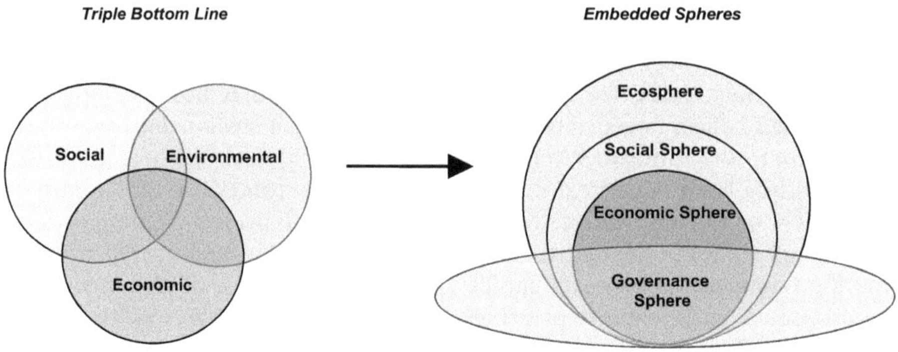

Figure 10.1 Triple Bottom Line versus Embedded Spheres—representations of sustainability framings.

(adapted from South African Government, Department of Environmental Affairs and Tourism, National Framework for Sustainable Development, 2008)

This framing was particularly important given that the innovation under review in the Western Cape was a food and nutrition programme introduced by a governance actor, the Western Cape Provincial Government, South Africa. This actor released its Draft Household Food and Nutrition Security Strategic Framework (WCHF&NSSF) in 2016 (WCG, 2016). The operational name of the framework, predominantly used, was Nourish to Flourish (N2F).[1] This was the governance innovation that the Cape Town UFIL reviewed.

10.3 A description of the methodology

Urbal research calls for insights from many experts and practitioners to better understand the structure and development of the innovation. Following this approach, the Cape Town UFIL involved different stakeholders of the innovation's development throughout the necessary conceptual, developmental, preliminary approval, truthing, and later refinement processes. This research relied primarily on key informant interviews, and was further supported by a participatory research approach. This process built on the experience and insights of innovators and practitioners, including civil society actors and policymakers. The authors also played an active role in the development of the Nourish to Flourish strategy. Insights gained as a result of their involvement in the strategy development process were tested as part of the interview and engagement methods.

The interview process involved a tiered and sequential data collection process. The initial interviews involved key informant interviews with the primary process innovators (the curators)—the leaders of the framework document, the

Western Cape Household Food and Nutrition Security Strategic Framework (Nourish to Flourish). These key innovators were known as the leaders of the innovation's development. Following a review of the feedback and responses from these primary innovators, the secondary tier of actors, namely the consultants and researchers who had worked with the Western Cape Government to assist in the development of the strategy, were interviewed. Their feedback was again reviewed and processed. The third tier of interviewees was related but non-aligned actors: actors who had played a support and input role in the process but not a strategic role. Table 10.1 provides an overview of the types of interview participants aligned directly with the Urbal interviewee categories.

The goal of the interview process was to capture and document the innovation mission, the activities and the short-term, medium-term, and long-term changes produced by the innovation. In the case of the Cape Town UFIL, the innovation was assessed according to the three broad overarching UFIL categories:

1) Innovations that shift the discourse on, conceptualization of and approach to the issue, but have not resulted in practical implementation or on-the-ground activities
2) Innovations that have resulted in proactive programmatic change, both in terms of policy development and project activities
3) Innovations that have resulted in less tangible change in food system sustainability

With these three categories in mind, the Cape Town UFIL research sought to ask the key question: "what has changed?" These questions also linked back to other sustainability and food security dimensions, like food access.

Given the food system sustainability focus of the wider Urbal project, interviewees were asked to consider the Urbal food system sustainability framing and its relevance to this work. In addition to this, given that the intervention in question would potentially inform and generate new policy, alignment with the South African National Framework for Sustainable Development was also discussed, in this case the 2008 South African National Framework for Sustainable Development (SANF4SD) (see Figure 10.1).

Alignment with both sustainability approaches, namely the six dimensions of the Urbal food system's sustainability framing and the embedded spheres of the SANF4SD, was necessary both for comparison with other UFIL processes as part of the wider Urbal project, and as a means to ensure contextual relevance and focus, specifically given the high levels of inequity and social exclusion in South Africa detailed earlier. This is not to suggest that inequity is absent from the Urbal framing, but using the South African framing ensured alignment with local needs and priorities.

Table 10.1 Interview participants including roles

Participants	*Sample interviewed*	*Role*
Innovators	3	People who developed the initial innovation concept
Stakeholders and other actors*	2	People involved in enabling (or not) the urban-driven innovation for the food system
Policymakers and/or funders as appropriate	2	Actors interested in enabling (or not) the innovation through policy, programmes, tools and other forms of support
Experts	2	Sustainability experts, urban governance experts, planning and other technical experts, etc.

* These included a policy actor from another sphere of government and process facilitators who assisted in engagement processes associated with the innovation.

The interview process resulted in two further stages in this work. As part of the Urbal review process, a report (the Urbal Project Assessment Report) was drafted for submission to the Western Cape policy innovators, but also to be shared more widely with project partners at different UFILs. Once a draft of this report was completed, this draft was used as a truthing process where the lead innovators, the curators, were consulted and asked to act as reviewers of the draft Urbal Project Assessment Report. The report not only served to document the Nourish to Flourish strategy development process described, but also prompted reflection on aspects not captured in the interviews. Furthermore, the review enabled edits that offered nuance and more detailed clarification on certain actions described in the report. The feedback and review comments added significant depth to and refined our understanding of the process. Importantly, this iterative and consultative approach resulted in the emergence of aligned innovation support processes. These will be discussed later in this chapter. However, these aligned processes also informed a workshop where the results of the review process were presented to all the interviewees as well as additional participants.

Given the restrictions imposed as a result of COVID-19, the feedback workshop originally planned as part of the Urbal approach was not able to go ahead. As a result, an online virtual workshop was convened. The workshop comprised of three connected stages. First, the participants were provided with a revised copy of the Urbal Project Assessment Report as pre-reading. A summarized version of the report was then presented and responses were elicited from participants regarding both the report and the presentation. This stimulated active dialogue and feedback. Finally, the key innovators and authors of the Nourish to Flourish strategy were asked to share their thoughts on the conversations that had just taken place. These perspectives were also detailed and added greatly to the workshop and the final report.

From an ethical perspective, this research was authorized by the custodian of the innovation, the Western Cape Government (WCG). In addition to obtaining permission from the curators of the innovation, full ethical approval was sought and obtained from the University of Cape Town's Faculty of Engineering and the Built Environment. All interviews, workshops and related research complied with these ethics requirements.

10.4 Conventional policy trajectories and processes

Before describing the Nourish to Flourish process as a governance innovation, it is important to explain the traditional and more conventional route through which governance processes are normally developed in South Africa. Governance innovation is very different to activist or private sector innovation. It follows specific hierarchical and legal processes, within formal government structures that refer back to legal prescripts dictating areas of command and control, and these government policy and programming prescripts and conventions determine both legal mandates and, as a result, fiscal resourcing. These processes are rooted in a Weberian understanding of the function of the State: command and control. In the South African case, these structures are deeply siloed and stratified, with different government departments and spheres of government seldom engaging with one another, and unable to transgress into another's "governance turf". This is a significant impediment to innovation.

In more conventional policy formulation processes, a problem or challenge is identified, and is then investigated through research. Following a filtering and analysis process, a determination is made as to the cause of the problem and the appropriate policy response. This response is then drafted into a policy document and, if needs be, enacted into law.

The process of drafting the Nourish to Flourish strategy exemplified an innovative approach to policy-making, in which the concept of iterative adaptation forms part of the policy development process.

10.5 Description of the innovation

The Nourish to Flourish strategy represented a dramatic departure from South African food security policy and programming, calling for explicitly transversal governance approaches to address food security through food system interventions (Box 10.1). Not only was the approach within the document novel, but so was the approach to the development of the framework. The strategic framework was extensively workshopped within government and beyond, and even the terms of reference were altered as information emerged from the engagement processes and as participants responded to the developing framework approach (Durno, 2020).

Box 10.1 Foundations of the Household Food and Nutrition Security Strategic Framework

The Food Security Strategic Framework is transversal, evidence-based, and contributes to a more coherent and targeted approach to addressing household food and nutrition insecurity in the Western Cape. It has been supported by a wide consultative process. The Food Security Strategic Framework articulates appropriate outcomes and objectives linking programmes to the reduction of hunger, improvements in health, nutrition, and productivity, supporting the ability of all people to active and productive lives in the Western Cape.
The Strategic Framework:

- Balances social and economic issues—supporting social protection and support for households as well as enabling opportunities to empower individuals and households within the food system
- Identifies interlinked agendas which need to be targeted simultaneously to affect the food system
- Highlights existing programmes within the food security realm and identifies ways to maximize positive outcomes through a coordinated approach
- Recognizes gaps in current areas of focus of the WCG regarding food and nutrition and proposes responses
- Identifies the importance of improving the availability of appropriate data on key issues that assist in identifying and responding to key social, economic, and demographic trends to better serve communities currently at risk of food insecurity
- Proposes a "whole-of-society" approach that will seek strategic partnerships with other spheres of the State and sectors of society to improve responses to food insecurity.

The Strategic Framework requires that governance mechanisms be identified to support the achievement of identified objectives by galvanizing action and creating working relationships amongst all stakeholders. It therefore aligns with a "whole-of-society" approach to improving food security and nutrition in the province, deliberately involving a diverse range of individuals, organizations and departments in identifying strategic priorities and opportunities. This work will be pursued through the creation of governance mechanisms that will address specific challenges in the food system.

(adapted from WCG, 2016, p. 2)

The Western Cape Government Strategic Framework on Household Food and Nutrition Security (Strategic Framework) adopts a food systems approach to analysing, interpreting, and responding to the features of the wider food system that create and contribute to food insecurity.

The Nourish to Flourish strategic framework document also required carefully and generally seamlessly navigating political and wider societal approval and acceptance processes. Importantly, we argue here that it is these processes, which accompanied the development and wider consultation processes associated with Nourish to Flourish, that represent a fundamental shift in policy development.

As the name denotes, the Western Cape Household Food and Nutrition Security Strategic Framework, or Nourish to Flourish, focused on food and nutrition security in the Western Cape province of South Africa. Some background into the state of food and nutrition security in South Africa and the Western Cape is provided here to highlight the importance of such a strategy.

> The food system is intricate and characterised by interaction and interdependence with other systems such as health, social security, resources, economic opportunity, spatial planning, the state of agriculture and the environment. The operation of this dynamic system determines the availability, access, utilisation and stability of the supply of food. Therefore, by taking a proactive food systems approach, the Western Cape Government (WCG) seeks to identify and promote sustainable household food security solutions and improve the nutrition of people living in the province.
>
> (WCG, 2016, p. 1)

Historical policy and political positioning mean that the policy orientation to address food security in South Africa falls to the National Department of Agriculture (currently the Department of Agriculture, Rural Development and Land Reform—DARD&LR). Nutrition is the responsibility of the National Department of Health and, to a lesser extent, the Department of Basic Education, specifically in terms of school feeding. These three national-scale ministries all delegate implementation powers to provincial departments. South Africa also has a robust and acclaimed social protection programme, with different components which, through operational policy imperatives and budgetary allocation, are delegated to implementing departments—housing to the housing departments, school feeding to the education departments, etc. The primary social protection component is channelled through the social grants system, facilitated by the National Department for Social Development and its implementing arm, the South African Social Services Agency (SASSA). Furthermore, the "right to food" is recognized as a right within in the South African Constitution, in Sections 27 and 28 of the Bill of Rights, binding all spheres of government to progressively realizing this Right (RSA, 1996, p. 11). Despite this legal and governance environment, food and nutrition security is one of South Africa's most pressing and stubborn developmental challenges.

South Africa has high food insecurity. A national survey conducted in 2013 found that 23.1% of households had inadequate or severely inadequate access to food: 26% of individuals were at risk of hunger, while 11,4% of individuals were experiencing hunger (Statistics South Africa, 2013).

The primary framing of food insecurity in South Africa has disproportionately focused on rural food insecurity, and any urban position has focused on poverty and not the systemic drivers of a specific urban food security challenge. For example, the Western Cape Department of Social Development's 2015 Strategic Planning document noted that

> According to the 2013 General Household Survey, 16.1% of households in the Western Cape have inadequate access to food, while 6.6% has severely inadequate access to food. In total 22.7% of households are food insecure. Food insecurity is more prevalent in rural areas where 27% of the rural population have inadequate access to food. The corresponding figure for urban areas is 20%.
>
> (WCG, 2015)

However, the province's population is approximately 90% urban. This means that 44,118 rural households are food insecure, while 294,120 urban households are food insecure. There are in fact over 6.5 times as many food insecure households in the province's urban areas as its rural areas.

The food system approach of the Nourish to Flourish strategy is useful as it shifts the framing of food insecurity beyond a simple issue of production to consider the entirety of the food system and its intersection with wider social, economic, and spatial systems. Importantly, Nourish to Flourish identified these connections and the intersections between systems as significant, framing its wider approach as a "whole-of-society approach" (Durno, 2020) which aligned with the Province's transition to such an approach. The intersection of society with the food system is a key conceptual framing of this innovation.

Nourish to Flourish emerged within this context, with an extremely unequal and unsustainable food system as well as a poorly framed and poorly implemented food and nutrition security governance regime. While novel, this framework did not, however, appear out of nowhere. Its development needs to be understood within the context of the food-related processes and policy approaches that preceded it.

10.5.1 Origins of the innovation

In the early part of the 2009 five-year governance cycle, various Provincial Strategic Objectives (PSOs) were formulated. One of these PSOs was Strategic Goal 3: Increase wellness, safety and tackle social ills. This required a variety of different departments to work together. Because of the complexity of governing a number of issues specifically relating to the extent of the food security challenge, a designated working group was convened, including different representatives or budget holders, to collectively address issues specific to wellness, education, social cohesion, sustainable communities, poverty reduction, and rural development. The group was referred to as the "Food and Society Working Group". Other groups were also convened to focus on other specific mandates. While group participants passionately presented their work, actions remained locked in silos. Despite the participants' best intentions, opportunities for integration and transversal systemic change were not realized.

> If you are not a budget holder and able to make decisions in such a forum, you cannot commit to anything and as a result, you talk and tell people what you are doing, but you cannot act in a strategic manner.
>
> (Respondent 4, Policy, 2020)

As a result, the Food and Society Working Group approached the strategic policy unit within the Department of the Premier, to seek ways to facilitate the development of a more strategic response to a number of key issues identified through the working group's deliberations. One of these issues was food and nutrition security. This formal request meant that the Department of the Premier had a formal mandate to initiate such work (see Figure 10.2).

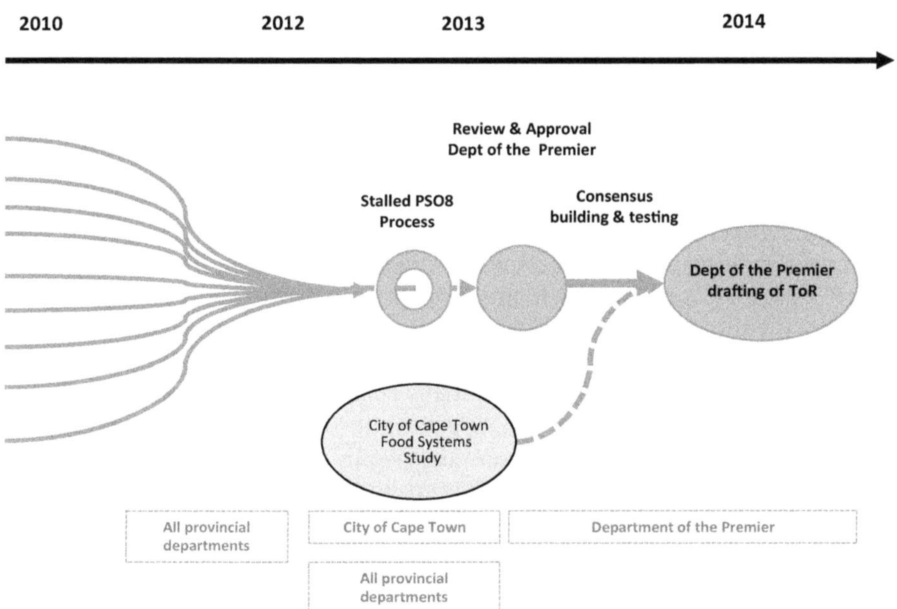

Figure 10.2 Initial activities associated with the stalled Provincial Strategic Outcomes (PSO) processes.

The PSO processes saw the Provincial Premier articulating a number of provincial strategic objectives: rural development and food security formed part of the third objective, PSO3.

With this formal mandate, key policy staff within the Department of the Premier were able to start formulating an approach, one that they knew was beyond their specific skillset. At the same time, a parallel process was underway in the City of Cape Town, which had commissioned a report on the city's food system and food security (Battersby et al., 2014). This process was co-funded by the City of Cape Town and the Provincial Department of Agriculture. The City of Cape Town's work, while ultimately not formally implemented in the city, provided fertile ground for reflection on food and nutrition systems. The effective co-ownership of this project meant that provincial departments had access to the suggestions in the report. Moreover, the City of Cape Town process made evident that responding to food insecurity was a "moving target" that could never be pinned down with traditional policy approaches. Food and nutrition security exemplified the concept of a "wicked challenge" (Lazarus, 2008; Rittel & Webber, 1973) in very clear and unambiguous ways. This meant that traditional policy processes were ill-equipped to effectively respond to the "wickedness" of the food and nutrition challenge. A different policy approach was required.

10.5.2 Initiating the Western Cape food and nutrition security strategic framework

The methodology adopted to develop Nourish to Flourish was consultative: many voices were encouraged across the wider food system. The drafters of Nourish to Flourish initiated processes that started with the identification and inclusion of different food system voices, from producers to informal vendors, formal food retailers, and activists working in the regional food environment. The processes of creating multiple spaces and moments for engagement, drawing out many diverse voices, filtering these without abstraction, and arriving at a coherent and robust policy document took time but developed in a slow and iterative manner.

A precondition of this process was the inclusion of as many voices as possible (R5, 2020). Care was taken to break down a number of challenging concepts and ideas without the process becoming patronizing or diluted. Developmental and facilitation techniques, such as using breakout groups, flipping knowledge hierarchies,[2] and facilitating equitable engagement processes were used to curate attendees' engagement and to get all participants to have their say, to take a vote and to arrive at a position that would ensure that the conversation could move forward, rather than circling around deadlock issues. This approach was not without its challenges. Unresolved dissonance remained. In the contested space that is food, opposing positions persisted. For example, some actors, specifically private sector participants, foregrounded economic development imperatives, or the market, as a means to enable greater access to food—following more traditional liberal economic approaches—based on the assumption of greater trickle down benefits, while others held more developmental and distributive positions. Some participants highlighted the ecological foundations necessary for a sustainable food system. Furthermore, issues linked to food but separate from it (such as land reform and water rights) were frequently conflated with the food issue by a number of attendees, particularly those without land tenure or working in the informal sector. Mediating these conflicting rationalities (Watson, 2003) made this process all the more complex. Central to both the Urbal approach and the goals of Nourish to Flourish was the drive to address the range of sustainability issues and focus areas without prioritizing one constituency's needs over those of another.

> An overarching philosophy behind the drafting process was a desire to not only arrive at a policy or strategy document, but to use the drafting process to build a community around what we ultimately wanted to implement.
>
> (Respondent 2, Innovator, 2020)

Aligning with the mandates of the provincial government and preventing a proverbial shopping basket of mismatched and unmandated ideas was a process that needed to be managed. A central facilitation function consisted in ensuring that the ideas and solutions proposed fell within the mandate of the provincial government rather than municipal or national government (Adelle et al., 2020). The policy drafting process remained largely participatory, with the consultants drafting the key document but with constant iterative feedback being sought through the Department of the Premier. Care was taken to focus on positive actions and research that already existed, rather than re-doing the same work (R2, 2020). The close collaboration with the policy team meant that both the wording and the content of the policy document were aligned to political priorities (Adelle et al., 2020).

The provincial authorities played an important strategic role. As the drafting process evolved, they were mobilized for feedback, consultations, awareness raising, and consensus building. These processes were led by the key innovators from the Department of the Premier. The Department of the Premier is a specific government department which plays a coordinating and convening role. While the Premier might be from a particular political party, this department is not aligned with their party affiliation. It is a bureaucratic department and not a political one. One of the key roles of the department is to develop such processes to embed change. The Nourish to Flourish strategy falling within this department's remit was essential, given its role in bridging mandates and organizational siloes. Of critical importance, this process also served to both keep various provincial officials informed of the processes and, in doing so, de-politicized the process. This may seem obvious, but it was essential to engaging in a transversal policy (or strategic framework) development process in a field like food and nutrition. Such an approach necessitated a far more subtle and consultative process that started with building awareness of how the system functioned (and of the fact that it concerned more than just agriculture, as the food system intersects with other systems—and political mandates).

This process was also of an inductive nature. Areas of possible resistance were identified by the convenors of the process within the Department of the Premier, through the consensus building process. During these consultations, when resistance or concerns were raised, these were investigated by the drafting team, the proposed framework responses were re-formulated, and strategies were then deployed, reflecting the integration of the concerns. In so doing, understanding and consensus were built. These inductive processes worked across scales and hierarchies within the regional governance structures. This iterative but carefully curated process is deemed to have been equally as important to the overall outcome of the innovation as the final Nourish to Flourish strategy.

While time will be the judge, a particularly interesting fact that emerged during the final process of public consultation on the finalized framework was that very little feedback or comments had been received from the public. When the research team enquired about this with relevant stakeholders, it was advised that given how broad and encompassing the consultation process had been, and how the outputs from those processes had been effectively captured, there was little need for comments and feedback (R2, 2020).

This led to a second stage of the innovation, upholding the same philosophy of broad consultation and listening. An important aspect of the innovation was the fact that while certain key areas of focus were identified and operational plans were developed in accordance with these needs, other areas of concern that were identified did not have clear operational hierarchies or champions and therefore, while important, were not actively pursued.

Building on the consultative processes that preceded the drafting of Nourish to Flourish, specialist facilitators were asked to convene key thematic groups in order to formulate actionable projects to test the viability and limitations of Nourish to Flourish. Although this preceded the Urbal process, it already aligned with a number of the features of Urbal, specifically in this case innovation and collaboration as well as wider stakeholder engagement. The second stage of the innovation brought together over 120 key individuals from different spheres of government, civil society and the private sector as well as other actors to:

- Establish specific areas of cross-sectoral collaboration (social innovation) on specific food security projects within the province
- Identify a clear way forward to continue developing collaboration and partnerships
- Elicit high-level feedback from provincial officials and other societal actors
- Secure the political support of various provincial departments as well as others with influence in the food system.

(SAFL, 2017a; R1; R3, 2020)

Through this consultation process, drawing on concepts and needs identified in the earlier stakeholder processes, initial key intervention areas were identified.

These processes brought together diverse and influential stakeholders with interest in and knowledge of the regional food system. It also aimed to creatively inspire change in how the Province, as well as other food system governance spheres, could address complex challenges pertaining to food and nutrition security. A further task was to conceptualize approaches in a way that would secure operational and political support from a wider pool of actors in the food system.

The reflection that took place as part of this process led to the formulation of six project ideas that were presented to a group of political stakeholders, who endorsed a process to take these projects to the design stage (SAFL, 2017b)[3]:

1) Securing wider consensus and political buy-in for the sale of nutritious food on informal markets
2) Early Childhood Development (ECD) support services in the Western Cape
3) Piloting a local smallholder farmer-focused agri-hub
4) The potential of school food gardens as community hubs
5) Promoting breastfeeding through workplace interventions
6) Realizing the social and economic potential of food waste in WCP

These projects were initiated with varying levels of success, but the process demonstrated the importance of Nourish to Flourish in a number of ways. It brought different groups together and served as a platform for further innovation around food and nutrition security. The process also involved other actors in these processes, including non-governmental specialists, activists and researchers, many of whom did not naturally embrace a food and nutrition security focus. This second phase led to a further process of internal governance alignment, ensuring the necessary authorization environment and the formulation of options for the eventual implementation (with associated governance) of the Nourish to Flourish strategy (see Figure 10.3).

The COVID-19 pandemic impacted the roll-out and finalization of the strategy. COVID-19 however, also demonstrated in shocking and visceral ways how important it is for the provincial government to pay far greater attention to food system issues.

In mid-2020, measures were taken to finalize Nourish to Flourish and for its implementation to be handed over to the overarching food system governance custodian in the Western Cape, the Provincial Department of Agriculture. However, as a result of these preliminary consultative and consensus-building processes, it was agreed that the wider programmatic development processes would be co-led by the Department of the Premier and the Department of Agriculture. The structure that emerged to drive the implementation of the Nourish to Flourish strategy was the multi-department Western Cape Provincial Food Systems Working Group.

As the work of Nourish to Flourish evolved, other aligned processes were taking shape, with their own governance and leadership processes. These were

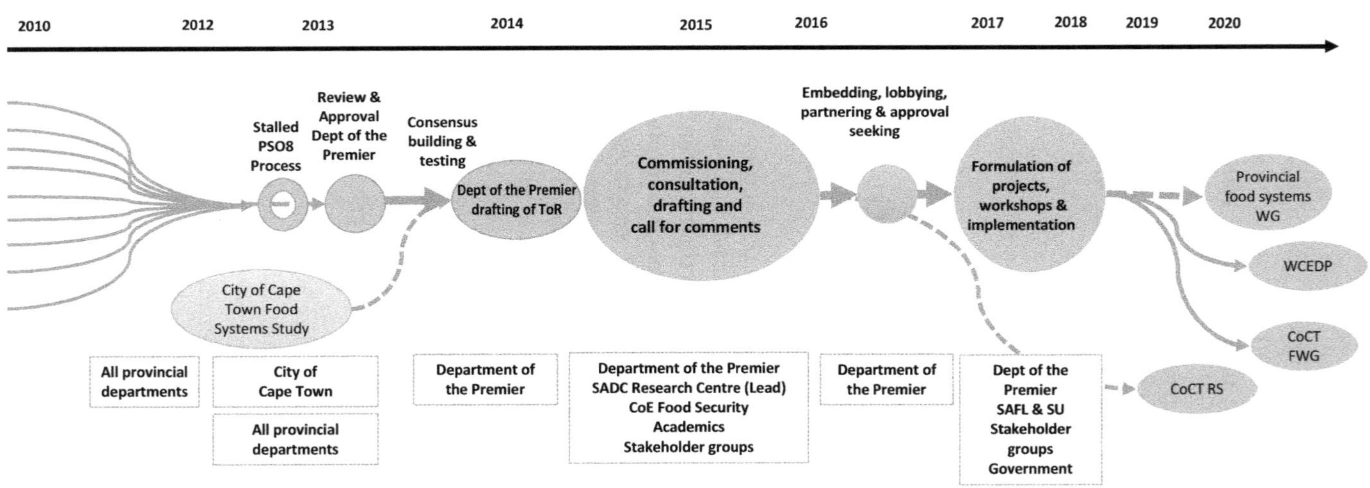

Figure 10.3 Evolution of the Nourish to Flourish process and other outcomes that emerged.

PSO	Provincial Strategic Objective
ToR	Terms of Reference
SADC	South African Development Centre
CoE	Centre of Excellence
WG	Working Group
WCEDP	Western Cape Economic Development Partnership
CoCT	City of Cape Town
CoCT FWG	Food Working Group
CoCT RS	Resilience Strategy

playing out in different sectors—State and civil society, mostly at the city scale. All were building on one another, feeding off and mutually supporting one another. Understanding these emergent processes and their links to the Nourish to Flourish strategy offers fascinating insights. These emergent actions were later catapulted into action as a result of COVID-19.

10.6 Aligned innovations and policy processes

As noted earlier, at the time when the initial conceptual ideas for Nourish to Flourish were being developed in 2013, the City of Cape Town had commissioned a city-wide food system and food security study. For reasons beyond the scope of this chapter, once completed, the city-scale food strategy did not gain the traction anticipated and was caught in a political process that resulted in city officials being directed not to participate in deliberate urban food processes (Olver, 2019). This point alone makes Nourish to Flourish an important innovation for three reasons. First, food and nutrition security retained an important place in aligned stakeholder engagement processes. Second, the active networks that had been brought together to draft the Cape Town study remained active. Finally, city officials who appreciated the importance of a more systemic food and nutrition approach were able to engage in the Nourish to Flourish processes without running the risk of overstepping their "mandate". However, over time and as the importance of urban food security and food systems emerged in connection with food-related issues such as the Western Cape drought (Faragher & Carden, 2023),[4] outbreaks of xenophobic violence (Scalabrini Centre, 2018), trucking strikes (WCG, 2019), and a listeriosis outbreak (Smith et al., 2019),[5] to name but a few, it was deemed essential that food be a key component in the City of Cape Town Resilience Strategy (CoCT, 2019). This process saw food re-emerging as an area of focus led by the City Resilience Department. It is important to note that the processes and concepts that were initiated as part of the Western Cape Household Food and Nutrition Security Strategy provided an important backdrop or foundation for the inclusion of food in the transversal governance processes of the City of Cape Town.

We should also point out that the Centre of Excellence in Food Security (CoEFS), co-led by the University of Pretoria and the University of the Western Cape, convened the initial team of consultants, from the SADC Research Centre, who drove the consultation processes and ultimately drafted the initial Nourish to Flourish document. The inclusion of the Centre of Excellence in Food Security was important, as it was independent from the government but had legitimacy in the eyes of the State because as a Centre of Excellence it was funded through the National Department of Science and Technology/National Research Foundation. At the time of drafting Nourish to Flourish, the CoEFS was itself developing its operational and research strategies. As this was one of the Centre's first active research projects, the processes associated with the development of the Nourish to Flourish strategy were key to informing the development of processes that the CoEFS has maintained, such as the collaborative consultation forum, the Community of Practice which emerged out of the wider network convened to support the development of Nourish to Flourish, or research activities linked to key aims of the strategy but driven by the CoEFS. These include work on nutrition, local government food mandates, food-sensitive planning, and food charters, to name but a few activities (De Visser, 2019; Even-Zahav et al., 2020; Haysom et al., 2020).[6]

Building on the initial conceptual ideas presented in earlier drafts of the Nourish to Flourish strategy, the Centre of Excellence in Food Security initiated the Western Cape Food Systems Community of Practice (WCCoP) on Food Systems Governance. A Community of Practice is a group of people who share a common interest or concern and who deepen their knowledge and expertise in this area by interacting on an ongoing basis (Wenger et al., 2002). The concept of a CoP involves a collective of competing "experts" and the organizations and institutions through which they bring their knowledge and experience into the deliberative spaces that constitute the CoP while also providing a space for "jostling publics" (Nowotny, 2003). The Western Cape Food Systems CoP is precisely that: a group that seeks to bring diverse voices and political views into a space that enables collective conversation, discourse, dialogue, and debate. Consensus is not the aim of the WCCoP. Rather, the aim is to conscientize a wide variety of food system actors on the positionality, politics, and needs of other food system actors. Through the initiatives associated with the development of the Nourish to Flourish strategy, the WCCoP also deepened actors' knowledge and supported Nourish to Flourish through the commissioning of research to align with and further develop concepts that emerged over the course of the Nourish to Flourish processes. Moreover, the curation of the WCCoP enabled officials from different spheres of government, different governmental silos that intersected with food (but might not have had an explicit food mandate), to engage in a "safe space". The concept of the WCCoP meant that participants were present in their personal capacity, not representing departments. This gave the City of Cape Town and a diverse group of Provincial officials the freedom to participate and build knowledge about regional food system processes "without working on food". Inputs, conversations, and tensions that arose through the WCCoP and its processes further fed into ongoing emergent regional food and nutrition system discussions.

COVID-19 resulted in renewed food system-related action, and the crisis prompted the formation of a City of Cape Town Food Systems Working Group. This group convenes multiple stakeholders from across the City food system, but with a specific focus on food and nutrition system processes that have a direct bearing on the roles and responsibilities of the City of Cape Town. Beyond this stakeholder working group, the City's Resilience Strategy team has identified a number of City of Cape Town food system areas and actors, building a valuable resource aligned with the Resilience Strategy but with wider relevance. Through the development of this working group, the Nourish to Flourish authors/custodians have offered direct inputs and proactively sought to align actions.

A further outcome of COVID-19 emerged as a product of the massive societal response to the dire food security situation brought on by both the lockdowns initiated in April 2020 and the drastic loss of livelihoods as a result of the economy shrinking due to COVID-19. In order to ensure effective coordination of the relief effort across the city and wider provincial areas, the Western Cape Economic Development Partnership (WCEDP) was asked to act as a coordinator and organize a variety of food system processes to facilitate the necessary support. While the initial work focused on direct support, as COVID-19 continued and as lockdown restrictions were lifted, the work of the WCEDP shifted from immediate relief responses to strategic planning and programmatic alignment. Through this process, the Western Cape Food Forum was established, bringing together a wide variety of actors, from individual actors to faith-based organizations, Community Action Networks, etc. A central part of the longer-term strategic planning of this work involves drawing on the Nourish to Flourish framings.

These different innovations and food system actions are detailed in Table 10.2, which outlines parameters including the scale of action, the food systems focus, the key actors, whether or not the processes were open to all or invitation-based, and the mandate of the group.

The custodians of Nourish to Flourish do not claim direct links to these actions nor alignment with their causes. However, given the development of various processes associated with these emerging structures, for the casual observer there is a clear trend, towards an iterative set of separate but affiliated processes that are building, aligning (albeit within their mandates) and deepening the food system governance processes within the province. While direct causality between the development of Nourish to Flourish and that of other projects and programmes should not be overstated, the relationship and mutual alignment between them all is clear. This is a further dimension of the innovation, one that is hard to quantify but distinctly observable. What can be quantified is the active interaction between the different processes, with information sharing and collaboration growing and building alignment across all processes.

10.7 The Urbal approach as a tool to support emergent processes

An unexpected outcome of the Urbal consultations with key informants associated with the Nourish to Flourish journey was that the respondents were able to see their work as connected, and contingent on a collection of processes, including Nourish to Flourish. In addition to this, the iterative Urbal approach, premised on inquiry, follow up, and wider group feedback, served to bring together groups whose initial work, aligned with but separate from Nourish to Flourish, had progressed significantly further since the start of the Nourish to Flourish process. As a result, through the presentation of findings from the Urbal inquiries, food system actors developed new connections between their work, Nourish to Flourish and other food projects, thereby deepening food system action in the region.

Table 10.2 Aligned innovations and policy processes—Western Cape

Action	*Western Cape food and society working group*	*Western Cape Community of Practice*	*City of Cape Town resilience strategy*	*City of Cape Town food systems working group*	*Western Cape food forum*	*Western Cape food and nutrition working group*
Year of Action	2009–2014	2017–ongoing	2019	2020–ongoing	2020–ongoing	2020–ongoing
Scale of Action	Western Cape Province	Western Cape Province	City Of Cape Town	City Of Cape Town	Western Cape Province	Western Cape Province
Food System Focus	Food and nutrition security – mostly production (food) and education (nutrition)	Food system democracy and voice, inclusion and processes to address "wicked problems"	Wider resilience, and resilience strategies with a specific food focus	Urban system and wider flows into the Cape Town system that arise from food but also flows that impact food system outcomes on a city scale	Initial (and maintained) coordination of food system-related crises and responses, but evolving to adopt systemic food system actions	Food and nutrition in connection with Nourish to Flourish goals
Open or by invitation	For officials only	Open but processes can be exclusionary as a result of how and where they are enacted	Internal CoCT process	Open but wider events and processes are invitation-based. The purpose is knowledge building, not debate.	Open but voices that are amplified are those active in the food relief space and those focusing on the transition to systemic change	For officials only
Actors/ voices	Government officials	All actors, but academics and officials from all sphere of government play an active role.	Local government officials	City officials and aligned provincial and para-statal agencies with academics	All actors are active but the forum is closely led by WCEDP	Government officials
Mandate	Societal wellness	Dialogue and knowledge sharing, pluralistic	Resilience and longer-term planning	Knowledge generation and dialogue	Food system failure response coordination and food system change	Food and nutrition security

When the Nourish to Flourish process entered its final stage, setting out to build the Western Cape Food and Nutrition Working Group, the Urbal researchers were asked to join the Working Group as independent specialists. Not only were the voices of the Urbal researchers included in the process, but the figures and tables derived from the methodology were key tools used to build consensus, to shift away from overly simplistic views, and to demonstrate the long-term evolution of the process.

Furthermore, the methodological tools designed in order to report on the Urbal process were used directly by key actors of the region's food system in their consultations, to demonstrate the different processes and project focus areas. The Urbal tools were specifically useful in demonstrating how the different components of the project aligned, as illustrated in Figure 10.4. Figure 10.5 was also useful, as it captured the iterative processes associated with the development of Nourish to Flourish and the outcomes.

Beyond the value of these tools, an additional benefit emerged, one that perhaps added even more weight to the importance of the Urbal processes and aligned methodologies. Limited budgets and the previously mentioned mandate disputes all make for a particularly fraught and contested policy and strategy development landscape. The work of the Nourish to Flourish strategy was not immune to these issues. Leadership changes, diverging views about who is responsible for food and nutrition, and importantly budget allocations all meant that achieving acceptance of a specific strategy remained challenging. As a result of initial consultations, and later review processes, the Nourish to Flourish authors presented the Urbal review to the emerging Provincial Food Systems Working Group as an external and independent review. The Urbal researchers were asked to draft a summary version of the Urbal Project Assessment Report that further supported the Nourish to Flourish consultation processes. The Urbal approach and methodological process again proved to support the needs for strategy refinement and transition from conceptual process to implementation.

In addition to the utility that Urbal offered for the Nourish to Flourish strategy, groups such as the City of Cape Town Food Working Group, the WCCoP, and the Western Cape Food Forum all used the Urbal report both as an internal working document and to support their own processes to refine their analysis and further develop their mandate.

10.8 Conclusion

The Urbal approach sought to map the impact of the Nourish to Flourish innovation and capture the emergent impact pathways. The Urbal process offered great utility, both as an analytical tool in and of itself, and through the use of the outputs and outcomes of the methodology by research participants to give the work an after-life.

The importance of Nourish to Flourish is significant in that drastic but innovative measures are required to address the stubborn negative (and unsustainable)

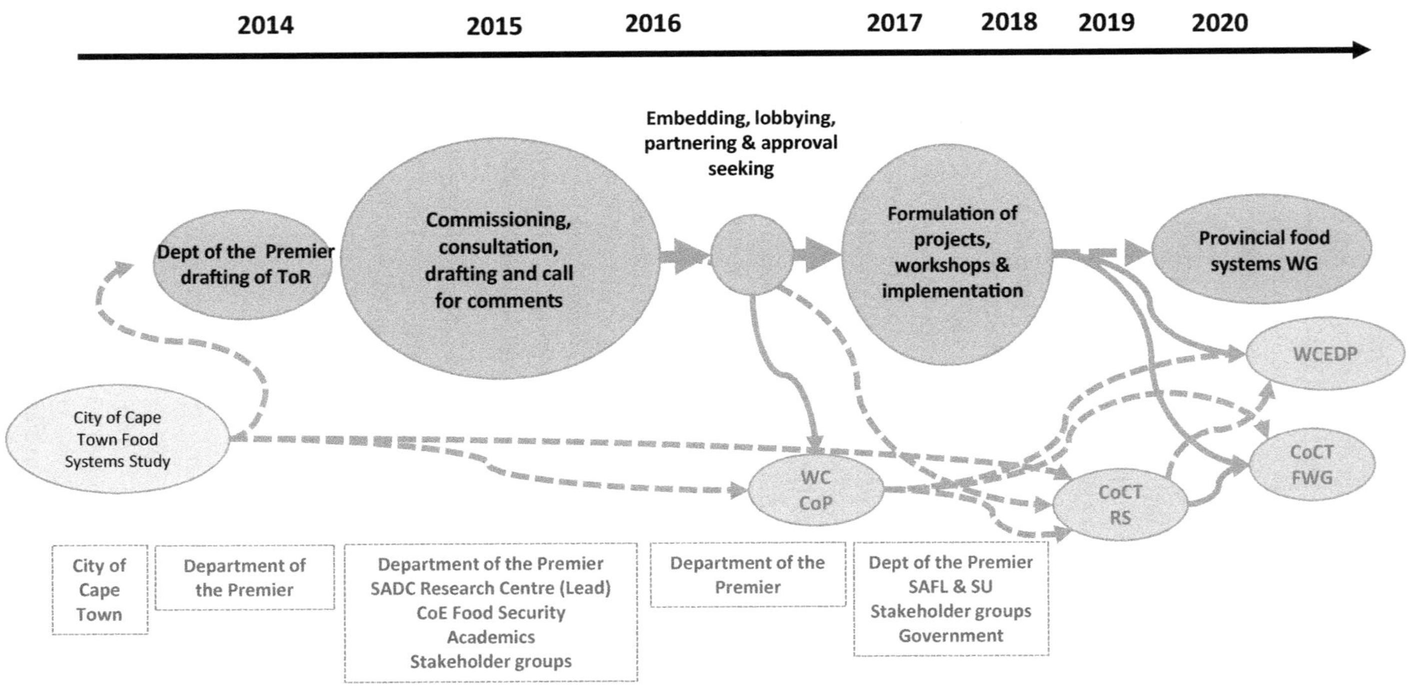

Figure 10.4 Diagram informed by Figure 10.3. Aligned emergent processes and flows are evident.

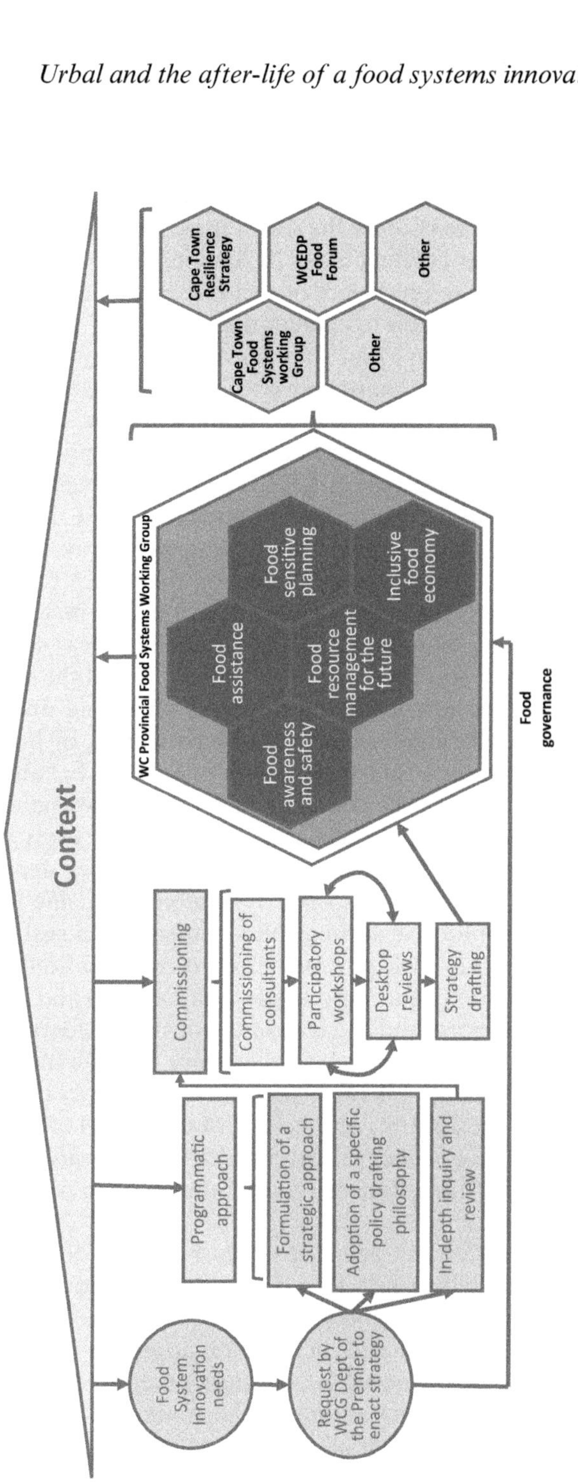

Figure 10.5 Representation of the evolution of the Nourish to Flourish process, drawn from the Urbal process.

(adapted from Urbal (n.d., p. 11))

food system outcomes of the Western Cape (and South Africa), evident in the high levels of stunting, high levels of food insecurity, and rise in diet-related non-communicable diseases observed. Existing policy frameworks and delegated authority have been unable to counter the rise in these negative food system outcomes. In addition to longer-running issues of food insecurity, South Africa has experienced a rapid rise in the prevalence of diet-related non-communicable diseases, with policy seemingly unable to counter this surge.

The impact of the Nourish to Flourish process is still to be tested fully. However, it could be argued that the teams convened through the process described above indirectly served as an important foundation for the convening of an array of food system actors who proactively engaged in the process to respond to the food system-related outcomes of COVID-19 and the associated hunger. New work is emerging, and the Nourish to Flourish plans are now being operationalized through explicit site-level activities. This new work has been made easier as a result of the conversations and reflection enabled by the Urbal activities, and the value of the Urbal approach for describing an innovation and its subsequent processes. The Nourish to Flourish document was seen as important, and a small group of food system actors rallied around the strategy.

COVID-19 saw further actors seeking to get involved and understand the multiple connections, made highly evident by the pandemic, of both food and non-food issues to governance and sustainability issues. Urbal and the methodologies used served to make the connections between governance and food security far clearer, and the reports generated became key tools used by the curators of Nourish to Flourish when trying to lobby other departments to join the process. The Urbal work also clearly demonstrated the intersections between the Nourish to Flourish strategy and elements of a sustainable food system. The Nourish to Flourish process helped draw attention to the interconnections between food systems (and their sustainability) and food security outcomes. Subsequent reports and engagement with stakeholders helped make this evident. Thinking about food security has since become more integrated into systemic ways of thinking. Likewise, there have been shifts in the way food security is understood, specifically with the High Level Panel of Experts' articulation of the six pillars of food security, which include sustainability and agency (Clapp et al., 2022), two dimensions that the Nourish to Flourish innovation sought to amplify.

The evolution of the Western Cape Household Food and Nutrition Security Strategic Framework (or Nourish to Flourish) from a stalled provincial working group unable to formulate a cohesive inter-departmental response to becoming a strategic framework and, beyond, an approach and a philosophy that has served as a reference point for multiple other emergent sustainable food system actions, is something unique in the context of both the Western Cape and South Africa. Innovation often requires new thinking, specific politics, and even courage to break away from convention and take the risk of developing a policy that is constantly evolving, one that is carefully curated and must navigate policy and stakeholder approval processes. This requires a thorough understanding of the trajectory that any policy document must follow, from conceptualization to approval and later implementation.

Three broad overarching factors underpinned the Nourish to Flourish innovation. Each was central to the success of the process and was mentioned in different ways by each of the interviewees consulted. These factors are all aligned and intertwined but are mentioned here as separate components for clarity.

First, the overarching philosophical approach to Nourish to Flourish was informed by the view that system-level change, specifically "change needed to embed sustainability and related material shifts in policy, requires a far longer innovation process, one that builds both institutional muscle and political consciousness across scales and spheres of government" (R2, 2020). The importance of this was amplified by the fact that "the state has such blunt and limited levers in food systems interventions" (R2, 2020). This required a process that was deeply inclusive, spanning a diverse range of actors and interest groups (R1, R3, 2020). Engagement with these groups needed to be honest and respectful (R5, 2020). The whole-of-society philosophy meant that every stakeholder had key insights on the process and these insights needed to be taken into account.

The second factor lay in the interplay between provincial management and leadership operated by those developing the Nourish to Flourish Strategy, the custodians of the process in the Department of the Premier. The Nourish to Flourish authors were very careful to ensure that senior management in the Department of the Premier and in other departments contributed to allowing the development of the strategy, ensuring that the necessary authorizing environment was maintained at all times (through lessons learnt from the Problem Driven Iterative Adaptation approach (R1, 2020)). This approach, linked to the overarching philosophical approach, meant that "processes were iterative, responding to the ever changing nature of a complex system, embracing the complexity, rather than trying to contain this" (R5, 2020).

Finally, both the underpinning philosophical approach and the management of the process unfolded within an environment of deep trust (R1, R3, R5, 2020), but also provided the environment for wider food system learning and alignment with other processes.

As mentioned earlier, while this innovation was implemented at the provincial scale, other actions both supported and drew on the Nourish to Flourish process. It is worth reiterating here that the City of Cape Town had also initiated a city-scale food system review which, for various reasons, was not operationalized. This City of Cape Town project heavily informed the initial development of the terms of reference of the Nourish to Flourish process. Importantly, when the political landscape of the city changed, a food systems focus was included in the City's Resilience Strategy. As both the Resilience Strategy and Nourish to Flourish evolved, the "curators" of both strategies collaborated, even if informally, to deepen and at times align processes, rejecting notions of governance turf and mandate-ism. This cross-scale collaboration and mutual cooperation was made evident by the Urbal process.

This innovation was a governance approach, but one that went well beyond traditional managerial notions of governance. The levels of trust involved, together with the ability to sit in the "disquiet of process", meant that the tensions between the different components and actors of a sustainable food system were able to find a voice, a certain alignment, and most importantly a place in the wider food system innovation space.

Importantly, two additional factors were observed through this inquiry. First, the Nourish to Flourish work, as well as the City of Cape Town food systems work, commenced well before COVID-19 struck. The impact of COVID-19 on food system outcomes is well documented. However, both the Province and City processes had built networks of food system actors that were known. The engagement with stakeholders had built trust and agency between partners and different actors felt free to speak and present their views. When the COVID-19-related food systems challenges became apparent, the pre-existing networks, built through these processes, were vital in activating appropriate responses to these challenges. The value of these networks cannot be overstated.

Second, various different food system researchers had been active in researching and understanding the urban and provincial food systems for a number of years. Equally, policy actors had been navigating food system actions, at times in subtle ways and in other instances more overtly, through the complex and sometimes politically fraught political and bureaucratic structures of government. Both groups of actors played a "long game". While there is always urgency in food system change actions, the importance of a slow but steady process of quiet engagement that builds while waiting for the appropriate implementation moment is a further key learning. Key policymakers' and food systems researchers' leadership role over an extended period of time was central to this process.

As a methodology, the Urbal process provided a unique tool to capture these processes and was of great value to the innovators themselves, both as an external validation of their novel and arguably high-risk work, and as part of their working processes, to support their lobbying and consensus building, supporting the constant work of maintaining the authorizing environment.

The Urbal process of documenting, but not assessing or judging, offered a particularly powerful tool to capture unique processes, to allow innovators to expose themselves and their work without the risk of critique, and to co-produce an assessment of the innovation. In the contested and at times highly politicized fields of governance and food systems politics, the Urbal process enabled a robust but open assessment of the innovation. Documenting sustainable food systems is essential if others are to be able to replicate these systems and the work of food system innovators. If this process can both document and deepen innovation processes, it is of critical importance.

Notes

1 See: https://www.westerncape.gov.za/food
2 In many instances knowledge holders, such as academics, are given primacy of place in such engagements. The detailed knowledge of food system actors is often granted less importance and can even be disregarded due to the racial, gendered and other hierarchies that remain present in South African society. This work sought to champion knowledge holders who had not always been given the same platform as traditional knowledge holders, thus flipping power and voice roles.
3 Links to these projects are listed here: https://www.southernafricafoodlab.org/western-cape-incubator-lab/
4 See: https://en.wikipedia.org/wiki/Cape_Town_water_crisis
5 See: https://en.wikipedia.org/wiki/2017–2018_South_African_listeriosis_outbreak
6 See: https://foodsecurity.ac.za/wp-content/uploads/2020/10/FINAL_CoEFS-Working Paper_007FoodSensitivePlanning_29Oct.pdf; https://foodsecurity.ac.za/wp-content/uploads/2019/04/CoE-FS-WP5-Multilevel-Government-Municipalities-and-Food-Security-17-Apr-19.pdf; https://foodsecurity.ac.za/programmes/understanding-the-national-and-global-food-system-systems/

References

Adelle, C., Pereira, L., Görgens, T., & Losch, B. (2020). Making sense together: The role of scientists in the coproduction of knowledge for policy making. *Science and Public Policy*, *47*(1), 56–66. https://doi.org/10.1093/scipol/scz046

Battersby, J., Haysom, G., Tawodzera, G., McLachlan, M., and Crush, J. (2014). Food System and Food Security Study for the City of Cape Town. https://www.researchgate.net/publication/305496094_Food_System_and_Food_Security_Study_for_the_City_of_Cape_Town#fullTextFileContent

City of Cape Town (CoCT). (2019). City of Cape Town Resilience Strategy. https://resource.capetown.gov.za/documentcentre/Documents/City%20strategies%2C%20plans%20and%20frameworks/Resilience_Strategy.pdf

Clapp, J., Moseley, W. G., Burlingame, B., & Termine, P. (2022). The case for a six-dimensional food security framework. *Food Policy*, *106*, 1–10. https://doi.org/10.1016/j.foodpol.2021.102164

De Visser, J. (2019). *Multilevel Government, Municipalities and Food Security*. Centre of Excellence in Food Security. https://foodsecurity.ac.za/wp-content/uploads/2019/04/CoE-FS-WP5-Multilevel-Government-Municipalities-and-Food-Security-17-Apr-19.pdf

Department of Environmental Affairs and Tourism. (2008). *National Framework for Sustainable Development in South Africa*. Department of Environmental Affairs and Tourism, Pretoria. https://www.dffe.gov.za/sites/default/files/docs/2008nationalframeworkfor_sustainabledevelopment.pdf

Durno, D. (2020). Interview: Darryn Durno, SADC Research Centre, Green Point, Cape Town, 21 February 2020.

Even-Zahav, E., Drimie, S. & Haysom, G. (2020). *A Food Charter for the Western Cape? A Critical Inquiry and Scoping Study*. Centre of Excellence in Food Security. https://foodsecurity.ac.za/wp-content/uploads/2020/10/Final_006FoodCharter.pdf

Faragher, T. and Carden, K. (2023). Groundwater governance for improving city water resilience in Cape Town, South Africa, *Frontiers in Sustainable Cities*, *5*. https://www.frontiersin.org/articles/10.3389/frsc.2023.1062661/full

Haysom, G., Battersby, J., & Park-Ross, R. (2020). *Food Sensitive Planning and Urban Design – A Blueprint for a Future South African City?* Centre of Excellence in Food Security. https://foodsecurity.ac.za/wp-content/uploads/2020/10/FINAL_CoEFS-WorkingPaper_007FoodSensitivePlanning_29Oct.pdf

Lazarus, R. J. (2008). Super wicked problems and climate change: Restraining the present to liberate the future. *Cornell Law Review*, *94*(5), 1153. https://scholarship.law.georgetown.edu/facpub/159/

Nowotny, H. (2003). Democratising expertise and socially robust knowledge. *Science and Public Policy*, *30*(3), 151–156. https://doi.org/10.3152/147154303781780461

Olver, C. (2019). *A house divided: Battle for the mother city*. Jonathan Ball Publishers.

Provincial Government of the Western Cape (WCG). (2015). *Department of Social Development Strategic Plan 2015–2020*. https://www.westerncape.gov.za/assets/departments/social-development/strategic_plan_2015-20.pdf

Provincial Government of the Western Cape (WCG). (2016). *Western Cape Government Household Food and Nutrition Security Strategic Framework*, September 2016, Draft approved by Cabinet for public comment. Cape Town.

Provincial Government of the Western Cape (WCG). (2019). Minister Madikizela condemns truck drivers' strike action. https://www.westerncape.gov.za/news/minister-madikizela-condemns-truck-drivers-strike-action

Republic of South Africa (RSA). (1996). *Constitution of the Republic of South Africa*, Number 108 of 1996. www.info.gov.za/documents/constitution/1996/a108-96.pdf

Rittel, H. W., & Webber, M. M. (1973). Dilemmas in a general theory of planning. *Policy Sciences*, *4*(2), 155–169. https://doi.org/10.1007/BF01405730

Scalabrini Centre. (2018). *Written submission to the South African Human Rights Commission for the National Hearing on Social Cohesion and Xenophobia South Africa*. https://scalabrini.org.za/wp-content/uploads/2019/05/Scalabrini-Centre-of-Cape-Town-South-African-Human-Rights-Commission-National-Panel-submission-2018.pdf

Smith, A. M., Tau, N. P., Smouse, S. L., Allam, M., Ismail, A., Ramalwa, N. R., … Thomas, J. (2019). Outbreak of Listeria monocytogenes in South Africa, 2017–2018: Laboratory activities and experiences associated with whole-genome sequencing analysis of isolates. *Foodborne Pathogens and Disease*, *16*(7), 524–530.

Southern Africa Food Lab (SAFL). (2017a). *Workshop Report: Designing a smallholder farmer-focused agri-hub*. https://www.southernafricafoodlab.org/wp-content/uploads/2017/03/Report_WCSmallholderFarmerHub.pdf

Southern African FoodLab (SAFL). (2017b). *Western Cape Government Food and Nutrition Design Lab Proposal*, submitted by the Southern African FoodLab (SAFL) of the University of Stellenbosch—Implementation period: February 2017–March 2017

Statistics South Africa. (2013). *Statistics South Africa General household survey 2013*. Statistics South Africa, Pretoria. https://www.statssa.gov.za/publications/P0318/P031 82013.pdf

URBAL. (n.d.). *Urban-Driven Innovations for Sustainable Food Systems, Methodology guide - draft V7*. www.urbalfood.org

Watson, V. (2003). Conflicting rationalities: Implications for planning theory and ethics. *Planning Theory & Practice*, *4*(4), 395–407. DOI: 10.1080/1464935032000146318.

Wenger, E., McDermott, R. A., & Snyder, W. (2002). *Cultivating communities of practice: A guide to managing knowledge*. Harvard business press.

11 Using Urbal to develop metrics for evaluation

Beatrice Intoppa and Élodie Valette

11.1 Introduction

This chapter focuses on the challenges that innovations face in structuring their project assessment in line with food system sustainability (FSS) regulatory frameworks at different scales. It argues that the Urbal approach (see Chapter 1) can be used as a preliminary step in the process of identifying and implementing indicators in a project's food sustainability assessment. Indicators produce relevant knowledge for both internal and external actors, enable knowledge transfer, and facilitate sharing the results of assessments guided by local and global FSS recommendations. Urbal can help frame the choice of indicators by prioritizing key factors that support or hinder the achievement of sustainability and by taking into account the context-dependent, place-based, subjective ranking of priorities. Furthermore, it can facilitate the interpretation of an innovation's contribution to sustainability according to multi-scale benchmarks, through the co-design of metrics drawing on local and global recommendations for FSS.

11.2 Developing meaningful indicators to assess the impact of innovations on food system sustainability

11.2.1 On the use of indicators: How to evaluate the systemic complexity of sustainability with indicators

Quantification is considered the most objective and rigorous method for assessing any human practice, yet it is also highly contested. Since the 19th century, the statistical sciences have spread to the point of shaping today's social world, providing tools to express and coordinate human activities. While statistical indicators initially only measured natural science objects, they gained ground between the 1930s and the 1950s with the rise of national accounting systems, to evaluate economies' performance and social well-being (Desrosières, 2008), and ultimately evolved into standards of consistency and exhaustiveness, used as quantitative descriptors of any social topic.

DOI: 10.4324/9781003285441-11

Indicators, which are continuously refined and adapted to better consider real objects based on contemporary governments' socio-environmental targets, are likewise recognized as a tool to support intended transformations. Indicators can be described as "the quantification of social and ecological conditions and can be used to assess the historical and current state of affairs, and predict future trends" (Levkoe & Blay-Palmer, 2018, p. 51). Although research suggesting alternative evaluation methods are multiplying, indicators are still widely praised for their ability to summarize and condense the complexity of our dynamic environment into a manageable amount of meaningful information (Singh et al., 2012) that can support policy and management decision-making (Ramos, 2019).

There are however limitations inherent to quantification methods, namely surrounding the selection and use of indicators, especially in the field of sustainability assessment. Scholars have pointed to the inadequate quality or the unequal availability of data, and the loss of information in the aggregation process (Bell & Morse, 2013; Schader et al., 2014). In FSS assessments, for example, gaps can involve missing or insufficiently detailed data about gender, health and socioeconomic status, ethnicity, nutrition adequacy, sociocultural well-being, geospatial location, food environments, agroecological conditions, production patterns, eating and purchasing habits, or even awareness of sustainability practices (Deconinck et al., 2021). Moreover, the streamlining and standardization operated by indicators through what can be described as a mechanistic worldview "reduces complexity and embellishes certainty" (Reid & Rout, 2020, p. 2), overlooking part of the peculiarity of local contexts (Molle & Mollinga, 2003) as well as the systemic intricacies surrounding sustainability, such as hidden feedback mechanisms and trade-offs (Grace & Pope, 2015; Wiek & Binder, 2005).

Another main limitation of the use of indicators is the false assumption regarding the objectivity of metrics and indicators, underestimating their social and political dimension. Indicators only provide information about the issues that they have been designed to measure (Bell & Morse, 2013). Indicator development is not just a technical exercise, since deciding to evaluate an outcome influences the allocation of human and financial resources towards its accomplishment, at the expense of other potentially relevant outcomes (Carlsson et al., 2017). The issue thus lies with taking responsibility for the choice of indicators. Since indicators are effective tools for public decision-making processes, the selection of indicators should be fully understood as a political process, focusing on the potential of indicators' use and influence to impact policy decisions (Lehtonen et al., 2016). According to Kaur and Lodhia (2018), it is paramount that indicator development involves understanding the specific needs, competences, and sustainability vision of local communities and, more generally, that it take into account the end users' needs and expectations. Several scholars also support the conclusion that local users have a more nuanced understanding of the variability of natural phenomena compared to the often overly polarized approach of scientific assessment, which favours positive or negative results (Fraser et al., 2006; Thomas & Twyman, 2004).

In line with Shen et al. (2011), we argue that indicators should be designed or selected following a collective process to reach an agreement based on a shared understanding, and subsequent revisions informed by emerging needs and the experience gained in individual cases should be welcomed. This is key to the sustainable development approach: first, it creates value for the actors and empowers them, and second, involving stakeholders in the indicator development process can foster the utility, transparency, and longevity of the tools chosen for evaluation (Ramos, 2019).

11.2.2 The challenges faced in the choice of indicators for food system sustainability assessments

In the field of FSS specifically, indicators have also taken on a growing role in benchmarking and tracking FSS, along with priority increasingly being given to including food in cities' and regions' planning agendas (Blay-Palmer et al., 2019). In 2015, the United Nations' 2030 Agenda for Sustainable Development issued a set of 17 Sustainable Development Goals (SDG) to be achieved by 2030, implying the development of indicators able to measure progress towards sustainability. The process involves data collection from 193 countries and is based on a set of 244 indicators. At the local level, the Milan Urban Food Policy Pact (MUFPP), fully dedicated to developing sustainable food systems, was also signed in 2015 by more than 200 cities. This international agreement includes a monitoring framework to support the implementation of the SDGs at local level, listing 37 recommended actions, organized into 6 categories. For each recommended action, there are specific indicators to monitor progress in the implementation of the Pact. As of 2017, the MUFPP offers 44 indicators, with 4–10 indicators per category. Other sets of indicators have also been developed in sub-national and more local contexts (for more information, see Blay-Palmer et al., 2019).

These SDG or MUFPP recommendations represent desirable objectives to avoid uncontrollable consequences for ecological, socio-economic, or even food systems, and valuable aspirational guidelines to refocus institutions worldwide towards a common strategy. However, there is a lack of planning and regulatory instruments for cities (Blay-Palmer et al., 2019). Furthermore, each region requires approaches tailored to its specific local subsystems, and the values of the actors bringing about change need to be taken into account (Meadowcroft, 2010).

Indicators are indeed context-dependent, yet they often remain disconnected from the specificities of local contexts. Global initiatives can thus be misaligned with local specificities (Carlsson et al., 2017), as "localities may experience substantially different cause-and-effect dynamics between the ecological and social variables peculiar to each context" (Carlsson et al., 2017, p. 3), making it extremely complicated to match national and international exercises with local-level specificity (Moragues-Faus & Marceau, 2018, p. 5). This is particularly concerning, as this

> disconnect between the design and operationalization of global, regional, or national level measurement and analysis, and the requirements of local-level stakeholders attempting to respond to these challenges on a daily basis inhibits communities' ability… to engage in strategic action that supports both sustainable community development, and a global sustainable food system.
>
> (Carlsson et al., 2017, p. 3)

Thus, specific challenges surrounding the evaluation of food innovations' impact on FSS need to be addressed. These include the difficulty of interpreting the interactions between sustainability goals within the local context using indicators (Halla & Binder, 2020), and the need for consistency between sustainability targets at different scales. In fact, irrespective of the specific implementation instruments chosen, when looking at the situation on the ground at local level, the misalignment with the SDG framework is often obvious: urban innovations go further than these targets and develop concrete needs and knowledge which often have not yet been integrated into food policy strategies.

Moreover, in the field of food system assessment, indicators tend to be designed according to the dominant political economy of food and wielded by dominant actors. In 2016, the International Panel of Experts on Sustainable Food Systems (IPES-Food) warned that "current systems will be held in place insofar as these systems continue to be measured in terms of what industrial agriculture is designed to deliver, at the expense of many other outcomes that really matter in food systems" (IPES-Food, 2016, p. 57). IPES-Food also called for more coherent approaches to assessment, pointing to the importance of breaking down disciplinary silos in order to understand the interactions between FSS sub-sectors, and stressed the need for FSS assessment to be inclusive, multidimensional, reflective, and continuous (IPES-Food, 2015). Although recommendations have consistently called for reconceptualizing the sustainability assessment process, what is required is not just an accumulation of indicators (Grainger, 2012) but a sustainability reframing, starting afresh with a focus on local stakeholders' diverse range of specific needs and visions of sustainability (Brockwell, 2019). Many scholars and practitioners have thus called for a better understanding of both power dynamics in the assessment of food systems and local contexts in the definition and use of indicators (Levkoe & Blay-Palmer, 2018).

Furthermore, in order to map the effects of innovations pursued on sustainability transformations, local-level food policies need to overcome the predominant reliance on pre-existing data, with no prior deliberation on what data would be most relevant for ascertaining an innovation's actual contribution to sustainability.

Given the limited accessibility of disaggregated local data (especially on food systems) (Blay-Palmer et al., 2019) and the considerable cost of data collection and management, it is essential to design the indicator identification process as a forum where different stakeholders can reflect on how to communicate the meaning of and reasons for their actions, before assessing these actions with quantitative parameters designed to monitor intentions other than those of the stakeholders (Alrøe et al., 2017). Moreover, taking into account multiple observers' points of view affords key insights not visible from a single perspective (Meter, 2010). In the three cases in a study conducted by Fraser et al. (2006), the participatory consultations with stakeholders to identify sustainability indicators provided a space to draw on the knowledge of local stakeholders and a wide range of views. This operation broadened the perspective and the knowledge of the individual participants and contributed to their empowerment (commensurate with the level of inclusiveness of the participation process itself). It also led to the identification of indicators not yet used that would be valuable to the stakeholders, and the continuous re-design of the indicators ensured that the assessment remained relevant as the stakeholders' needs evolved (Fraser et al., 2006). Despite the complexity and uncertainty surrounding the process of translating the results of participatory processes into strategy improvements or actual policy, these authors argue that when data are collected at the finest resolution possible, when aggregation is transparent, and when the interpretation of data is flexible, local participation in the identification of indicators can provide valuable material to enable decision-making to take local perspectives into account. Of course, the inclusiveness of this process depends on the nature and extent of actors' participation.

Positing that there are many challenges involved in measuring what is measurable in the context of innovation, Brockwell makes an interesting proposition to shift "from a convenience-driven technical approach ('what can be measured', using the methods and datasets that are currently available), towards a normative approach based on creative and critical thinking ('what should be measured')" (Brockwell, 2019, p. 105). Given these various challenges, we considered it worthwhile to explore a potential use of the Urbal approach in completing an impact pathway analysis for a follow-up evaluation using metrics. Urbal can enable reflection on the selection of indicators based on the specificities of local contexts, involving stakeholders in the process and taking broader sustainability assessment frameworks into consideration (SDG, MUFPP).

11.3 A framework to support the design of assessment metrics and orient stakeholders in a multi-level regulatory framework using Urbal results

Urbal is a qualitative and participatory evaluation method that provides innovators, decision makers, and donors with information on how innovations contribute to or impede the development of more sustainable food systems, thus assisting them in determining which actions should or should not be taken (see Chapter 1). The main outputs are cognitive maps showing the impacts of innovations on sustainability. The evaluation process focuses on participatory reflection on impact pathways that allow for identifying a systemic theory of change for each innovation evaluated. Urbal is a qualitative method. It does not provide metrics or indicators. Yet we argue that it can prove very useful for the process of selecting relevant indicators prior to an evaluation and for addressing the main difficulties involved in selecting indicators.

In order to structure the choice of indicators in such a way that they reflect sustainability recommendations and are tailored to the innovation context, practitioners following the Urbal approach can undertake a collaborative exercise to articulate the Urbal results with local and international sustainability guidelines, building on the knowledge co-created in the workshop.[1]

The output of this articulation provides groundwork on which urban-driven innovation practitioners can draw—it allows them to choose metrics from the large number of existing options, to develop their own customized metrics, or to improve their existing assessment system. We have formalized this exercise into a practical tool that can be represented in the form of an analytical framework.

11.3.1 Co-creating the tool with stakeholders

To develop this framework, the Urbal research team carried out a study drawing on foundations from a literary review on FSS indicator frameworks, and on an Urbal impact pathway analysis applied to the case study of Ma Cantine Autrement (MCA) the school catering improvement programme of the city of Montpellier, France (see Chapter 5). This programme draws on the sustainability targets set out in the Food Policy of Montpellier (P2A),[2] and was initially designed to reduce food waste and promote a sustainable diet for children.

At the request of the city's Food Policy Department, the results of this participative in-depth analysis of the change process generated by the MCA initiative were used to guide a metrics-based evaluation of the programme. The purpose of this evaluation was to revise the existing set of indicators used, so as to design an evaluation framework more in line with the specific issues identified by Urbal. It also aimed to better align the programme with existing normative frameworks. We thus undertook a collaborative exercise with the main stakeholders of the Montpellier school catering programme. In this exercise we were able to build and test a practical tool to structure the choice of indicators, taking in account priorities specific to the context and to local, national, and international sustainability guidelines. This tool is fully usable by urban-driven innovation practitioners. The exercise relied on meetings with small groups of innovators and experts.[3] We adopted a co-design approach, guided by the principle that "users of goods or services are experts of their own needs and experiences, and therefore can usefully contribute to their [re]design" (Mackenzie & Davies, 2019, p. 6). By enabling a better understanding of users' needs, co-design affords better-informed decision-making and greater motivation among the participants designing and using a tool or service (Moser, 2016).

11.3.2 A practical tool to support innovation assessment design

The analytical framework provides the basis for identifying appropriate indicators to assess the performance of the activities and resources used in support of the innovation and, in keeping with the theory of change, distinguishing between indicators relating to resources (inputs), indicators of short-term change or the results of activities (outputs) and indicators of medium-term change (outcomes).

The analytical framework is structured around the various elements based on which each selected innovation activity[4] was evaluated as part of the Urbal process. The tool can serve as a roadmap and can be adapted depending on the users' priorities, needs and context.[5] Figure 11.1 shows the logical sequence which was followed to feed the content boxes in the pilot case study and the stages of the process, which were supplemented with frequent information exchange. The boxes are grouped into six sections (Columns A to F), and each section indicates the data source, as outlined in the key. Boxes with a dashed border present the results of the interviews and the participatory workshop conducted in Urbal Steps 1, 2, and 3.

This is ideally a collaborative process involving the workshop participants, that is, the innovators, different stakeholders, and a researcher or expert.

The "Initial documentation" stage consists of an analysis of the FSS themes that emerged from the interviews and the participatory workshop (Urbal Steps 1, 2, and 3) in order to establish a knowledge base for subsequent meetings and a starting point for the identification of indicators.

The second stage consists in setting the objective of the framework. This can be to standardize the collected data to develop a set of indicators for the project's evaluation, to improve the project's current set of metrics, to select or adapt a number of existing sustainability indicators, or to prove the contribution of the project's actions to align with sustainability recommendations. The "Tool development" stage involves populating the first four columns:

1) Column "A" outlines the reasons for which each activity has been implemented in relation to the Urbal sustainability dimensions
2) Column "B" reports the positive and negative changes and impacts associated with each activity, as well as factors fostering or impeding change
3) Column "C" identifies the sustainability dimensions impacted and the ways in which the activity and other project activities mutually influence each other
4) Column "D" provides evidence regarding the activities, in the form of testimonials and accounts shared by stakeholders directly involved

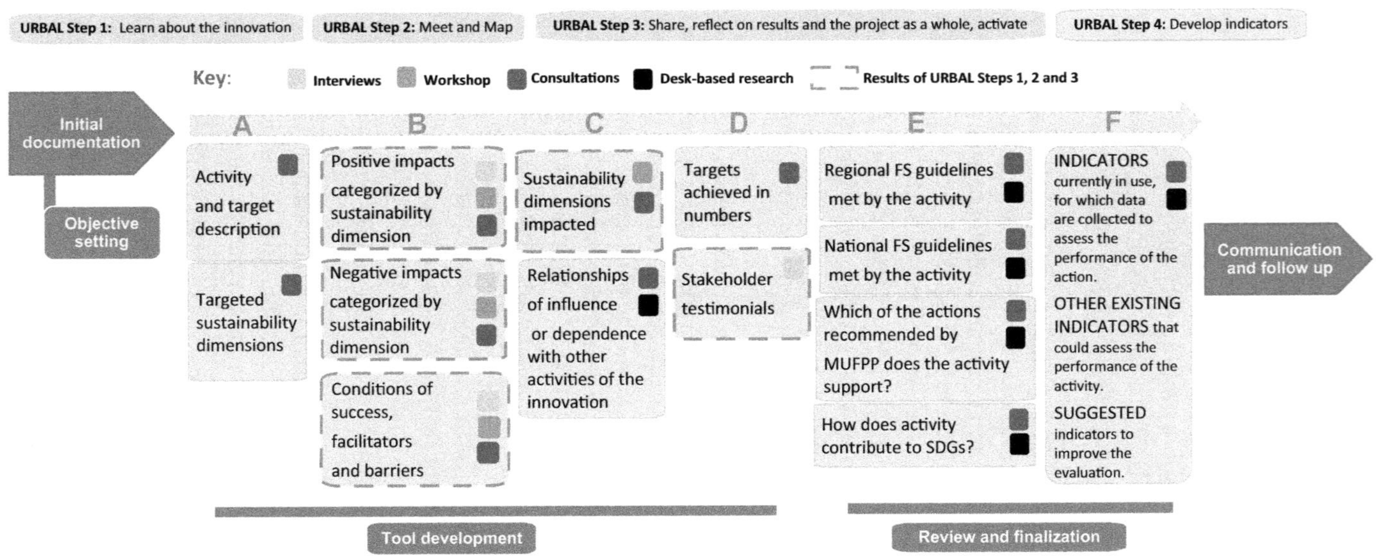

Figure 11.1 Analytical framework development process, content of the sections, and source: example of the content established for a single innovation activity.

The feedback and knowledge collected serve to model the analytical framework to develop a new draft for the "Review and finalization" stage. During this fourth stage, participants reflect on how the activity relates to different FSS guidelines, thus populating Column E, and proceed to identifying indicators. This involves reviewing the activity's pathway, outlining topics of interest based on the activity's objectives and contributions to different FSS frameworks, defining questions to ask in order to explore the topics, and identifying appropriate metrics through which to actually address these questions based on factual capabilities and the viability of data collection (Section F). Once completed, this process results in an analytical framework that provides the basis for continuously improving the innovation's assessment.[6]

The criteria informing the selection of indicators should be established according to the context and scale of the innovation. These criteria include the indicators' relevance to the needs of the people involved in the innovation, the accessibility and affordability of data collection, and the extent to which the indicators align with local, national, or international FSS guidelines (Carey & Cook, 2021).

11.3.3 Application to the Ma Cantine Autrement programme

We can look at a few examples from MCA's school catering programme to learn more about the value of the Urbal approach for setting up a quantitative evaluation. Previously, the MCA's evaluation system was based on a set of indicators reflecting the overall impact of the programme, without a distinct evaluation of each of the actions comprising the programme, nor of the stages of the innovation process. Identifying these stages and characterizing the obstacles or facilitators along the impact pathway allowed MCA to choose indicators that account for specific stages of the innovation pathway. These can be material or contextual resources that enable the action, activities implemented to generate change, any levers or obstacles encountered, or long-term effects on the system. For instance, the MCA action "Finer allotment by product or family of products" aims to split the procurement process into a larger number of batches to encourage applications from a more diverse pool of producers and processors, particularly small, local businesses. The impact pathway mapped collectively with Urbal showed that "sourcing" (i.e., the consultations carried out to identify potential suppliers), is a favourable precondition for the success of the action. An ad hoc indicator was therefore added to the existing set of indicators.

The analysis of the impact pathways thus allowed indications to be identified in order to improve the evaluation of the programme's sustainability, drawing on existing and new data sources. In particular, multi-stakeholder dialogue yielded insights that made it possible to include indicators in the evaluation that took into account the interests of the diverse range of actors involved, beyond the project leader alone. For example, during the participatory workshop, the agents who facilitate the children's meals at the canteens indicated that the tools in the "Cutting kit"—designed to facilitate the agents' cutting work and reduce fruit waste—could entail a risk of injury. Taking this into account will ensure better working conditions and prevent an increase in healthcare costs. In this case, as tracking these incidents' occurrence would be difficult for privacy reasons, anonymous questionnaires with a mixture of closed- and open-ended questions could be envisaged to take into account the agents' perspectives, so as to monitor the improvement of the safety process.

The Food Policy Department had also decided to reflect on the articulation of the programme's monitoring-evaluation system with normative sustainability frameworks at different scales (P2A Charter, EGalim national law, MUFPP, SDG). The characterization of change proposed by Urbal through the mapping of impact pathways facilitated this articulation by highlighting the programme's contribution to the different dimensions of sustainability (economic, social, environmental, health/nutrition, and governance).

The activity "Generalization of waste sorting and recovery of biowaste" was previously evaluated using the indicator "Number of school restaurants sorting bio-waste", generally associated with SDG 11 "Sustainable cities". The Urbal results allowed for identifying the impact of this activity on the creation of renewable energy sources from bio-waste and on the reduction of waste through prevention, recycling, and reuse. This resulted in a more accurate evaluation by highlighting a connection with SDG 7, which aims to ensure access to reliable, sustainable and modern energy services for all and SDG 12, which aims to establish sustainable consumption and production patterns.

11.3.4 Variables to consider for an effective use of the framework

Regarding participation in the indicator identification process, a few factors need to be taken into account. The configuration of the group of participants, including the number of participants, the different levels of interest in presenting results, and power dynamics between participants, may influence the level of collaboration among the stakeholders and their appropriation of the assessment tool. To ensure that the co-design process is effective and inclusive, it is necessary to provide sufficient time and appropriate information material to enable each participant to understand the process and make a valuable contribution.

Despite the many benefits of this approach, potential barriers to the use of the Urbal process are the small number of participants involved (15–20 maximum) and the necessary involvement of external facilitators. Moreover, monitoring an innovation project's impact over time implies strong stakeholder engagement, with a commitment—primarily on the part of the project leader—to continuously improve the evaluation system.

For this case study, the results obtained through the Urbal process not only helped the innovation project leader (the Food Policy Department of Montpellier) to communicate about the project to internal and external stakeholders but also contributed to the creation of a monitoring committee for the city's school catering system. This committee aims to ensure transparency in the actions taken and the choices made by the municipality regarding school catering, and will be comprised of elected municipal representatives, technicians, researchers, farmers, teachers, parents, and a dedicated children's council.[7] Such collective involvement has a strong positive impact on the continuity of engagement and funding for long-term project assessment, since periodic meetings can support actors' knowledge and the setting of priorities, common goals, and strategies for monitoring implementation as well as improvement. Moreover, the existence of a multi-actor committee to monitor progress provides more guarantee of a lasting commitment to monitoring and evaluation, irrespective of any changes in the project leadership.

11.4 Discussion: What solutions do Urbal results offer to address issues surrounding the assessment of innovations' FSS?

The dialogue around place-based knowledge stemming from the Urbal approach provides stakeholders with a better understanding of the process and context of the innovation by shedding light on different perspectives regarding internal or external practices that interact and facilitate or hinder the implementation of innovation activities, and which relate to multiple unexpected dimensions of FSS in its broadest sense. This allows practitioners to develop the ability to identify, develop, and carefully use a set of indicators tailored to the specificities of the innovation, including the subjectivity of the actors involved and the innovation's evolution process.

Thanks to the analytical framework developed to use Urbal results, instead of selecting metrics that measure a situation or characteristic abstracted from its context, practitioners can identify metrics that capture complexity and specificity where they work and are making change, thus enabling the results to be place-specific. This is crucial both for framing problems and for guiding decision-making.

With regard to benefits for evaluation, the proposed framework helps to avoid a standardization of indicators, embedding them instead in the narrative process of the innovation, taking into account social, physical, economic, and cultural intervening or interacting factors (Cohen, 2019). In practice, this allows for better matching of indicators to specific stages of the innovation changes and impacts pathway, based on material or contextual resources that enabled implementation (input indicators), activities implemented to generate change and their effects (activity and output indicators), and long-term effects on the system (outcome indicators), as shown in Figure 11.2.

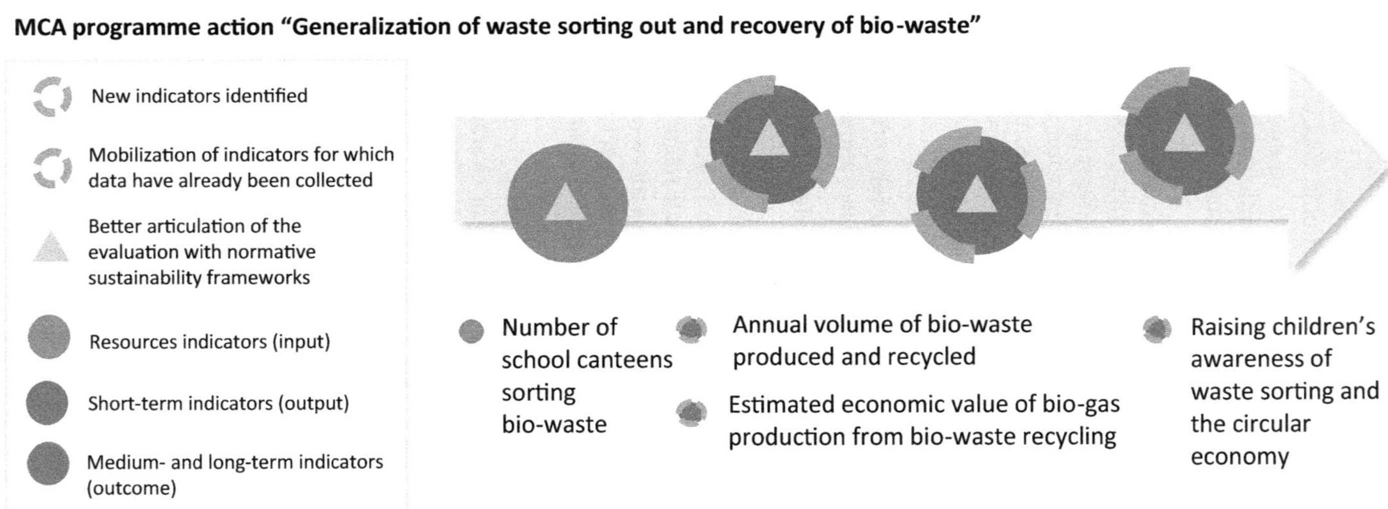

Figure 11.2 Example of how the Urbal approach can facilitate the elaboration of quantitative evaluation.

The articulation of Urbal with local, national, and global targets requires reflection on the connections between specific sustainability issues, as identified by official declarations at different scales, and the concrete ways in which these issues are addressed by the actions carried out as part of the innovation. Such reflection sheds light on the variety of approaches to and points of focus surrounding sustainability issues that can be adopted for different scales, and thus allows:

1) identification of missed parameters by envisaging the creation of metrics informed by "unstructured" place-based data, and inclusion in the evaluation not only what is expected to change, but also the conditions required for impact pathways to occur, unforeseen changes, and stakeholder feedback
2) extension or improvement of the application of indicators already in use
3) improved targeting of the indicators' contribution to meeting the SDGs as well as local and national guidelines

By providing support to frame the interpretation of standardized FSS objectives, the Urbal approach enables practitioners to situate the innovation action within the regulatory evaluation systems established at local and international level, thus facilitating project communication. This could allow for a degree of comparison across study sites.

Thanks to the Urbal approach's context-specific interpretation regarding the fulfilment of FSS objectives and the nuanced understanding it affords of the innovation process, ideas and best practices can be more effectively disseminated, a wider range of actors can use and interact with this knowledge, and integration into urban FSS programmes is more accessible.

Moreover, documenting this diverse range of data on resources, practices, processes, and orientations can provide a valuable resource for similar innovations operating on a different scale and in a different context to compare the dynamics of change, detect criticalities, and improve their strategy. Indicators developed following the Urbal process allow for comparing the ways in which different innovations conduct activities, based on the vision guiding the innovation, the change and impact pathway, the people involved, the resources available, the institutional and cultural context, and the approaches used.

Figure 11.3 summarizes the field of application in which Urbal results can help address the challenges that FSS innovations face in assessment design, and how local and global FSS recommendations articulate with this process.

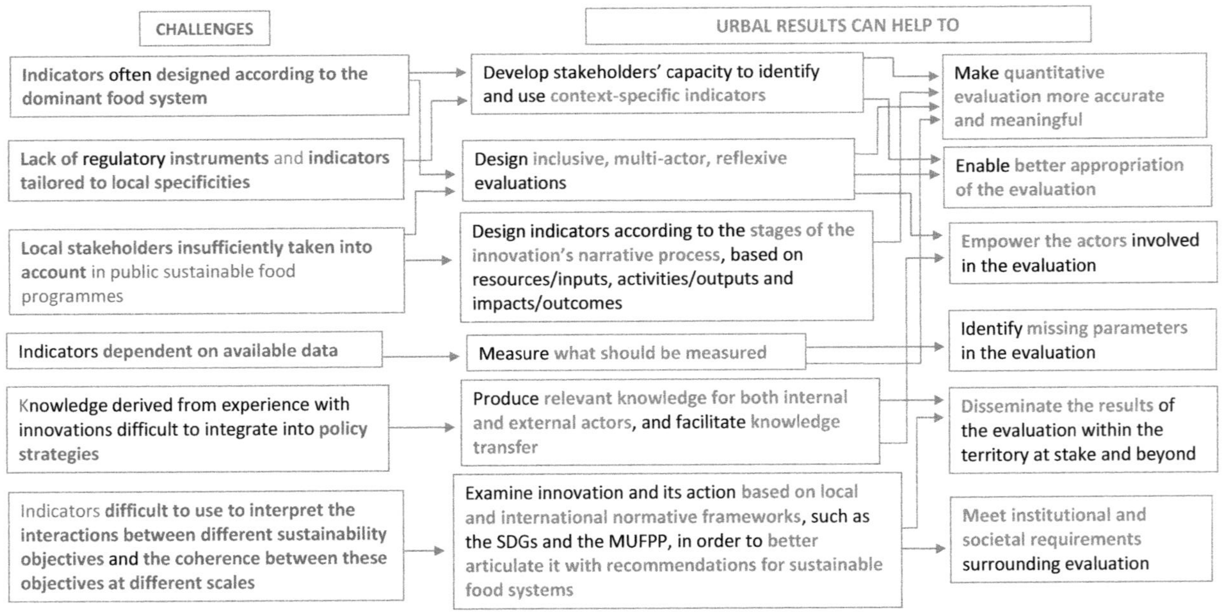

Figure 11.3 The potential contribution of Urbal to address the planning and evaluation challenges of innovations.

11.5 Conclusion

Developing methods for collectively designing indicators with or in agreement with local users proved to be crucial to the effectiveness of quantitative evaluation. We have addressed this need by proposing a framework to build on the change and impact pathways captured by the Urbal approach. This framework helps select relevant indicators for innovators and future users seeking to improve and communicate their long-term impact on sustainability, while orienting their action in the sustainability frameworks established at local and international level, such as the SDGs, MUFPP, FAO-SAFA, etc.

The application of this framework involves using the results produced by the Urbal approach in a process of collaboration between the innovators and stakeholders. It allows for inclusiveness and multidimensionality, embracing the subjectivity of the stakeholders participating in the evaluation, a subjectivity which reflects the variability of the needs at play in a local food system. It also unlocks a number of potentials, including the potential to enhance the actions carried out within the framework of innovations and to support the joint action of interconnected and multi-scale processes at work to reshape the food system. Finally, it shows one of the possible uses of Urbal as a way to prepare quantitative assessments or to select indicators, laying the foundations for future applications of the Urbal approach.

Notes

1 If the conditions needed to run the workshop cannot be met for various reasons (power imbalances between actors, hierarchical relationships, social and cultural context, etc.), several other options involving participative methods can be used (see Chapter 1 of this book or the Urbal guide on this topic).

2 The Food Policy of Montpellier, known as P2A ("*politique agroécologique et alimentaire*"), aims to improve access to sustainable food for all by developing an agroecological food system and redirecting local products towards local supply chains. As of 2019, the school catering improvement programme is a mandatory requirement set out in the French Food law, EGalim, the outcome of the "*États généraux de l'alimentation*" (French National Food conference) held from 20 July to 21 December 2017. The EGalim law seeks to provide fair remuneration for producers, to guarantee the safety, environmental and nutritional quality of food products, and to promote healthy, safe, and sustainable food for all.

3 It is however important to note that the process could also rely on bigger meetings, using focus groups. The focus groups would ideally include the stakeholders of the innovation project, some participants from the Urbal workshop, and a researcher/expert in the field or a member of the Urbal research team to facilitate the indicator identification process.

4 The Step 2 of the Urbal process involves the selection of six to nine of the activities included in an innovation project, to be evaluated during the workshop. The selected activities are those that are most innovative or most likely to generate the greatest impact on FSS. For more information on the activities collectively evaluated as part of the MCA programme, see Chapter 5 this volume.

5 To find out more about the Urbal approach used to identify or modify existing or future impact indicators and to establish the articulation with various normative

FSS benchmarks, please see the results “Booklet” and “Poster” produced for the MCA programme in the “Resources” section of the Urbal website.

6 Ibid.

7 For more detail on the City of Montpellier’s school catering monitoring committee project, see https://www.montpellier.fr/evenement/25242/3624-lancement-du-comite-de-suivi-de-la-restauration-scolaire.htm

References

Alrøe, H. F., Sautier, M., Legun, K., Whitehead, J., Noe, E., Moller, H., & Manhire, J. (2017). Performance versus values in sustainability transformation of food systems. *Sustainability*, *9*(3), 332. https://doi.org/10.3390/su9030332

Bell, S., & Morse, S. (2013). Towards an understanding of how policy making groups use indicators. *Ecological Indicators*, *35*, 13–23. https://doi.org/10.1016/j.ecolind.2012.12.023

Blay-Palmer, A., Conaré, D., Meter, K., Di Battista, A., & Jonhston, C. (2019). Sustainable food system assessment lessons from global practice. In A. Blay-Palmer, D. Conaré, K. Meter, A. Di Battista, & C. Johnston (Eds.), *Sustainable food system assessment lessons from global practice* (pp. 1–19). Routledge. https://doi.org/10.4324/9780429439896

Brockwell, A.J. (2019). *Measuring what matters?: Exploring the use of values-based indicators in assessing education for sustainability*. Wageningen University. https://doi.org/10.18174/476056

Carey, J., & Cook, B. (2021). *The Milan urban food policy pact monitoring framework: A practical handbook for implementation*. FAO. https://www.fao.org/3/cb4181en/cb4181en.pdf

Carlsson, L., Callaghan, E., Morley, A., & Broman, G. (2017). Food system sustainability across scales: A proposed local-to-global approach to community planning and assessment. *Sustainability*, *9*(6), 1061. https://doi.org/10.3390/su9061061

Cohen, N. (2019). Integrating upstream determinants and downstream food metrics. In A. Blay-Palmer, D. Conaré, K. Meter, A. Di Battista, & C. Johnston (Eds.), *Sustainable food system assessment lessons from global practice* (pp. 216–223). Routledge. https://doi.org/10.4324/9780429439896

Deconinck, K., Giner, C., Jackson, L.A., & Toyama, L. (2021). Overcoming evidence gaps on food systems. OECD Food, Agriculture and Fisheries Papers, 163. https://doi.org/10.1787/44ba7574-en

Desrosières, A. (2008). Pour une sociologie historique de la quantification : L’Argument statistique I. Presses des Mines. http://books.openedition.org/pressesmines/901

Fraser, E.D., Dougill, A.J., Mabee, W.E., Reed, M., & McAlpine, P. (2006). Bottom up and top down: Analysis of participatory processes for sustainability indicator identification as a pathway to community empowerment and sustainable environmental management. *Journal of Environmental Management*, *78*(2), 114–127. https://doi.org/10.1016/j.jenvman.2005.04.009

Grace, W., & Pope, J. (2015). A systems approach to sustainability assessment. In A. Morrison-Saunders, J. Pope, & A. Bond (Eds.), *Handbook of sustainability assessment* (pp. 285–320). Edward Elgar Publishing.

Grainger, A. (2012). Forest sustainability indicator systems as procedural policy tools in global environmental governance. *Global Environmental Change*, *22*(1), 147–160. https://doi.org/10.1016/j.gloenvcha.2011.09.001

Halla, P., & Binder, C.R. (2020). Sustainability assessment: Introduction and framework. In C.R. Binder, R. Wyss, & E. Massaro (Eds.), *Sustainability assessment of urban systems* (pp. 7–29). Cambridge University Press.

IPES-Food International Panel of Experts on Sustainable Food Systems. (2015). The new science of sustainable food systems: Overcoming barriers to food systems reform. International Panel of Experts on Sustainable Food Systems. http://www.ipes-food.org/_img/upload/files/NewScienceofSusFood.pdf

IPES-Food International Panel of Experts on Sustainable Food Systems. (2016). From uniformity to diversity: A paradigm shift from industrial agriculture to diversified agroecological systems. http://www.ipes-food.org/images/Reports/UniformityToDiversity_FullReport.pdf

Kaur, A., & Lodhia, S. (2018). Stakeholder engagement in sustainability accounting and reporting: A study of Australian local councils. *Accounting, Auditing & Accountability Journal*, *31*(1), 338–368. https://doi.org/10.1108/AAAJ-12-2014-1901

Lehtonen, M., Sébastien, L., & Bauler, T. (2016). The multiple roles of sustainability indicators in informational governance: Between intended use and unanticipated influence. *Current Opinion in Environmental Sustainability*, *18*, 1–9. http://dx.doi.org/10.1016/j.cosust.2015.05.009

Levkoe, C., & Blay-Palmer, A. (2018). Food Counts: Food systems report cards, food sovereignty and the politics of indicators. *Canadian Food Studies / La Revue canadienne des études sur l'alimentation*, *5*, 49–75. https://doi.org/10.15353/cfs-rcea.v5i3.277

Mackenzie, S.G., & Davies, A.R. (2019). SHARE IT: Co-designing a sustainability impact assessment framework for urban food sharing initiatives. *Environmental Impact Assessment Review*, *79*, 106300. https://doi.org/10.1016/j.eiar.2019.106300

Meadowcroft, J. (2010). Who is in charge here? Governance for sustainable development in a complex world. *Journal of Environmental Policy & Planning*, *9*(3–4), 299–314. https://doi.org/10.1080/15239080701631544

Meter, K. (2010). Metrics from the field: Letting food systems emerge. *Journal of Agriculture, Food Systems, and Community Development*, *1*(1), 23–26. https://doi.org/10.5304/jafscd.2010.011.006

Molle, F., & Mollinga, P. (2003). Water poverty indicators: Conceptual problems and policy issues. *Water Policy*, *5*(5–6), 529–544. https://doi.org/10.2166/WP.2003.0034

Moragues-Faus, A., & Marceau, A. (2018). Measuring progress in sustainable food cities: An indicators toolbox for action. *Sustainability*, *11*(1), 45. https://doi.org/10.3390/su11010045

Moser, S.C. (2016). Can science on transformation transform science? Lessons from co-design. *Current Opinion in Environmental Sustainability*, *20*, 106–115. https://doi.org/10.1016/j.cosust.2016.10.007

Ramos, T.B. (2019). Sustainability assessment: Exploring the frontiers and paradigms of indicator approaches. *Sustainability*, *11*(3), 824. https://doi.org/10.3390/su11030824

Reid, J., & Rout, M. (2020). Developing sustainability indicators–The need for radical transparency. *Ecological Indicators*, *110*, 105941.

Schader, C., Grenz, J., Meier, M. S., & Stolze, M. (2014). Scope and precision of sustainability assessment approaches to food systems. *Ecology and Society*, *19*(3), 42. http://dx.doi.org/10.5751/ES-06866-190342

Shen, L. Y., Ochoa, J. J., Shah, M. N., & Zhang, X. (2011). The application of urban sustainability indicators–A comparison between various practices. *Habitat International*, *35*(1), 17–29. https://doi.org/10.1016/j.habitatint.2010.03.006

Singh, R.K., Murty, H.R., Gupta, S.K., & Dikshit, A.K. (2012). An overview of sustainability assessment methodologies. *Ecological Indicators*, *9*(2), 189–212. https://doi.org/10.1016/j.ecolind.2011.01.007

Thomas, D.S.G., & Twyman, C. (2004). Good or bad rangeland? Hybrid knowledge, science, and local understandings of vegetation dynamics in the Kalahari. *Land Degradation & Development*, *15*(3), 215–231. https://doi.org/10.1002/ldr.610

Wiek, A., & Binder, C. (2005). Solution spaces for decision-making: A sustainability assessment tool for city-regions. *Environmental Impact Assessment Review*, *25*(6), 589–608. https://doi.org/10.1016/j.eiar.2004.09.009

Index

Pages in *italics* refer to figures, pages in **bold** refer to tables, and pages followed by 'n' refer to notes.

For Product Safety Concerns and Information please contact our EU
representative GPSR@taylorandfrancis.com
Taylor & Francis Verlag GmbH, Kaufingerstraße 24, 80331 München, Germany

www.ingramcontent.com/pod-product-compliance
Ingram Content Group UK Ltd.
Pitfield, Milton Keynes, MK11 3LW, UK
UKHW020010200926
475702UK00015B/2572
* 9 7 8 1 0 3 2 2 5 8 8 3 6 *